SHAKESPEARE IN PRODUCTION

TROILUS AND CRESSIDA

This edition is the first to offer a detailed account of the theatrical treatment
of *Troilus and Cressida* on the British and North American stages from
its first revivals at the beginning of the twentieth century to the present.
The illustrated introduction also briefly traces the play from its earliest
printings and adaptation in the seventeenth century through its period of
theatrical neglect in the eighteenth and nineteenth centuries and notes some
important Continental productions. Frances A. Shirley gives an overview
of the conceptions behind the important revivals, and responses to those
revivals, as well as noting the critical trends that helped shape a great variety
of more recent theatrical approaches.

The authoritative New Cambridge Shakespeare text, edited by Anthony
B. Dawson, is accompanied by detailed commentary on stage business,
actors' interpretations, specific use of settings and properties, and substantial textual alterations. The introduction also shows the close ties between
theatre and the political, social and cultural contexts of productions. This
edition will be useful to students of Shakespeare in performance and to
those intrigued by the rise in popularity and change in reputation of what
is still considered one of Shakespeare's less well-known plays.

FRANCES A. SHIRLEY is Professor of English Emerita, Wheaton College,
Norton, MA. Her publications include *Shakespeare's Use of Off-Stage
Sounds*, *Swearing and Perjury in Shakespeare's Plays*, an edition of
Webster's *The Devil's Law-Case* and a collection of critical essays on *King
John* and *Henry VIII*.

SHAKESPEARE IN PRODUCTION

SERIES EDITORS: J. S. BRATTON AND JULIE HANKEY

This series offers students and researchers the fullest possible stage histories of individual Shakespearean texts. In each volume a substantial introduction presents a conceptual overview of the play, marking out the major stages of its representation and reception. The commentary, presented alongside the New Cambridge Shakespeare edition of the text itself, offers detailed, line-by-line evidence for the overview presented in the introduction, making the volume a flexible tool for further research. The editors have selected interesting and vivid evocations of settings, acting and stage presentation, and range widely in time and space.

ALREADY PUBLISHED

A Midsummer Night's Dream, edited by Trevor R. Griffiths
Much Ado About Nothing, edited by John F. Cox
Antony and Cleopatra, edited by Richard Madelaine
Hamlet, edited by Robert Hapgood
The Tempest, edited by Christine Dymkowski
King Henry V, edited by Emma Smith
The Merchant of Venice, edited by Charles Edelman
Romeo and Juliet, edited by James N. Loehlin
Macbeth, edited by John Wilders
The Taming of the Shrew, edited by Elizabeth Schafer
As You Like It, edited by Cynthia Marshall
Othello, edited by Julie Hankey

FORTHCOMING VOLUMES

Twelfth Night, edited by Elizabeth Schafer

TROILUS AND CRESSIDA

EDITED BY
FRANCES A. SHIRLEY

Professor Emerita,
Wheaton College, Norton, Massachusetts, USA

CAMBRIDGE UNIVERSITY PRESS
Cambridge, New York, Melbourne, Madrid, Cape Town, Singapore, São Paulo

Cambridge University Press
The Edinburgh Building, Cambridge CB2 2RU, UK

Published in the United States of America by Cambridge University Press, New York

www.cambridge.org
Information on this title: www.cambridge.org/9780521796842

© Cambridge University Press 2005

First published 2005

Printed in the United Kingdom at the University Press, Cambridge

A catalogue record for this book is available from the British Library

ISBN-13 978-0-521-79255-4 hardback
ISBN-10 0-521-79255-X hardback
ISBN-13 978-0-521-79684-2 paperback
ISBN-10 0-521-79684-9 paperback

CONTENTS

ILLUSTRATIONS

SERIES EDITORS' PREFACE

It is no longer necessary to stress that the text of a play is only its starting-point, and that only in production is its potential realized and capable of being appreciated fully. Since the coming-of-age of Theatre Studies as an academic discipline, we now understand that even Shakespeare is only one collaborator in the creation and infinite recreation of his play upon the stage. And just as we now agree that no play is complete until it is produced, so we have become interested in the way in which plays often produced – and pre-eminently the plays of the national Bard, William Shakespeare – acquire a life history of their own, after they leave the hands of their first maker.

Since the eighteenth century Shakespeare has become a cultural construct: sometimes the guarantor of nationhood, heritage, and the status quo, sometimes seized and transformed to be its critic and antidote. This latter role has been particularly evident in countries where Shakespeare has to be translated. The irony is that while his status as national icon grows in the English-speaking world, his language is both lost and renewed, so that for good or ill, Shakespeare can be made to seem more urgently 'relevant' than in England or America, and may become the one dissenting voice that the censors mistake as harmless.

'Shakespeare in Production' gives the reader, the student and the scholar a comprehensive dossier of materials – eye-witness accounts, contemporary crit-icism, promptbook marginalia, stage business, cuts, additions, and rewritings – from which to construct an understanding of the many meanings that the plays have carried down the ages and across the world. These materials are organized alongside the New Cambridge Shakespeare text of the play, line by line and scene by scene, while a substantial introduction in each volume offers a guide to their interpretation. One may trace an argument about, for example, the many ways of playing Queen Gertrude, or the political transmutations of the text of *Henry V*; or take a scene, an act, or a whole play, and work out how it has succeeded or failed in presentation over four hundred years.

For, despite our insistence that the plays are endlessly made and remade by history, Shakespeare is not a blank, scribbled upon by the age. Theatre history charts changes, but also registers something in spite of those changes. Some productions work and others do not. Two interpretations may be entirely dif-ferent, and yet both will bring the play to life. Why? Without setting out to give absolute answers, the history of a play in the theatre can often show where the energy and shape of it lie, what has made it tick, through many permutations. In this way theatre history can find common ground with literary criticism. Both will find suggestive directions in the introductions to these volumes, while the commentaries provide raw material for readers to recreate the living experience of theatre, and become their own eye-witness.

J. S. Bratton
Julie Hankey

ACKNOWLEDGEMENTS

Research for this edition has been made possible by generous help from the librarians and staffs of many institutions, including the British Library, the Westminster Reference Library, The Library of Congress, Harvard's Houghton Library, The Boston Public Library, The Yale University Library, The New York Public Library, and the Wheaton College Library. I have been assisted in innumerable ways by Georgianna Ziegler and her staff at the Folger Shakespeare Library; Niky Rathbone and her staff at the Birmingham Central Library (The Birmingham Shakespeare Library); Annette Fern and Kathleen Coleman at the Harvard Theatre Collection; Marion Pringle, Karen Brown, Helen Hargest and the staff of the Shakespeare Centre Library; Janet Birkett and others at the British Theatre Museum; Sarah Cuthill, Keeper, University of Bristol Theatre Collection; Richard Mangan, Administrator of the Raymond Mander and Joe Michensen Theatre Collection; and Louise Ray, Archivist of the Royal National Theatre. Theatres and their publicity departments have also provided information about promptbooks and production photographs. They include The Royal Shakespeare Theatre, The Royal National Theatre, Trinity Repertory Company, Amy Richard at The Oregon Shakespeare Festival and Ellen Charendoff at The Stratford Festival Canada. Edward Brubaker has furnished many insights on productions of the Oregon Shakespeare Festival. Jill Levenson, Robert Ormsby and especially M. J. Kidnie have made accessible details and opinions about the 2003 Stratford Canada production that I did not have a chance to visit. Sister Agnes Fleck provided notes and a tape of a Terry Hands discussion. During the whole process, I have been grateful to the series editors, J. S. Bratton and Julie Hankey, for their guidance and patience, and to Sarah Stanton of the Cambridge University Press for her continuing assistance.

Finally, I am most appreciative of the permissions given by the copyright owners of the illustrations.

EDITOR'S NOTE

I have silently corrected occasional misprints in quotations from newspaper articles, especially some reprinted on the Internet. Where details of costumes, sets and stage business have come from three or more reviews, a promptbook or production videotape, or, in the case of many Stratford, London and North American revivals I have seen since 1956, the sort of notes Arthur Colby Sprague taught me to keep, I have not footnoted extensively, but merely mentioned the company and date, especially in the commentary to the text.

The play text used is The New Cambridge Shakespeare *Troilus and Cressida*, edited by Anthony B. Dawson, Cambridge University Press, 2003.

ABBREVIATIONS

ASF	American Shakespeare Festival
BBC	British Broadcasting Company
BET	*Boston Evening Transcript*
BOV	Bristol Old Vic
BR	Birmingham Repertory Company
CF	Cambridge Festival
CSM	*Christian Science Monitor*
DM	*Daily Mail*, London
DT	*Daily Telegraph*, London
FT	*Financial Times*, London
FTG	Folger Library Theatre Group
GC	Glasgow Citizens' Theatre
Gdn	*Guardian*
HSSR	Harvard Summer School Repertory
ILN	*Illustrated London News*
In	*The Independent,* London
LM	London Mask Theatre
LT	*The Times*, London
MS	Marlowe Society
NAO	National Arts Centre Ottawa
NS	*New Statesman*
NT	Royal National Theatre
NYEP	*New York Evening Post*
NYHT	*New York Herald Tribune*
NYS	*New York Sun*
NYSF	New York Shakespeare Festival
NYTh	National Youth Theatre
NYT	*New York Times*
OA	Open Air Theatre, Regent's Park
Obs	*Observer*, London
OSF	Oregon Shakespeare Festival
OX	Oxford Stage Company
OV	Old Vic
PI	*Plays International*

PMLA	*Publications of the Modern Language Association of America*
PP	*Plays and Players*
RSC	Royal Shakespeare Company
RST	Royal Shakespeare Theatre
SCL	Shakespeare Centre Library
SFC	Stratford Festival Canada
SMT	Shakespeare Memorial Theatre
SQ	*Shakespeare Quarterly*
SR	*Saturday Review of Literature*
SS	*Shakespeare Survey*
ST	*Sunday Telegraph*, London
St	*The Standard*, London
SuT	*Sunday Times*, London
TA	*Theatre Arts*
TLS	*Times Literary Supplement*
TR	Trinity Repertory Company, Providence
TS	*Theatre Survey*
TW	*Theatre World*
YR	Yale Repertory Theatre

Note

Journal references appear in an abbreviated form in the text, but can be found in full in the bibliography. References to newspaper and periodical reviews are found only in footnotes and the commentary.

PRODUCTIONS

The following is a selective chronological list of productions of *Troilus and Cressida* in English. Where amateur or semi-professional productions are noted, they were either pioneering or considered important enough for substantive reviews in major newspapers. All productions between 1679 and 1733 are of the Dryden adaptation. The first name after the title of the company is the producer or director (early producers were the equivalent of today's directors). Where principal actors are listed, 'T' stands for Troilus, 'C' for Cressida, 'P' for Pandarus, 'U' for Ulysses, 'TH' for Thersites, 'A' for Achilles, and 'H' for Hector. SMT represents The Shakespeare Memorial Theatre and its company. It became the Royal Shakespeare Company (RSC) in 1961, and RST stands for their main Stratford theatre. All locations are in Great Britain, most often in London, unless otherwise indicated by company name or the notation of a city.

A chronology that includes many Continental revivals, but omits some of the British and American productions listed below, can be found on the Theatre for a New Audience web site http://www.tfana.org/2001/troilus/chronprt.htm as of this writing.

Theatrical productions

Date(s)	Company/Director; Principal actors	Venue(s)
1602?	Lord Chamberlain's Men?	Globe or Inns of Court?
1679	Duke's Men/Davenant; Betterton T, Leigh P, Underhill TH	Dorset Garden
1697	Betterton P, Wilks T, Quin H	Lincoln's Inn Fields
1709	Betterton TH, Wilks T, Quin H	Drury Lane
1720	Quin H, Leigh A	Lincoln's Inn Fields
1723	Quin TH, Hippisley P	Lincoln's Inn Fields
1733	Quin TH, Hippisley P, Ryan T	Covent Garden

Date(s)	Company / Director; Principal actors	Venue(s)
1907	Charles Fry TH, Lewis Casson T	Great Queen Street
1912, 1913	Elizabethan Stage Society/William Poel; Edith Evans C, Elspeth Keith TH, Robert Speaight U	King's Hall; Stratford
1916	Yale Shakespeare Association/E. M. Woolley	Hyperion, New Haven, CT
1922	Marlowe Society/Frank Birch	Cambridge; Everyman
1923	Old Vic/Robert Atkins; Ion Swinley T, D. Hay Petrie TH	Old Vic
1927	Rockford College	Rockford, IL
1928	Norwich Players/Nugent Monck	Maddermarket
1932	Cambridge Festival/Frank Birch; Anthony Quayle H	Arts Theatre
1932	Players Theatre/Henry Herbert; Otis Skinner TH, Edith Barrett C, Eugene Powers P	Moss's Broadway Theatre, NY
1934	Carnegie Institute of Technology/B. Iden Payne	Little Theatre, Pittsburgh, PA
1936	SMT/B. Iden Payne; Donald Wolfit U, Randle Ayrton P, Pamela Brown C	SMT
1936	York Settlement Community Players/Kenneth Muir	Harrogate Festival Opera House
1938	London Mask/Michael Macowan; Robert Speaight U, Max Adrian P, Robert Harris T, Ruth Lodge C	Westminster
1938	Oxford University Dramatic Society/Neville Coghill	Exeter College Garden
1940	Marlowe Society Cambridge Revels/George Rylands	Cambridge Arts Theatre
1941	Princeton Theatre Intime	Princeton, NJ

Date(s)	Company / Director; Principal actors	Venue(s)
1941	Civic Theatre/Leon Askin; Murray Sheehan P	Washington, DC
1946	Open Air Theatre/Robert Atkins	Regent's Park
1948	Marlowe Society/George Rylands	ADC Theatre, Cambridge
1948	SMT/Anthony Quayle; Paul Scofield T, Noel Willman P	SMT
1948	Norwich Players/Nugent Monck	Maddermarket
1948, 1950	Brattle Theatre Company/Jerry Kilty U, Thayer David P	Cambridge, MA
1953	Oxford University Dramatic Society/Merlin Thomas	St John's College Gardens; Paris
1953	Antioch Area Theatre/Arthur Lithgow; Elias Rabb T	Yellow Springs, OH
1954	SMT/Glen Byam Shaw; Anthony Quayle P, Laurence Harvey T, Leo McKern U, Keith Michell A	SMT
1954	University of Colorado/J. H. Crouch	Boulder, CO
1954	Marlowe Society/George Rylands	Cambridge
1955	Portsmouth Southern Shakespeare Players	St. Peter's Hall
1955	Sloane School	Sloane School
1956–7	Old Vic/Tyrone Guthrie; Paul Rogers P, John Neville T, TH, Rosemary Harris C, Jeremy Brett T	Old Vic; US tour
1956	Marlowe Society/John Barton, George Rylands	Cambridge Arts
1958	Oregon Shakespeare Festival/James Sandoe	Ashland, OR
1958	Youth Theatre/Michael Croft	Lyric, Hammersmith; Moray House, Edinburgh

Date(s)	Company / Director; Principal actors	Venue(s)
1960, 1962	SMT-RSC/Peter Hall, John Barton; Denholm Elliott T, Ian Holm T, Dorothy Tutin C, Max Adrian P, Michael Hordern P, Peter O'Toole TH, Gordon Gostelow TH	SMT; Edinburgh Lyceum; Aldwych
1961	American Shakespeare Festival/Jack Landau; Carrie Nye C, Ted van Greithuysen T	Stratford, CT
1961	Richmond Shakespeare Society	Terrace Garden; Fulham Open Air; George Inn
1963	Birmingham Rep/John Harrison; Derek Jacobi T, Arthur Pentlow TH, Philip Voss A	Repertory Theatre
1963	Stratford Festival Canada/Michael Langham; John Colicos H, William Hutt P, Eric Christmas TH, Peter Donat T	Festival Theatre Stratford, Ont.
1964	Marlowe Society/Robin Midgley	Cambridge Arts
1964	Victoria University Drama Club	Wellington, N.Z.
1965	National Youth Theatre/Michael Croft	Old Vic
1965	APA Repertory/Richard Watts, Jr	Phoenix, NY
1965	N. Y. Shakespeare Festival/Joseph Papp	Delacorte, Central Park, NY
1966	Nottingham Theatre Club	Hutchinson St.
1968	University of Michigan, Ann Arbor	Lydia Mendelssohn Theatre, MI
1968	Guildhall School of Music and Drama/Edward Argent	Guildhall School
1968–9	RSC/John Barton; Norman Rodway TH, Michael Williams T, Helen Mirren C, David Waller P, Alan Howard A, Patrick Stewart H, Sebastian Shaw U	RST; Aldwych,
1969	John Fernald Company/John Fernald	Rochester, MI
1969	Great Lakes Shakespeare Festival/Lawrence Carra	Lakewood, OH

Date(s)	Company / Director; Principal actors	Venue(s)
1970	Princeton Repertory/Arthur Lithgow, Tom Brenner	McCarter, Princeton, NJ
1970	Champlain Shakespeare Festival/James J. Thesing	Burlington, VT
1971	Belgrade Coventry	Studio Theatre
1971	Royal Academy of Dramatic Art	Vanbrugh Theatre
1971	Trinity Square Repertory/Adrian Hall; Richard Kneeland U	Providence, RI
1971	Yale Repertory	New Haven, CT
1972	Oregon Shakespeare Festival/Jerry Turner	Bowmer Theatre, Ashland, OR
1972	Olney Theatre/Ellie Chamberlain	Olney, MD
1972	Bristol Old Vic/Howard Davies; Anna Calder-Marshall C	Theatre Royal
1972	New Jersey Shakespeare Festival	Madison, NJ
1973	NY Shakespeare Festival/David Schweitzer	Lincoln Center, NY
1973	Marlowe Society/Richard Cottrell	Cambridge Arts; Nuffield, Southampton
1973	Merseyside Unity Theatre/Jerry Dawson	Liverpool Everyman
1973	Glasgow Citizens'/Philip Prowse; Mike Gwilym A	Citizens' Theatre
1976	Yale Repertory/Alvin Epstein; Jeremy Geidt P	New Haven, CT
1976	Old Globe Theatre Co./Edward Payson; John Doolin U, Sandy McCallom T, Pamela Payton-Wright C	San Diego, CA
1976	National Theatre/Elijah Moshinsky; Robert Eddison P, Denis Quilley H, Philip Locke U	Young Vic

Date(s)	Company / Director; Principal actors	Venue(s)
1976-7	RSC/John Barton, Barry Kyle; Mike Gwilym T, Tony Church U, Michael Pennington H, Robin Ellis A, David Waller P, Francesca Annis C	RST; Aldwych
1977	Round House Downstairs/Ronald Hayman	Roundhouse, Chalk Farm
1978	National Arts Center/John Wood; Edward Atienza U, Erik Donkin P	Ottawa, Ont.
1978	The Changing Space	New York
1979	Bristol Old Vic/Richard Cotrell	Edinburgh Festival; Theatre Royal
1980	New York Theatre Ensemble	East 4th Street, NY
1981	Oxford University Dramatic Society	Oxford Playhouse; Cambridge Arts
1981	RSC/Terry Hands; David Suchet A, Tony Church P, Joe Melia TH, Carol Royle C	Aldwych
1983	Manchester Umbrella	Bretton Hall College
1983	Folger Library Theatre Group/John Neville-Andrews	Washington, DC
1984	Oregon Shakespeare Festival/Richard E. T. White	Ashland, OR
1984	Utah Shakespeare Festival/Libby Appel	Cedar City, UT
1985-6	RSC/Howard Davies; Anton Lesser T, Juliet Stevenson C, Peter Jeffries U, Alan Rickman A, Alun Armstrong TH	RST; Barbican
1987	Stratford Festival Canada/David William	Avon Theatre, Stratford, Ont.
1987	National Youth Theatre/Matthew Francis	Christ Church, Spitalfields
1987	Chicago Shakespeare Rep/Barbara Gaines	Ruth Page Theatre, Chicago, IL

Date(s)	Company / Director; Principal actors	Venue(s)
1988	Berkley Shakespeare Festival/Michael Addison	Hinkle Park, Berkley, CA
1990	Yale Repertory/Andrei Belgrader; John Turturro TH, Ethyl Eichelberger P, Bill Camp T, Cindy Katz C	New Haven, CT
1990–1	RSC/Sam Mendes; Norman Rodway P, Simon Russell Beale TH, Ralph Fiennes T, Patterson Joseph T, David Troughton H	Swan; Barbican Pit
1992	Shakespeare Company/Bill Alexander	Washington, DC
1992	Shakespeare and Company/Dennis Krausnick	The Mount, Lennox, MA
1993	Contact-Tara Arts Co./Jatinder Verma	Manchester; Stockport
1995	London Theatre Base	Diorama, Camden Town
1995	New York Shakespeare Festival/Mark Wing-Davey	Delacorte, NY
1996	RSC/Ian Judge; Joseph Fiennes T, Philip Quast A, Clive Francis P	RST
1996	Georgia Shakespeare Festival/Tom Markus	Atlanta, GA
1997	Colorado Shakespeare Festival/Tom Markus	Boulder, CO
1997	Wisconsin Shakespeare Festival/Thomas Collins	Platteville, WI
1998	Open Air Theatre/Alan Strachan	Regent's Park
1998–9	RSC/Michael Boyd; Jayne Ashbourne C, Darrell D'Silva A, Alistair Petrie H, William Houston T	Pit; Tour (UK, US), Swan
1999	National Theatre/Trevor Nunn; David Bamber P, Sophie Okonedo C, Peter de Jersey T, Dhobe Oparei H	Olivier
1999	Alabama Shakespeare Festival/Kent Gash	Montgomery, AL
1999	Utah Shakespeare Festival/Paul Barnes	Cedar City, UT

Date(s)	Company / Director; Principal actors	Venue(s)
1999	Washington Shakespeare Co./Joe Banno	Arlington, VA
1999–2000	Oxford Stage Co./Dominic Dromgoole; Matt Lucas TH	Oxford Theatre; Tour; Old Vic
2000	Playhouse/Peter Bogdanov	Sydney, Australia
2001	Theatre for a New Audience/Peter Hall	American Place, NY
2001	Oregon Shakespeare Festival/Kenneth Albers	Ashland, OR
2003	Tobacco Factory/Andrew Hilton; Lisa Kay C, Ian Barritt P, Andrew Kaye U, Jamie Ballard TH	Bristol
2003	Stratford Festival Canada/Richard Monette; Bernard Hopkins P, Claire Jullien C, Peter Donaldson, U	Tom Patterson Theatre, Stratford, Ont.
2004	Publick Theatre/Steve Barkhimer	Boston, MA

Radio, television and recordings

1935	BBC Radio/Val Gielgud; Ion Swinley H, Angela Baddeley C
1955	BBC TV/George Rylands, Douglas Allen, Frank Pettingell P, Walter Hudd U, Richard Wordsworth TH
1966	BBC TV/Michael Croft, Bernard Hepton, Paul Hill
1981–2	BBC Shakespeare Plays Series/Jonathan Miller; Anton Lesser T, Charles Gray P, 'The Incredible Orlando' TH, Suzanne Burden C
1948	Marlowe Society audio recording/George Rylands
1961	Caedmon audio recording/Howard Sackler
1981	BBC/Audio Forum recording
1998	Arkangel/Clive Brill; Norman Rodway P, David Troughton TH, Julia Ford C, Ian Pepperell T

INTRODUCTION

Troilus and Cressida is described by scholars, critics and directors as Shakespeare's play for the twentieth century. They point out features of style and content that make it more accessible to modern audiences than to those a century or two ago. The cynical, reductive railing of Thersites about the war and its participants, the scheming of the Greeks, the debate of the Trojans about Helen and value, and the unflattering glimpses of some combatants undercut the long-accepted epic status of the Trojan War and reflect modern concerns. The aura of social malaise has its current parallels. Moreover, Cressida has gradually been viewed with increased understanding as she responds to her male-dominated wartime society. Although ambivalence remains about whether she is a victim of masculine power and politics, a helpless responder to her own shifting urges, or an opportunistic young female seeking her main chance first with romantic Troilus, then with pragmatic Diomedes, there is at least argument, rather than outright dismissal of her as the villain. Conversely, flaws have been discovered in Troilus, Ulysses, and even Hector, who used to be treated with unquestioning sympathy.

The play's comments on people and events from differing viewpoints speak to a modern lack of absolute values. Like the Greeks bogged down before Troy, we have endured the effects of stalemated war. In an anti-heroic age, we accept Thersites' cynical comments on subjects the nineteenth century regarded as high tragedy. During the Second World War, the escapism of a romanticized *Midsummer Night's Dream*, or the heroism of Olivier's *Henry V* resonated, but in that war's aftermath and even more during later conflicts, the debates and attitudes of *Troilus and Cressida* seemed truer. Furthermore, we now talk frankly of sex and disease, topics polite Victorians and Edwardians considered taboo. We accept uncut a broadly played Helen scene, Pandarus' jokes and closing speech, homoerotic elements and Thersites' scurrility. Finally, we are accustomed to plays that are not neatly comic or tragic, but dark satire without closure.

All these aspects are revealed in reading, but the play comes fully alive only in production, as visual images, actions and the spoken word coalesce to empha-sise new meanings. The stage history of *Troilus and Cressida* is also essentially twentieth century, but theatre never occurs in a vacuum, and productions have changed radically over a hundred years, reflecting evolving theatrical practice, new critical approaches and shifting tastes and expectations of audiences during a period of wars and cultural revolution. When first revived in England in 1907 and

1912, and in the United States in 1916, the play was treated as newly discovered Shakespeare. Except for conjectured early seventeenth-century performances and Dryden's 1679 revision, which held the stage fitfully for half a century, *Troilus and Cressida* had no documented stage history until 1890s German revivals. The first twentieth-century producers were consequently free of precedents established by eighteenth and nineteenth-century actor-managers regarding character delineation and set and costume design. Nor did audiences and critics have memories of prior productions to shape their expectations as they responded to the work of Fry, Poel and their early followers.

Traditions have developed, but the text remains the starting point for fresh approaches, especially since 1960, as professional performances rival Shakespeare's more famous works in frequency. Concomitantly, approaches to dramatic literature have changed. Scholars and critics have given directors and performers a wider theoretical and interpretive base and Continental influences have been felt. Occasional later productions or performances stand out as high points in various styles or have been particularly successful in coming to grips with the play's difficulties. Others highlight problems that arise if the treatment of this complex work is too idiosyncratic or not carefully controlled. Unlike much Shakespeare, *Troilus and Cressida* is not a star vehicle and I shall often concentrate more on the overall conception, rather than a single actor's work.

From Shakespeare to Dryden

There are no production records of the play from Shakespeare's lifetime. The Stationers' Register entry of 7 February 1602/3 says 'as yt is acted by my lord Chamberlen's Men'. When registered and finally printed in 1609, the play's title page claim of performance by 'The Kings Maiesties servants at the Globe' was replaced during the press run by 'Excellently expressing the beginning of their loues, with the conceited wooing of Pandarus, Prince of Licia'.[1] The Quarto 'b' includes the 'Epistle' to the reader proclaiming it 'a new play, neuer stal'd with the Stage, neuer clapper-clawd with the palmes of the vulgar, and yet passing full of the palme comicall'. Numerous scholars, including Peter Alexander, Gary Taylor and W. R. Elton, have proposed the Inns of Court as the first venue, while Robert Kimbrough has supported the public theatre.[2] The satiric tone and long reasoning speeches do seem appropriate to a sophisticated audience, but evidence is conjectural, and presumably the company would have followed

---

1 Documents are reprinted in Schoenbaum and details are given in *The New Variorum*, pp. 321ff. Alice Walker discusses the textual problems quite fully, and Anthony Dawson's edition provides analysis and specific details.
2 Peter Alexander and Nevill Coghill also had an ongoing debate about public vs. private venues in *TLS* during January and February 1967.

a special performance with presentations at the Globe, rather than staging the play just once.

One variant between Quarto and Folio texts may indicate revision during performance. Troilus' dismissal of Pandarus: 'Hence brother lackie; ignomie and shame / Pursue thy life, and liue aye with thy name' appeared at 5.3.112–13 in the Folio, as well as almost word for word at the Quarto position in 5.11.[3] This suggests that in some early performances Pandarus may have left in 5.3, and the action ended on Troilus' resounding couplet: 'Strike a free march to Troy, with comfort goe: / Hope of revenge shall hide our inward woe'.

Ambivalence about classification also began early. The Quarto title page mentions 'comicall' elements. The Folio printers planned to bind it after *Romeo and Juliet*, but inserted *Timon of Athens* there and moved *Troilus and Cressida* to an unpaginated place between the Histories and Tragedies, with an added Prologue filling the blank page before the title and Act 1. The Folio 'Catalogue' of plays omits it, and ownership problems presumably caused some of the printing anomalies with the Folio and the 1603 registration.[4]

Shortly after the Restoration of Charles II in 1660, two patent theatre companies were established in London, and divided the extant repertory. On 28 August 1668, *Troilus and Cressida* was assigned to Davenant's Duke's Company. There is no record of a production in the 1660s or 1670s, however, and by 1679 Dryden added his adaptation to the 'improved' versions that supplanted Shakespeare's originals.[5] Adaptation has been described as a form of criticism, and Dryden enumerated his reasons for reworking the original in his prefatory essay 'On the Grounds of Criticism in Tragedy'.[6] He felt Shakespeare lost interest in developing the most fascinating characters, Pandarus and Thersites, and let the play decline into a series of fights that resolved nothing. The major flaw in this potential tragedy was the failure to kill Cressida for her falsehood and give Troilus closure. Shakespeare hadn't dwelt on Cressida's inner responses to temptation and frailty, and Dryden wanted to create a clear, noble motive for her actions. The result is a comparatively uninteresting Cressida who met Harold Matthews' later dictum that a character in a play should not be as inconsistent as a real person.[7] Pandarus' speeches are often less clever and more vulgar, and Cressida's responses less witty and wanton. Before her night with Troilus, she insists on the promise of a priest to unite them later, though nobody mentions marriage in the original.

---

3 First Folio, facsimile prepared by Helge Kökeritz.

4 *The New Variorum*, pp. 321–34, summarizes many of the arguments and conclusions about the printing.

5 See Hazelton Spencer, *Shakespeare Improved*, for a survey of the revised plays.

6 Dryden, II, 201–9.   7 Harold Matthews, *TW*, October 1960, p. 38.

Dryden believed he strengthened the play by cutting some characters, including Helen and Cassandra, and expanding scenes between others. A 'due proportion was allowed for every motion', rather than Shakespeare's vignettes. Toward the end of 3.2, after Pandarus' musicians serenade the lovers, Hector tells Troilus of the trade in a long passage where tempers flare, giving a foretaste of their later quarrel. Dryden was proudest of their meeting that replaces many of the battle scenes. Like Shakespeare's Brutus and Cassius, Hector and Troilus make accusations, then reconcile before going to their deaths.

The most important plot changes come at the end. Cressida's father wants to return to Troy, and suggests she pretend to yield to Diomedes so he will relax his guard and they can escape. She is aghast at feigning infidelity, but obeys. Troilus is ready to take revenge on Diomedes, but she pleads for his life. Troilus, of course, misinterprets and curses her. Given no chance to explain, she commits suicide, another wronged tragic heroine forgiving her lover as she dies in his arms. Troilus is distraught and in the ensuing battle slays Diomedes. Achilles and his Myrmidons destroy the Trojan war party, including Troilus. Hector's death is merely reported, and Ulysses' closing speech voices political sentiments current during the succession crisis:

> Now peaceful Order has resum'd the reins,
> Old Time looks young, and Nature seems renew'd,
> Then, since from homebred Factions ruine springs
> Let Subjects learn Obedience to their Kings.[8]

Dryden made other changes to meet neoclassical aesthetic standards. His simpler, more ordered structure had fewer shifts between Troy and the Greek camp. A 'heap of rubbish' hid many excellent things, and rubbish removal included most of the long, highly imaged speeches in a play he considered 'so pester'd with Figurative Expressions, that it is as affected as obscure'. He shortened and focused those passages he retained, especially in his first scene, where the Greeks discuss the war.

Dryden's version was entered in the Stationers' Register on 14 April 1679, and soon staged by the Duke's Men. Leading actors originated roles and continued to play them, or moved on to older characters in subsequent revivals. Betterton spoke Dryden's Prologue as Shakespeare's ghost and acted Troilus. By 1709, he was Pandarus, then Thersites, while Wilks and Quin, respectively, played Troilus and Hector. In 1723, Quin took over Thersites, a role originated by Cave Underhill.[9] Dryden's adaptation was relatively seldom played, but the repertory

---

8 Dryden, *Troilus and Cressida*, p. 256.

9 Details of performances, mainly cast changes and box office receipts, can be found in *The London Stage*, Parts 1, 2 and 3. Lucyle Hook pointed out that Dryden's text refers to

system and stock sets allowed short revivals. On 2 June 1709, for example, it was staged 'At the Desire of several Ladies of Quality'. By the 1720s, songs, dances and afterpieces were added, following current theatrical fashion, though at odds with the tone of Dryden's tragedy. In December and January, 1733/4, after a decade's hiatus, the final documented performances occurred at Covent Garden. Quin still played Thersites, Hippisley repeated his Pandarus of 1721 and leading romantic actor Lacy Ryan was Troilus in a version embellished by the dancing of Malter and Mlle Salle.

I found no descriptions of the staging, but typical Restoration and early eighteenth-century theatrical practice would have dictated scenic backgrounds on quickly shifted wings and shutters, with action mainly on the large forestage. Properties were restricted to those called for in the action. Men's costumes would have classical military touches, while Cressida wore contemporary dress with plumed headgear to indicate her tragic status. A 1709 engraving, illustrating Shakespeare's play, shows Cressida in such a costume handing the sleeve to Diomedes in Greco-Roman armour, with short sword, breastplate, plumed helmet, knee length tunic, and a cloak. Similarly garbed, Ulysses and Troilus stand in curtained shadows representing an upstage right tent. Thersites, in a dark, nondescript costume and small, plain helmet, points from upstage left.[10]

The eighteenth and nineteenth centuries

Negative comments by Dryden, Johnson and others may have been partially responsible for reluctance to stage Shakespeare's original, though far less was said about it in prefaces, essays and lectures than about the more popular works. Johnson's remarks in his edition of Shakespeare are typical. Except for textual notes, he was brief: the play 'is more correctly written' than most, but lacks 'invention'. Presumably he approved beginning *in medias res*, covering a few days, and using locales in and near Troy. Apparently self-contradictory, he declared the comic characters 'superficial', yet 'copiously filled and powerfully impressed'. Most significant, he dismissed Cressida and Pandarus. Shakespeare's 'vicious characters sometimes disgust, but cannot corrupt, for both . . . are detested and contemned'.[11] In 1754 Charlotte Lennox, one of the first women to write about

specific actors. Thersites is described in terms of Underhill's nose, mournful eyes and great size, Mistress Betterton's heroic style was suited to the rewritten Andromache, and Mary Lee, Dryden's Cressida, generally declaimed on themes of love and honour ('Shakespeare Improv'd', p. 295).

10 Nicholas Rowe's edition; also reproduced in Tonson. The sleeve marks it as Shakespeare's, for Dryden substituted a ring, but the artist portrayed stage conventions of the time.

11 Johnson, VII, 547.

the play, commented in terms that were echoed well into the twentieth century: 'Troilus is left alive, and *Cressida*, too scandalous a Character to draw our Pity, does not satisfy that Detestation her crimes raise in us by her Death, but escaping Punishment, leaves the play without a Moral, and absolutely deficient in poetical Justice.'[12]

Coleridge admitted puzzlement. He was certain of Cressida as a 'portrait of vehement passion'. Her 'sudden and shameless inconstancy' sinks her into 'infamy below retrieval', while Troilus' 'moral energy snatches him aloof from all neighborhood with her dishonor . . . [and] rushes with him into other and nobler duties'. He perceived Thersites' 'intellectual power deserted by all grace', and was G. Wilson Knight's precursor in citing the 'purer morals' of the Trojans as opposed to the policy-oriented Greeks.[13] William Hazlitt, though no fan of the play, made some of the most cogent early remarks. He saw in its looseness an approximation of the way things happen, noting the 'barbarity and heroism' of Hector's death and the blend of the 'stately and impassioned' with the 'ludicrous and ironical'. He recognized the originality in Pandarus and Cressida, and characterized her as thoughtless and 'giddy' rather than villainous.[14] During the nineteenth century, a number of German scholars also discussed the play as part of their methodical study of Shakespeare. Beyond textual matters, however, their predominant focus was on the satire and irony, especially as it was aimed at the Greeks.[15]

While essayists and lecturers puzzled over *Troilus and Cressida*, apparently no one had a chance to judge it on stage. The sale of a Third Folio copy among plays performed at Dublin's Smock Alley Theatre may indicate a performance in the 1660s.[16] John Philip Kemble began a promptbook, undated and based on a cheap 1791 edition, but never produced it.[17] His pencilled partial cast, listing no women, suggests a date of 1800,[18] and his preparations tell us much about aesthetic taste and theatrical practicality of the period.

12 'The Fable', pp. 92–3. Lennox also dismissed the plot as 'only a Succession of Incidents'.

13 *Shakespearean Criticism*, I, 98–100.   14 Hazlitt, IV, 221–5.

15 Schlegel, Goethe, Heine and Ulrici are representative. *The New Variorum* reprints substantial extracts.

16 James McManaway found the listing in a sale catalogue of 1827 as part of a group of Third Folio copies from the Theatre, but did not examine it (pp. 64–5).

17 Newlin, 'The Darkened Stage', p. 191. Dr Newlin examines Kemble's proposed changes and their relationship to Francis Gentleman's suggestions for staging the play in Bell's 1776 edition.

18 The list included his brother Charles as Troilus, John Hayman Packer as Priam, Richard Wroughton as Hector, and John Bannister, Jr as Thersites. All were in the Drury Lane Company in 1800, and the Kembles left for Covent Garden in 1803. See Highfill, who notes Packer's retirement before the Kembles returned to Drury Lane.

Kemble repeated many of Dryden's structural changes, probably to avoid shifting Drury Lane's increasingly elaborate scenery. His Greek council opening emphasized the military story. There was no shortage of actresses, but he cut Helen, although Shakespeare's portrayal of the mythic beauty, with her banter and adaptation to life with Paris, creates interesting parallels to Cressida. Cressida's role was diminished, making her less able to match Pandarus' repartee. Kemble cast himself as Ulysses, yet shortened his long speeches, especially in the council scene. Like Dryden, he excised many similes and highly imaged lines, focusing on facts to speed the action, a practice Poel and many others followed in the twentieth century. In 1800, sentimental novels were popular, their long-suffering heroines so different from Cressida and Helen. People wanted absolutes, soon embodied in the heroes and villains of melodrama. *Troilus and Cressida* satisfied neither of these tastes. Although poorer plays were popular, it was apparently not time to revive Shakespeare's original.[19]

Reading was another matter. The play was available in cheap printings such as Dick's, and in good collected editions. Occasional 'acting' editions included extra stage directions and a frontispiece purporting to be a scene in production or a portrayal of a character. The Folger has a number of 'theatrical' engravings, including Robert Dighton's depiction of 'Mr. Brereton in the character of Troilus' for Bell's 1776 edition and Edward Francis Burney's 'Mrs Cuyler in Cressida', printed by Bell in 1785.[20] Ironically, Cressida, so forcefully criticized, was a favourite of artists.

Although George Bernard Shaw insisted that the play was stageable (in a paper delivered to the New Shakespeare Society in 1884), it was the Germans, perhaps spurred Schliemann's Troy excavations, that began modern revivals with a heavily cut translation in Munich in 1898, and others in Berlin in 1899 and 1904.[21] A Viennese 1902 staging had leading actors in a much-revised text that ennobled Ulysses and puzzled reviewers.[22] These productions and one in Hungary may have influenced Charles Fry to present the play in London in 1907, determined that all of Shakespeare's plays could boast a modern English production.

---

19 The Folger Library owns R. J.'s manuscript from this era that combines Shakespeare and Dryden in another effort to 'improve' the play, but there is no indication that it was ever produced.

20 Most numerous among the prints at the Folger are the lovers, sometimes with Pandarus, sometimes with the sleeve; Cressida giving a glove or sleeve to Diomedes; Troilus tearing her letter; and portrayals of Cassandra, Andromache and Hector, alone or with others. Angelica Kauffman painted Cressida and Diomedes.

21 *The New Variorum* comments rather fully on these pioneering Continental productions.

22 W. von Sachs, *Commercial Advertiser*, 14 February 1902.

Pioneering productions

Early revivals in Britain and the United States were single performances or very brief runs, acted by amateurs and semi-professionals, and widely reviewed as curiosities. Not dogged by nineteenth-century scenic conventions, the play could be presented without long breaks to shift 'archaeologically correct' representations of Troy or the Greek camp. Two styles dominated. There were Renaissance costumes before an approximation of an Elizabethan tiring house, with a few properties suggesting locales, (Poel, 1912; The Shakespeare Memorial Theatre, 1936), or 'classical' costumes in front of draperies or columns and screens, with properties resembling Greek artifacts (Yale University, 1916; The Marlowe Society, 1922). Despite speedy staging, the early productions seem to have lacked the coherence and vigour of some later revivals, and critics often declared the play better read than seen.[23]

A new daring was transforming the British theatre by 1907, replacing the moralizing of the melodramas and the neatness of the well-made plays. Shaw and Galsworthy had tackled unpleasant subjects, and Ibsen aroused conservative anger by undercutting society's sacred institutions. Charles Fry imbedded a performance of *Troilus and Cressida* in a week of familiar works at the Queen's Theatre.[24] The play's satiric treatment of an epic event, and its heroine's conduct didn't fit preconceived notions of 'divine Shakespeare', and the audience was shocked, puzzled and often bored. Reviewers found the action confusing and the long discussions tedious. The predominately amateur cast aimed at 'elocutionary adequacy' rather than 'histrionic interpretation'. E. A. Baughan stayed away, feeling that Fry lacked adequate resources to do the work justice, although he thought Thersites 'quite modern'. Another critic agreed with Henry Irving that the work should be shortened and 'fumigated' despite Fry's extensive cuts, including Pandarus' last speech.[25] Walkley commented 'Pandarus and Thersites cannot possibly be played in full in the present era', adding that the play is better read 'as a corrective for romanticism'.[26]

The production was visually simple, with green velvet curtains rather than illusionistic scenery. Classical helmets, breastplates and swords created atmosphere. This departure from pictorial staging may have increased audience confusion, although the programme listed locations, with a quick curtain fall between each

---

23 Strangely, Daniel Seltzer was still concurring in 1963: 'Probably no modern production of this play can make it a satisfactory theatrical experience.'

24 The other six plays were *The Comedy of Errors, The Winter's Tale, As You Like It, The Merchant of Venice, Henry VIII* and *Much Ado About Nothing*.

25 E. A. Baughan, *News*, 3 June 1907; 'Caradus', *Referee*, 2 June 1907.

26 'Great Queen St. Theatre', 22 June 1907. James O'Donnell Bennett also mentioned a current 'higher standard of propriety than the Elizabethans observed'.

of Fry's twelve scenes. He began with the Greek council and Hector's challenge, then conflated Troy scenes 1.1, 1.2 and 2.2. The rearrangement highlighted and provided exposition about the war, focused attention on the Greeks, and subordinated the love story and Cressida. She was barely established before Helen, better known to the audience, became the topic. Scenes 2.1 and 3 were run together, then Shakespeare's order was followed, minus 4.1 and 3, until Act 5. Though Helen (Mrs E. J. Way) was 'comely and seductive', her scene was bowdlerized. Focus after the interval was on the lovers' parting in 4.2 and 4, and the Hector/Ajax combat, arranged by Mortlake Mann. The last act began with Troilus watching Cressida and Diomedes, followed by Andromache and Cassandra's pleas, and gave only a hint of the final battle scenes. Pandarus departed early and there were no Myrmidons. Hector's death was reported by Troilus and given tragic definition by a final mourning tableau occasionally repeated by later directors. Nineteenth-century actor-managers generally cut and rearranged Shakespeare's texts, and Fry followed their example.

The Telegraph's reviewer wondered 'what was Shakespeare aiming at?' though he praised some individual performances, including Fry's 'character drawing' as Thersites. He was unimpressed by Lewis Casson and Olive Kennett in the title roles and felt people were laughed at in an 'aborted and ill-natured' play. Edwardian propriety pervades the review. Hector argued too practically for Helen's return, Ulysses 'manipulated the weaknesses of others', Achilles and Ajax were not generous and Thersites, 'mean in body and mind', 'derides his betters'. The play lacked the gallantry and romantic feeling people expected of Greek heroes and proper respect for social position, and exhibited un-Shakespearean bitterness and wantonness.[27]

Changing taste was important. A French production was 'received and enjoyed' in 1912 and 1913, when, Adolphe Bressen declared, it would have been rejected in 1900. Bressen appreciated the mix of 'lyricism, buffoonery, triviality, heroism and irony', recognized Pandarus as 'a gin-soaked Londoner', and likened Thersites to a 'splenetic Parisian cabbie'.[28] Although social change on the eve of the First World War made the English slightly more receptive to the second English revival, also in 1912 and 1913, reviewers still struggled with the play.

William Poel had presented Shakespeare in a non-illusionistic 'Elizabethan' fashion since the 1880s, with a tiring house façade, simulated thrust stage and English Renaissance costumes. His speedy productions earned him a reputation when Harley Granville-Barker and Gordon Craig were also experimenting

27 'Troilus and Cressida. A Strange Experiment', *DT*, 3 June 1907.
28 Originally in *Tempe*, reprinted in *DT*, 22 March 1912. *The New Variorum* describes many of the continental productions before 1950 and The Birmingham Shakespeare Library has photographs of more recent revivals.

with simplified staging for a wide range of plays. Poel lacked money to build an equivalent of today's Southbank Globe, and adapted to the available hall. Each production ran a few days with amateur and semi-professional actors. Poel's fascination with the play began when he was warned against reading it and *Measure for Measure* because they were 'not proper' for schoolboys.[29] Shaw encouraged him and, though he usually presented more popular works with his English Stage Society, he chose *Troilus and Cressida* as his final offering.

Poel's methods were not so consistently 'Elizabethan' as later commentators assumed. Archer said one revival was 'staged after the manner of the sixteenth century and acted after the manner of the nineteenth-century amateur'.[30] The *Troilus and Cressida* promptbooks reveal Edwardian and late Victorian touches, including atmospheric electric lighting, rather than an approximation of the daylight or candlelight of a Globe or Blackfriars production.[31] S. R. Littlewood described 'all sorts of lighting experiments against an enormous spread of black and purple draperies; now Rembrandtesque effects of warm glow, now cold streaks of limelight'. A small recessed area at the rear of the stage was lit from the opposite prompt (right) side.

At the King's Hall, three steps led from the main platform to the constructed forestage, providing downstage entrances as well as those from the tiring house.[32] The programme records Poel's solution to the identification problem besetting later 'Elizabethan' productions: his 'heavy bourgeois' Greeks dressed as Elizabethan soldiers; the more romantic, 'flippant, graceful' Trojans wore flamboyant masque costumes. The result must have been a strange mix of the realistic and highly artificial. Poel also indulged in the tableaux so popular on proscenium stages. He hung dark curtains between the stage pillars and opened or closed them on visually impressive character groupings, eliminating the need for Elizabethan entrance and exit processions. Littlewood found 'the whole thing designed in the modernest of modern ways, to work upon the nerves instead of upon the free imagination'.

Poel followed the 1889 Cassell Edition, with its final tableau of Troilus mourning Hector's corpse, and made further excisions after 5.2, but retained Hector's death. He once said his method was to 'rehearse the whole play as it was originally written, and only when the author's point of view was realized to make such omissions and revisions as are absolutely essential', generally cutting lines

29 Speaight, *William Poel*, p. 192.   30 Ibid., p. 102.

31 The two copies of Poel's promptbook in the Enthoven Collection are very similar, but each has a few unique stage directions and light cues.

32 Littleton, in *The Daily Chronicle*, recalled details of Poel's production when writing of the Yale revival, 25 June 1916.

rather than whole scenes.[33] For speed and clarity he cut much of the poetry, as well as pruning the Achilles/Ulysses discussion he felt Shakespeare had inserted merely for its current political reverberations. Contrasts were lost, like Diomedes and Paris' frank scene (4.3) that interrupts Cressida's response to her exchange. *Troilus and Cressida* is Shakespeare's third longest play, and is almost always cut, but removing a third of the lines seems extreme.[34]

The casting also raises questions. Herbert Ranson recalled that Poel didn't have enough 'light, graceful, handsome men' for the Trojans and used women, who 'were too self-conscious'.[35] Madge Whitman (Aeneas) and May Carey (Paris) weren't mentioned in reviews, nor were minor roles, including Alexander. There were apparently none of the issues cross-gender casting raises today. But one choice – Elspeth Keith as Thersites – seemed perverse and got attention. Pole feared a man would play him too vigourously, but critics who knew the play said Keith lacked the necessary venom, becoming 'a ludicrous cross between Touchstone and Puck'. Unfortunately, reviews omit details. How did Ajax handle the beatings? How did the audience react to Thersites' language? Did they suspend disbelief, taking this figure in motley, with clay pipe and Scots accent, as a man? Hermione Gingold's Cassandra and Poel's Pandarus also received scant attention.

Some felt Poel allowed individual actors too much leeway. Earlier, he had written that with no precedent, actors must develop their own interpretations.[36] He considered the early scenes pure satire and played Pandarus as a slightly cockney comic. Edith Evans, still an amateur, aroused controversy with her Cressida. George Moore praised her 'winsomeness of the pure animal redeemed from thought, ideas, prejudices and conventions', and Bridges-Adams called her 'classic'.[37] Others dismissed her as a Restoration coquette, with singsong voice and mincing walk, who missed the youth, innocence and internal conflict of Cressida. Littleton described her as 'a rusee spinster of about 30' with the 'languid voice familiar in modern flats and dressing rooms'. Her impatient donning of a hat in 4.4 was merely seen as action, with no perception that here was a 'new woman', disappointed with Troilus' repeated exhortations and failure to defend her. Poel approved her interpretation because Chaucer's Cressida had been a widow. He wrote Evans: 'critics don't read the play and only look

---

33 Poel, p. 9; Lundstrom, p. 163.
34 Speaight, *William Poel*, p. 197, notes controversy over the treatment of the text.
35 Herbert Ranson, *NYHT*, 29 May 1932. He played Diomedes at Stratford-upon-Avon with Poel in 1913.
36 Poel, p. 70.
37 Forbes, p. 22. Evans wrote to Poel, thanking him for the opportunity and saying that after the exciting experience, she feared she would have to give up making hats (p. 199).

for something unreal'. Shaw was a stout supporter, having earlier proclaimed Cressida 'Shakespeare's first real woman'. He called this Shakespeare's one attempt 'to hold a mirror up to nature'.[38] Despite lukewarm critical response, the production went to Stratford in the summer of 1913 with essentially the same cast, so Stratford could claim a revival.

Two university presentations

University drama groups, spurred by interest rather than obligation to complete the canon, staged two important early productions. Although classically costumed and not consciously politicized, both gained from the First World War social upheaval. The Yale University Shakespeare Association, marking the tercentenary of Shakespeare's death, staged the first recorded American production during graduation week, 1916. In 1922, Cambridge's Marlowe Society first used an all-male cast, then reworked the production, with women in the female roles, for a brief London run.

Yale's all-male version attracted numerous critics, including Tucker Brooke, who praised the speedy treatment of this 'play of disillusionment'. He remarked on the 'fullness of costume' and 'nakedness . . . of language' in Elizabethan times, compared to Yale's 'very considerable under-clothing' and the 'over-modest veil [cast] over the frank mental vulgarity of Pandarus'.[39] Newspapers in Boston and New York published stiffly posed photographs. H. T. Parker noted the lack of 'tradition to check the imagination of the producers and actors, or to choke the answering fancy of the spectators'.[40] Director E. M. Woolley suggested the 'deleterious effect of the siege' by having Helen no longer 'the adorable winner of the famous beauty contest . . . but . . . a middle-aged woman of none too graceful form', though Parker found her 'of matured comeliness'.[41] Achilles and Hector were athletic, while Ajax was clumsier and oafish. Thersites was 'sharp and sour' with a 'churlish cringe' and Patroclus was 'obsequious and simpering'. Woolley considered irony the central force, and felt even Hector's death was intended to mock heroism.[42] Key speeches came across well and seriously, including Achilles and Ulysses' exchange on time and reputation.

38 Shaw, p. 238.
39 *Yale News*, 20 June 1916. Brooke's is one of the fullest, most understanding of early reviews, and considers the context of the play as well as the production.
40 'Strange New Shakespeare on Our Stage', *BET*, 19 June 1916.
41 'Yale Unearths a Play', *BET*, 16 June 1916. The Yale University Library has a complete collection of pictures from various publications as well as programs. J. S. P. Tatlock was one of the first to recognize Ajax as 'a capital acting part'.
42 Programme note.

Parker carefully described Grace Clark's colourful costumes that have had counterparts in later productions:

> Short tunics that ended at the hips and left arms . . . shoulders as well as legs bare, metal-like helmets bearing broad-arched crests, . . . occasional mantles for the elder kings and high-placed chieftains; spears, very long and willowy lances or short blunt swords, greaves and round shields, painted with many sorts of rude insignia, headbands, armlets and soft, blue tunic for the luxury-loving Paris, and a like suggestion of effeminacy in the garments of Patroclus.

Hector, Agamemnon, Nestor, Ulysses and Achilles wore six-inch bronze-painted wooden buskins. The stage resounded as they walked,[43] an artificial effect never repeated in later productions, and at variance with the indirect, naturalistic lighting.

Rain drove the company into the Hyperion Theatre, where they effectively used the 'simplest ways of the newer stagecraft'. Gordon Craig-inspired steps and 'pillar-like screens' were rapidly augmented with hangings suggesting various locales. Achilles' tent was 'a deeply colored cloth, decked . . . with a bold archaic ornament'. Lighting on a plain cloth backdrop indicated times of day and the shadows of Calchas' tent. Sixty student extras provided Greek and Trojan attendants: Hector's bowmen, Paris and Helen's fan-bearers. Guards and soldiers gave the council scenes a military air, while servants joined the civilian groups. A battle scene photograph shows at least thirty warriors on each side.

Dramatic criticism of the period often dwelt on the play's faults, and cutting was readily accepted. Parker approved when Woolley shortened debates that might suit an 'old ranting actor', but were not appropriate to 1916. The sanitized dialogue was suitable for the Yale audience, and one in Naugatuck, Connecticut, with 'ears too polite – or too miscellaneous – to listen in public to some of the coarser Billingsgate of Thersites or the whimsical skulduddery of Pandarus'. Like Poel's work, this moderately successful revival didn't inspire others. It was sixteen years before another American attempt.

Casting changes made the Marlowe Society's energetic, straightforward production notable. Frank Birch used all men before his predominately male, white, upper-class, well-educated Cambridge audience.[44] In response to critics and in anticipation of a broader London audience's reaction, he brought in actresses and made other changes before the transfer to the Everyman. Yale's production had gained resonance from the stalemated war in Europe. The Cambridge revival reverberated more strongly because of veterans in the cast and audience. The 'No Man's Land between the Greek Camp and Troy' helped create war's atmosphere

43 H. T. Parker.   44 Bowen, p. 40.

and a sense of 'many-sided truth'. Birch found reality in Shakespeare's picture of the Trojans 'fighting for no better an ideal than the retention of Helen . . . and the quarrelsome, policy-ridden Greeks, rotten and rotting after seven years in the trenches'.[45]

Contradicting the theory that modern dress heightens audience involvement, this classically garbed revival was repeatedly linked to the First World War by critics and playgoers. The *Manchester Guardian* declared that Troilus' loss of his brother Hector echoed what many English families had experienced.[46] Cressida was forgiven as 'a gracious lady made loose by the abandonment of war'. The concept of a prolonged conflict destroying standards and demoralizing a populace suffused a number of reviews. St John Ervine wrote: 'I doubt whether there is a young man in these islands to whom it is not a clear and simple play . . . A realistic picture of war-weariness'. He cited modern parallels among 'fat-headed cavalry generals enviously conspiring against each other', noted 'moral disintegration and social sourness', and commented that Thersites' 'impotency and cowardice render his sound judgments and clear sights useless to others and tortuous to himself'.[47]

But there was also puzzlement with this 'very post-war', 'very un-Shakespearean' work. The *Times*' reviewer, echoing then current biographical criticism, longed to know what in Shakespeare's life had occasioned such a play. The overhearing scene (5.2) 'is writing in blood, the expression of an agony experienced'. Birch had not guided his actors to sensitive realizations of their roles, and in Cambridge Helen and Cressida were played mainly for laughter. Cressida was well-meaning but unable to resist compliments, and became 'a mockery in her faithlessness'. The male parts were better conceived, but also drawn in broad strokes: conceited Ajax blustered and Nestor was an 'old bore'. Like many later student productions, this had speed and enthusiasm instead of depth or power. The carefully choreographed Myrmidon attack was effective, however, for Birch had told them to advance like vampires.[48] Unfortunately, the production was hampered by the small stage at the ADC Theatre. Gestures and movements were constricted and seemed 'irresolute'.[49] When teenaged John Gielgud saw it in London, there was still the problem of a 'production . . . irritatingly arranged for a bigger stage than the Everyman'.[50]

---

45 Marlowe Society production, Festival Theatre, Cambridge, programme notes, May 1932. Birch recalled the atmosphere for the 1922 production at length, in comparison to 1932.
46 Reprinted in *Boston Transcript*, March 1922.
47 St John Ervine, 'At the Play', *Obs*, 12 March 1922.
48 Quoted in Sprague, p. 82.   49 *LT*, 6 March 1922, p. 10.
50 Note on a programme in the Mander and Mitchenson collection.

Figure 1. Death of Hector in Frank Birch's Marlowe Society production, Everyman Theatre, 1922.

The sold-out week in London brought deepened interpretations. Actresses saved 'the Society from the errors of burlesque into which they were driven' in Cambridge. Still, Enid Clinton-Baddeley played Cressida as a spoiled child, and 'could not achieve . . . [the] dignity which is necessary to . . . the farewell to Troilus', which reviewers envisioned as a tragic scene. The men had settled into their parts and showed more variety and steadiness. Ulysses handled his rhetorical speeches with sureness, but only 'nominally addressed [them] to his companions on the stage'. The conversation with Achilles on time and fame in 3.3 was directed to the audience.[51] This theatricalized handling must have contrasted sharply with some of the more naturalistic characterizations long before theories were advanced on the way the words remind audiences that they are seeing a play.

Birch was more faithful to the text than some early directors, making cuts, but keeping Shakespeare's scene order. Alec Penrose's costumes immediately confirmed the period of the action, with conventional round shields, short tunics, capes, short swords and crested helmets.[52] Perhaps to remind his audience that this was an English Renaissance reworking of the story, Birch chose music by Byrd, Farnaby and their contemporaries as a prelude and to accompany 3.1, 3.3 and changes of locale.[53]

51 *LT*, 21 June 1922, p. 14.
52 Photographs in the Enthoven Collection show details of the military costumes.
53 Programme notes for the Everyman run.

Professional productions finally begin

In November 1923, the Old Vic staged the first fully professional English language revival, completing a nine-year plan to produce the First Folio plays plus *Pericles* with full texts and original scene order. Despite chronic financial difficulties, Lilian Baylis' company had resources unavailable to Poel or Fry. Recognized Shakespearean director Robert Atkins had a repertory cast. Ion Swinley, a promising English classical actor, and Poel's Troilus at Stratford, repeated that role, while D. Hay Petrie was Thersites. Princess Mary lent glitter by attending the celebration of the First Folio tricentenary, and a ninth performance was added because of popular interest. Although the promptbook and most materials were destroyed during the Second World War bombing, reviews and programmes survived. The programme credits sets and costumes to Hubert Hine, but many of the Elizabethan costumes probably came from stock. Rather than period music, however, the orchestra played Mendelssohn's 'Ruy Blas' as an overture, and later Nowques' 'Quo Vades'.

Despite 1920s social freedoms, many viewers remained uncomfortable. Hubert Griffith's preview article complained, 'The days are gone . . . when Shakespeare could be quoted as teaching any moral principle.' He found the arguments unconvincing, the characters extreme, the language not particularly beautiful.[54] Moral outrage peppered H. Chance Newton's comments. He asked why The Vic poured unexpurgated Shakespeare on young people, insisting that many passages were not for mixed audiences and could be omitted without damaging the play.[55] One *Times* reviewer was relieved to see the 'last of the . . . deeds of loyalty', lamenting the dullness and hoping in future to see Shakespeare done for pleasure rather than duty. He disliked the mix of 'splendor and triviality' and uncut debates, and deemed the final battle scenes a disaster. On the other hand, he felt Swinley and Florence Saunders succeeded as the lovers. She was intensely personal and passionate, if not musical, and he gave the part life and deep feeling. For this reviewer, however, Petrie's bitter conception of Thersites was too small and minutely detailed. He was not the essential chorus of the play.[56]

James Agate, a leading theatre critic, missed any First World War reverberations and felt there was little in the play to interest a modern audience. The full text had too much tedious talk, like an 'antique Senate House'. Only the makeup fascinated him. Revner Barton's Ulysses looked like Shakespeare, Ernest Mead's Agamemnon resembled Athos, and Wilfred Walter's Achilles recalled Lawrence's portrait of John Philip Kemble. Agate felt Cressida had an impossible part, while Troilus was 'giddy with expectation'. The difficulty of accurately sensing a

---

54 Hubert Griffith, 'At the Play: Out of School', 4 November 1923.
55 H. Chance Newton, 'The Old Vic Breaks all Records', 11 November 1923.
56 'Shakespeare at the Old Vic "Troilus and Cressida"', *LT*, 6 November 1923, p. 12.

performance from reviews becomes obvious as one compares *The Times'* and Agate's comments. For Agate, Petrie's 'misshapen dwarf ' Thersites dominated the stage, even when lurking in the shadows.[57]

Other reviewers, with preconceived notions of what Shakespeare should be, used phrases like 'genius hammering at the gates of Bedlam', ignored the play's many corresponding characters and actions, and lamented the lack of a neat resolution and balance between diverse elements. Thersites' savageness was that of 'a cur being kicked to death', and seemed beyond the pale. Pandarus (Neil Curtis) 'lurked' to make the love story obscene. One perceptive reviewer, however, deemed this The Vic's best production, grasping Shakespeare's stark, destructive realism and mocking of romantic virtues. Unlike most commentators during the first third of the century, he did not test the play against some 'standard', but accepted it as a 'comedy of disillusion'. He appreciated Cressida's 'mix of wantonness and protestations of fidelity', Thersites' 'blend of wickedness and laughter', and Pandarus' 'evil glee'.[58]

The first professional American production came almost a decade later, at Moss's Broadway Theatre in 1932. Otis Skinner's Thersites led The Players Theatre Company benefit week that Stark Young branded 'a handsome gesture'.[59] It showcased a number of actors, and Howard Lindsay's casting included Charles Coburn as Ajax and Blanche Yurka as Helen. A photograph shows Ajax with goatee, ruff and Renaissance helmet, snarling at a fleshy, bearded and moustached Thersites. Skinner, suggesting fool's motley with his striped costume, tights and feathered hat, looks unusually dashing despite a hunch. Sketches portray Cressida in a modest, square-necked dress with stand-up collar, beads decorating her hair and bodice. Eugene Powers' Pandarus was clean-shaven and like the other Trojans, looked Hispanic in a dark top with a white collar and a close-fitting cap with a small feather.[60] His acting, by contrast, was 'a marvel of oily enthusiasm'. Wilella Waldorf commented that the sixteenth-century costumes were easier to move in than classic drapery and Homeric armour, and preferable to modern dress, though Richard Skinner criticized them for hiding the satire.[61] Except for modern footwear, Charles B. Falls coordinated costumes and scenery well. The dark-garbed Trojans were easily distinguished from the Greeks in reds touched

---

57 Agate, 'The Dramatic World', *Sun*, 11 November 1923.
58 H. G., 'Genius Hammering at the Gates of Bedlam', and *LT*, 7 November 1923. Unfortunately, many of the reviews in the Harvard Theatre Collection and the New York Public Library lack dates and/or attributions.
59 'Have at thee, Hector', *The New Republic*, 22 June 1932, pp. 157–8.
60 *NYEP*, 10 June 1932.
61 Richard Dana Skinner, 'The Play: "Troilus and Cressida"', *The Commonweal*, 29 June 1932, pp. 246–7.

with yellow, a reversal of modern costuming where Greeks wear darker colours to emphasize their underlying pragmatism in contrast to Trojan romanticism.

Critics gave capsule descriptions of the characters, implying caricature rather than complex conceptions. Coburn indulged in 'legitimate exaggeration'. Skinner used good nature and humour to leaven his railing.[62] Cressida was played from Troilus' point of view. Edith Barrett made her 'a model of female treachery', blatantly encouraging Diomedes. The Players had numerous extras available: three dozen Trojan and twenty-two Greek soldiers, and a dozen 'court ladies and Trojan woman'. Two singers performed songs arranged by Robert Armbruster (well known to radio audiences) and offstage trumpeters provided fanfare. The production was lauded for visual effectiveness, with its suggestion of an Elizabethan setting where tapestry-like painted draperies were quickly changed for different locales.[63] Most of the speaking took place on the forestage, and was often orated rather than delivered naturalistically. Soldiers marched and fought on an elevated rear area. A 'dovetailing' technique linked the military figures to the lovers, one group leaving its space as the next came on in theirs.[64]

Unlike Atkins, Henry Herbert felt free to 'adapt' the text, omitting much bawdry, but retaining scenes that satirized war and the frailty of women. Some changes, including the addition of Hecuba to illustrate Alexander's comment in 1.2, have been retained in occasional later productions. Herbert wrote *The Sun* that he brought her back to lean, 'grief-stricken, over dead Hector' and 'convey by eloquent silence the impression of speech' as an effective end to the play. He grouped the episodes by locale, and eight scenes replaced the twenty-five modern texts suggest. The first act moved from Troy to the Greek camp. The second sandwiched a Greek camp scene between two in Pandarus' garden. The third opened in the Greek camp (4.5–5.2), moved to Priam's palace, then finished on a generalized 'Plains' locale for the retained parts of 5.4–11. Herbert may have encouraged Skinner to temper the bitterness of Thersites, and simplified Barrett's Cressida so the benefit performance audiences would have a pleasant theatrical evening at a play still considered strange 'new' Shakespeare.

By this time more critics and professional scholars were engaging with *Troilus and Cressida*. The Players' production occasioned numerous articles in anticipation and response. Some expressed old opinions, declaring it 'without plot, poetic justice, catastrophe or denouement' and saying satire dimmed everything but the poetry.[65] John Erskine joined Shaw and a few reviewers in emphasizing its modernity and portrayal of universal attitudes. They praised Shakespeare for

62 Percy Hammond, 8 June 1932.
63 Stephen Rathburn, 'Players Club Presents . . .', *NYS*, 7 June 1932.
64 Arthur Ruhl, 'Second Nights'.   65 Percy Hammond, *NYHT*, 6 June 1932.

shrinking mythic people to ordinary size and eschewing the grandeur of classical tragic treatments of the stories.[66] Arthur Ruhl deemed rhetoric and disillusion the uniting forces, with sensuality replacing higher love and military glory transformed into bunk. Joseph Wood Krutch, pondering biographical possibilities, joined those conservatives who explained that the play was neglected because the tone was not 'Shakespearean'. For him, only Troilus and Hector had integrity, and a worthy beginning went wrong when Cressida became more base than a coquette, and Hector ended up 'pig-stuck'.[67] Brooks Atkinson was sure he would never see another production and catalogued the play's faults. Paramount among them was the failure to develop the potential of the battle/love dualism, which he called 'badly proportioned and carelessly related'.[68] His review echoed his preview: too much talk, too little action, and only wit to create a modern sense of unity. Given the controversiality, The Players showed courage in choosing this for a benefit run.

Four years later the semi-professional Pasadena Playhouse introduced the play to America's West Coast in a season that included the Roman plays, *Timon of Athens*, *Cymbeline* and *Pericles* in a series of five-day runs. Only a dedicated repertory theatre dared mount such a season, but Pasadena, Stratford and The Old Vic were setting a pattern for later companies that drew specialized audiences and used subscriptions and sponsorship to underwrite productions unfeasible on Broadway or London's West End. The Pasadena revival, like many others, was faulted for inconsistency of character conception, but may have been pointing ahead to modern eclectic productions. Patricia Walsh, as Cressida, was called 'contemporary' in her movements and appearance, with her head and shoulders swathed in a scarf, while Henry Brandon played Troilus as the formal, classic warrior in his tunic and helmet.[69]

During the 1930s scholars were providing more keys to the play, although only occasionally did revivals seem influenced by these closer studies. E. K. Chambers was ahead of many in considering Cressida a victim of circumstances. She 'is not a psychological monstrosity like her uncle . . . It is in her humanity that the bitterness of it lies. She was not made of the stuff of heroines, but her vows and protestations were real enough when they were uttered.'[70] Caroline Spurgeon catalogued image patterns and found the play filled with references to food, spoilage and disease, underpinning later interpretations that present Helen and Cressida as morsels for men in a decaying society. In the past four decades, especially, some productions have made this visual, with baking in 1.1,

66 Erskine, 'When Shakespeare Went Modern and Gods Talked Like Men'.
67 Krutch, *The Nation*, 29 June 1932, p. 734.
68 Brooks Atkinson, 'Introducing a Play' *NYT*, 5 June 1932, x, 1.
69 The company's souvenir book for the season.   70 Chambers, pp. 193–4.

Helen brought in on a platter-like litter, and Thersites providing food for Achilles and Ajax. By 1968, Thersites often became covered in scabs, and Pandarus now is almost always ravaged by disease. Recently other scholars, including Tom McAlindon, have continued to investigate the language and the speech patterns Shakespeare gives different characters. Many of these linguistic subtleties are lost in the speed of production, and actors tend to employ a modern class or regional accent to help delineate character, though the details help directors and actors conceive roles and scenes.

G. Wilson Knight concentrated on dualism, contrasting Troy's emphasis on human beauty and worth with the Greek camp's stupid bestiality and 'barren intellect'. During the last half century, a number of directors have perpetuated this by choosing costumes suggesting a romantic country against an efficient one, or an underdog band of brothers against an army, often in the context of colonialism. Knight also emphasized time as a destroyer of values, further validating the conception of producers who attempt to unify the play by highlighting social collapse after seven years of war.[71] W. W. Lawrence and others sought patterns in social order versus individual will. Most important, following the lead of F. S. Boas, they treated *Troilus and Cressida* as a 'problem play', worthy of analysis and acceptance in its own right rather than a failed tragedy or comedy.[72] The term 'problem play' is outdated, but patterns continue to be found, interpretations advanced, and the complexities seen as challenges rather than structural weaknesses. Since the 1960s, productions have been informed by these analyses, as well as new theoretical approaches, but the nineteen thirties, forties and fifties, with a few exceptions, revisited old ground.

Payne brings Troilus to Stratford

Except for Poel's visit in 1913, Stratford had ignored the play, concentrating on popular favourites. In 1922 Ben Iden Payne, a Poel disciple, built an 'Elizabethan' stage within a proscenium arch at Pittsburgh's Carnegie Institute. In 1935, he produced an almost full text *Troilus and Cressida* there in Elizabethan costume. When Payne directed Stratford's 1936 season, he was often too scholarly to provide the excitement the public theatre needed, and his *Troilus* was not a

---

71 Knight, *The Wheel of Fire*, pp. 51–2.
72 Lawrence was originally published in 1934. Frederick Boas spoke of 'Problem plays' in 1896, but criticized Cressida as a 'scheming cold-blooded profligate', found fault with the travesties of the 'glorious paragons of antiquity' and likened Thersites to one of Swift's Yahoos (pp. 375, 377 and 383). *The New Variorum* gives a reasonably full sampling of criticism up to 1950.

success.[73] He again constructed an 'Elizabethan' set, with balcony and curtained inner recess behind the four-year-old Memorial Theatre arch, creating a picture of an Elizabethan production with additional downstage entrances. A flight of steps paralleling the arch was pushed on to provide access to the balcony, a device used earlier by Nugent Monck at the Maddermarket Theatre.[74] Minimal properties were employed as needed. Most of the action was cramped at the front of the stage, then much shallower than it is today, and production photographs give a sense of stiffness and constriction. The costumes, meticulously copied from Renaissance evidence, confused people unfamiliar with the play and made it seem less realistic.[75] Unlike Poel or Herbert, Payne and designer Barbara Heseltine did not create distinct styles for the Trojans and Greeks. Their careful work merely created an additional, unintentional level of parody of the classical heroes.[76]

Payne cut almost a fifth of the text,[77] but reviewers still found the play slow-paced and Baughan considered the speaking 'too deliberate'. The production didn't offend taste, but lacked the savagery and drive that made some more recent Stratford revivals exciting. Randle Ayrton's Pandarus was more paternal than lascivious. His wit seemed senile, kindly and only a bit vulgar, and 'his motive was simply to guide the young people to happiness'.[78] Geoffrey Wilkinson burlesqued Nestor, and Ajax became A-jakes in a mild gesture toward scatology. Pamela Brown was merely a flirt, rather than a believable woman, and her Cressida lacked 'sting'. One reviewer felt Shakespeare had lost control, an ongoing criticism. But he also faulted the portrayal. Brown's red lips, pink cheeks, and white and scarlet costume 'gave the impression of an Elizabethan doll', a hindrance as she parried the advances of the Greeks. She 'simpered and pouted'. Pronouncing 'r' as 'w' suited the conception, but handicapped her verse speaking. The most successful characters were James Dale's Thersites and Donald Wolfit's Ulysses.

73 Speaight, *Shakespeare on the Stage*. Payne ran Stratford until 1942, and finally returned more happily to a university setting.
74 Nugent Monck suggested that the Elizabethan theatre might have used such a device when people had to descend from the balcony area (*SS 12*, pp. 72–3). Monck, using a converted factory in Norwich's Maddermarket, followed Poel's lead with Elizabethan costumes. Like Poel, he operated on a shoestring, but his amateur Norwich Players mounted seasons of Shakespeare from 1921 through the 1950s. He produced *Troilus and Cressida* in 1928 and 1948 on his permanent thrust stage with balcony and inner stage.
75 *Birmingham Evening Dispatch*, 25 April 1936; *Birmingham Gazette*, 25 April 1936.
76 T. C. K., *Birmingham Post*, 25 April 1936.
77 In 1.3, for example, he excised 22–30, 59–74, 85–101a, 189–97, 340b–48a and an additional forty-five scattered lines – roughly a quarter of the scene.
78 M. F. K. F., *Birmingham Mail*, 25 April 1936.

Figure 2. Cassandra appears at the Trojan Council in B. Iden Payne's production, Shakespeare Memorial Theatre, 1936.

Thersites was an 'old soldier with a raucous voice' who directed his comments at the audience and emphasized the satire. Wolfit revealed the Machiavellianism in Ulysses' schemes, and 'was never a puppet figure mouthing lines'.[79] Characteristically, he was eloquent if a bit old-fashioned in his delivery, and treated what was left of the discussions of order and time with absolute seriousness. Dale and

79 *The Scotsman*, 10 June 1936.

Wolfit succeeded by playing from the characters' points of view and not inventing idiosyncratic touches.

Thersites' wicked humour helped offset the play's dullness, but overall the production was uneven and not illuminating. Opening seven plays in ten days probably exhausted the company, but the concept also seemed flawed. People were static, much 'like the latter-day Shaw with . . . characters just standing or sitting around arguing'.[80] *Troilus and Cressida*, relying too much on prior audience knowledge, would draw students, but not the general public.[81] In 1936, war was not close enough to make the play's anti-heroism reverberate as it had in 1922, although some saw the demolishing of reputations in keeping with the spirit of the decade. Greek costumes, however, would have more effectively emphasized the serious defects in the heroes and been less distracting.[82]

Experiments begin

As theatrical treatment of Shakespeare became increasingly flexible, directors tried to make the plays more accessible or startling, and to impose specific interpretations on the text. Modern-dress, period, or eclectic styles gradually became common. Analogy justifies modern-dress. Shakespeare's contemporaries saw the plays in Elizabethan costume; today's clothing theoretically gives lines the immediacy they originally had. Differences in class or occupation, and distinctions between Greek and Trojan soldiers are quickly perceived when current visual cues are sent. Macowan's 1938 production pioneered this approach to *Troilus and Cressida*, following Barry Jackson's experiment with *Hamlet*. Other directors believed a culturally important period or event could visually and emotionally enhance meaning. Tyrone Guthrie's Edwardian Old Vic production and Jack Landau's American Civil War revival relied on such reverberations. Many now embrace an eclectic style mixing swords, armour, period clothes and modern attire to lend universality to a four-hundred-year-old play about an ancient war coupled with a medieval romance.

Directors also began to emphasize political meaning, rather than leave the overtones to chance, as Birch had done. In 1932 Birch was concerned that his Cambridge Festival production would not reverberate as the 1922 revival had. Despite the Festival's often-experimental style, he stuck to classical costumes and used a curtain with horses' heads to bridge the stylistic gap between costumes and a clean-lined, modern set. A photograph shows dark-cloaked Myrmidons ringed around Hector on the symmetrical arrangement of steps and central arch that served as city walls and vantage point. With Anthony Quayle (Hector), George

80 *Birmingham Gazette*, 25 April 1936.
81 W. A. Darlington, *DT*, 25 April 1936.   82 E. A. Baughan, *News Chronicle*.

Howe (Diomedes), Jessica Tandy (Cressida) and V. C. Clinton-Baddeley (Nestor) the production was more polished than Birch's earlier revival, but drew less attention and seemed less relevant to the early 1930s. Programme notes recalling the First World War and likening Achilles to 'a jealous and temperamental flying ace' were not enough.

Growing tension in Europe with the rise of Naziism and two pointedly contemporary interpretations in 1938 again brought out the play's applicability. Continental productions in translation had outnumbered those in English in the twenties and thirties and gave German producers, especially, a way to criticize militarism without being overtly anti-Nazi, until the Third Reich banned it as 'too unheroic'.[83] In Zurich's Schauspielhaus, Oskar Wälterlin showed an actor in a Mussolini mask. People likened Ajax to Hitler and Goebbels, spouting their propaganda just across the border. Hans Mayer commented, 'Achilles doesn't have to get his hands dirty . . . there are always Myrmidons ready to do the dirty work'.[84] Hector's murder was seen as a warning to Switzerland not to be caught unarmed, a year before Swiss general mobilization.

With Guernica still fresh in people's minds and Picasso's painting on exhibit in London, Michael Macowan staged the first English modern-dress revival at the Westminster Theatre. Peter Goffin's skeletal frameworks against a dark backdrop suggested contemporary locales. Thersites occasionally spoke before the curtain during set changes in an under-three-hour production, while a drawing room, office, bedroom, or battlefield was speedily evoked, and gave an immediacy lacking at Stratford in 1936. Neville Chamberlain was making his second visit to Hitler, tension was high and Macowan underlined parallels in disillusionment, debates about a course of action and the contrast between drawing room and battlefield. Goffin added meaning by including signifiers of contemporary social life: a white piano, cigarettes, glossy magazines, cocktail glasses and stylish attire for Helen, Pandarus, Paris, and others at her party.[85] Swing music played on the radio. In uniform, Greeks wore blue and Trojans, British khaki.[86] They used anti-aircraft guns and field telephones. Barbed wire suggested no-man's land. Macowan justified his choice of period and political overtones in a programme note, declaring that what Shakespeare was saying 'can only be seen clearly by relating it to contemporary experience'.

Most critics reacted favourably even if, like Richard Prentice,[87] they came prepared to complain. *The Stage*, however, was reminded of Priestly and noted the

---

83 Hortmann, p. 121.   84 Quoted in Hortmann, p. 168.

85 Sixty years later Worthen codified much of what happened in this and other productions when modern cultural referents gave new meaning to texts and established new conventions (pp. 1097–8).

86 Gordon Crosse, Notebook, XVII, 30ff.

87 'Two Kinds of Shakespeare', *John O'London's Weekly*, 30 September 1938, p. 14.

disjunction between language and appearance. James Agate, ever conservative, titled his review 'Shakespeare and Schiaparelli', and declared this an invalid approach. Elizabethans might forget costumes and concentrate on the words. He, too, found a 'colossal discrepancy between dress and speech . . . you never stop thinking about the costumes, with the result that you have less attention to spare for what is being talked about'. He capped his remarks by asking how a horse could drag a body through a field of barbed wire.[88] Macowan's was, however, the most successful production to date because it had a unifying vision behind it, rather than merely a commitment to a visual style or an emphasis on comedy or irony.[89]

It set a pattern of contemporary reference for many later revivals, though today high society overtones are muted. Two years after Edward's abdication, however, the cocktail party suggested Wallis Simpson's lifestyle along with pleasures that appealed to Helen (Ariel Russ). Both outsiders had ensnared a prince, upset the equilibrium of a kingdom and occasioned fiery debates. Reviewers found it appropriate that the Greek generals should conduct 'their inordinate arguments with the aid of a decanterful of whiskey and a soda siphon'. The familiar costumes seemed to relax the actors and make their speaking less forced.[90] There was little ranting, more fluency, and apparently no urge to try lisps or exaggerated gestures, though some characterizations received mixed reviews. W. A. Darlington thought Ruth Lodge, aided by modern clothes and an air of sophistication, succeeded as far as possible with Cressida, an impossible role.[91] One reviewer found Lodge's 'manners hinting at fickleness', and thought Troilus (Robert Harris) foolish not to notice. Ivor Brown, resisting her modern reading, considered her miscast, and a theorist of free love rather than the naturally weak and bad person he believed the play demanded. On the other hand, Max Adrian's Pandarus was a cad 'of the glossily squalid night-club type', more threatening and representative of a sick society than an avuncular portrayal.[92] Robert Speaight's Ulysses reminded some of a professor called to war, comfortable with long verse lectures, but lacking dynamism. Ajax and Achilles resembled Germanic

88 *The Stage*, 29 September 1938; Agate, 'Shakespeare and Schiaparelli – Waggery at Westminster'.
89 The reviewer for *Reynolds Newspaper*, 25 September 1938, uniquely read the play from a Marxist viewpoint as a trade war for the Dardenelles, 'a bunch of toughs fighting for plunder', and said Macowan lacked a real modern viewpoint.
90 Peter Brook later commented that actors must find the impulse to use words and images related to life, in his Preface to Kott.
91 W. A. Darlington, 'A Modern Dress "Troilus", New Venture at the Westminster', *Daily Telegraph and Morning Post*, 22 September 1938.
92 Ivor Brown, *Obs*, 25 September 1938.

Figure 3. Helen's cocktail party in Michael Macowan's production, London Mask Theatre, 1938.

bullies, their respective stupidity and conceit not overdone. Cassandra was least successful, not reinterpreted in contemporary terms as a protestor with a mission. Darlington said her black velvet evening dress made Rosanna Seaborn 'dwindle from a frenzied prophetess to a young lady with fits'.

Audiences want to be able to place Thersites when the costumes of other characters immediately suggest social niches. In some 'Elizabethan' productions, he was a court jester, licensed to speak freely but, like Lear's fool, physically punishable. In modern-dress or post-Renaissance period revivals, trends have emerged. If military, he has been the army private, orderly, or scruffy camp follower; if civilian, a news reporter covering the expeditionary force as observer and commentator.[93] Ivor Brown described Stephen Murray as 'a mordant, maggoty product of New Grub Street', brilliant in his bitterness. Critics and audience didn't tire of the spleen of the war correspondent, more perceptive than his social superiors.

Modern-dress battle scenes present a problem when talk of swords and shields contradicts what the audience sees. In 1938, binoculars and a wireless in camp added atmosphere, but sword fights were not post-Guernica style, when the emphasis was on tanks, planes, and long-range guns. Crosse noted that the Ajax/Hector combat was among Macowan's many omissions, and that the final fights were the weakest point in the production.[94] Planes roared, bombs burst and machine guns rattled over the sound system. Words were lost and the short scenes became difficult to follow. The one-on-one matches lost their power in an otherwise admirable presentation. Despite flaws, the production occasioned letters to the *Times* editor from Una Ellis-Fermor and Dorothy Sayers, the former calling it 'more terrifying than Swift's Modest Proposal' and the latter declaring that 'The modern dress restores emphasis to the place Shakespeare put it.' She was glad not to be distracted by helmets or swords. Ellis-Fermor would soon write, 'The idea of chaos, of disjunction of ultimate formlessness and negation, has by a supreme act of artistic mastery been given form.'[95]

Post-war revivals

During the Second World War, theatre managers didn't risk scarce resources on a play debunking war and heroes. Audiences preferred the patriotic histories, real comedies and proper tragedies. Although some of Cressida's behaviour might be understood as women gained new freedoms, 'nice girls' did not write 'Dear John'

93 J. S. Bratton notes that the tradition of showing a reporter in a dramatization of war began with the Crimean conflict.
94 *LT* said the duel was not plausibly staged (25 September 1938) and there is the possibility that it had been cut by the time Crosse saw the production.
95 Ellis-Fermor, p. 72.

letters. Shortly after the war there were productions in Regent's Park's Open Air Theatre and at Stratford, but neither was particularly successful. They provide object lessons about the play's challenges.

The Open Air Theatre is a problematic venue for a play well-suited to cinema, with long, dense speeches and intimate love scenes that benefit from close-ups, and panoramic episodes such as the returning army, duel and final battles. Quiet scenes were lost on the large stage in Queen Mary's Garden,[96] and the *Times* reviewer commented on the difficulty of getting intricate thoughts across amid outdoor distractions, despite good individual performances.[97] The surrounding greenery lent a pastoral air at odds with a play that suggests interiors, city walls and a military camp on a desolate shore.[98] Robert Atkins also seemed to be sending two messages in 1946. He again used Elizabethan costumes, but focused on the play's content and modernity of tone. He regarded it as 'a precursor of *Arms and the Man* and *The Silver Tassie* . . . a satire on the romance of war and love and of life in general'.[99] Atkins emphasized 'the power of prolonged war to corrupt and degrade aspirations that were once genuinely noble', and heavy cutting clarified his message. It sat poorly with the typical Regent's Park audience, wanting pleasant Shakespeare while they coped with rationing, extensive bomb damage and personal loss after a war that had lasted as long as the Greeks had been camped near Troy.

Broad characterizations suited the venue and traditional expectations, though the actors sometimes achieved deeper readings. Cressida (Patricia Hicks) was 'attractive, but heartless and wanton'. Pandarus (Russell Thorndike) was 'an aged sensualist', Troilus (John Byron) 'an heroic green-horn', and Thersites (Ivan Staff) 'independent-minded', with a goal of tearing 'to final tatters the ideals of chivalry'. Atkins emphasized parallels between Troilus' senseless infatuation with Cressida and the mindless blood-letting by two nations infatuated with the idea of Helen. Despite open-air problems, the play was often well spoken, and Trewin(?) suggested that people should go to hear the verse.[100]

At Stratford, Anthony Quayle participated in two visually different revivals. In 1948 Motley, leading London theatrical designers, differentiated sharply between Greeks and Trojans. Reviewers criticized a lack of coherence when the Greeks appeared in winter sheepskins, rank patches and combat ribbons, while the Trojans were in 'Renaissance splendour'.[101] Photographs attest to even greater eclecticism. The Greeks resembled Fascists in practical camp wear while the

96 Gordon Crosse, Notebook, XIX,18.
97 *LT*, 29 June 1946.   98 Lincoln Hale, *DM*, 28 June 1946.
99 Robert Atkins, Programme Notes, Open Air Theatre, June 1946.
100 J. C. T. (John Trewin?), *Obs*, 30 June 1946.
101 Harold Hobson, *Theatre 2*, pp. 71–2.

Figure 4. Ajax and Thersites, with Achilles, Patroclus and Myrmidons in Anthony Quayle's production, Shakespeare Memorial Theatre, 1948.

Trojans at home had a variety of more luxurious garb. Paris, Hector and Troilus were Renaissance nobles; Pandarus looked Roman in a heavy decorated collar and layered, pleated skirt; Priam and Helenus seemed more Attic Greek in robes that gave dignity to king and priest. Cressida's low-cut, sleeveless gown could have been modern or classic.

Motley's set designs made better use of the Memorial Theatre stage than Payne's had. Photographs show striped hangings and angled poles pulled on to represent Greek tents furnished with light stools and tables. The Trojan locales, by contrast, were architectural and detailed, with columns, a frieze course and steps leading to a second level. Heavier, more elaborate furniture suggested permanence and none of the stress of war. At the end, however, Troy's collapse was forecast by broken blocks and tipped columns, a motif occasionally employed by later directors. Cutting and some scene rearrangement, such as the conflation of 2.3 and 3.3, reduced set changes.

Reviewers complained that the mix of costumes and set styles underlined Quayle's lack of a coherent overview. Paul Scofield's Troilus was most effective in his sadness after Cressida's betrayal. Noel Willman, an almost senile Pandarus, giggled when Paris held grapes over frankly sensual Helen (Diana Wynyard) as she lolled on a couch in a scarlet gown reminiscent of the 1930s. The Greeks kissed Cressida sedately, as was customary in earlier productions, except for

Patroclus, who pulled her to him. Pandarus' closing speech was kept, but spoken in 5.3 after the letter scene (3.4 in the promptbook). The battle among the ruins followed. At the end, recalling old tableaux, Troilus stood on a rock, the Trojan soldiers trudged past in defeat and the light slowly faded. Without explaining himself, Harold Hobson commented that the scene would have impressed in 1908, 1928, perhaps even in 1938. Presumably he was saying that in 1948 there must be emphasis on the bitter, anti-heroic values rather than an attempt at a quasi-tragic, highly theatrical ending. Quayle had rejected Atkins' harsh interpretation, and returned to the conservatism of gentler early productions. He also allowed actors to insert distracting details, and Hobson criticized Paul Hardwick's nose-blowing during his prologue.

By the 1950s reviewers increasingly appreciated the finer points of the play, and contextualized it in terms of modern drama. Where initially *Troilus and Cressida* had been criticized for its bitterness, now productions were faulted for not reflecting current disillusionment, though Eric Keown felt 'One can scarcely wait to have a bath' after the 'black glimpses of the human zoo'.[102] Philip Hope-Wallace declared the play 'as sharply realist as Giradoux's The Trojan War Will Not Take Place. [It] appeals far more strongly to a generation raised on Shaw and Bridie than it did to the Victorians who really could not "take" Cressida at all.'[103] But when Stratford mounted it in 1954, Glen Byam Shaw again mitigated the harshness, perhaps to appeal to the busloads of tourists who seldom chose what play they saw. Even Ivor Brown, introducing the Memorial Theatre's photographic record, admitted weaknesses. 'The poignant and tragical side of this label-evading piece miscarried through the inability of Laurence Harvey to rise to the poetry of the entranced, betrayed embittered Troilus.' Consequently Muriel Pavlov, 'strangely cast', played Cressida as a mere coquette. Richard David noted that she 'modeled herself from the start on Ulysses' description', which made him wonder why Troilus was fooled.[104] Brown praised the voice of William Devlin (Agamemnon), and David noted Leo McKern's skilful portrayal of Ulysses, 'patiently unrolling his comments' rather than mouthing a long, dry speech. His control in 5.2 in contrast to Troilus' wild passion unfortunately lessened the impact of the betrayal.[105] Despite some strengths, uneven speaking undermined Shaw's efforts to focus on the 'almost Shavian debates on the nature of value'. 'Keith Michell as Achilles was suitably handsome of mien and contemptible of conduct', but 'Tony Britten's charm made casting him as the ragged, gimpy Thersites "impolitic"'.[106]

102 'At the Play', *Punch*, 21 July 1954, p. 130.
103 Philip Hope-Wallace, 'Troilus at Stratford', *Time & Tide*, 24 July 1954, p. 993.
104 Richard David, 'Stratford, 1954', *SQ* 5, p. 390.
105 David, p. 391.   106 Brown, p. 5.

Neither Troilus and Cressida nor Thersites provided a centre, and Quayle's eccentric Pandarus seized the lead. He was 'a benevolent old woman of an uncle, something of a dandy, too, in his swathings . . . The meagre white hair floated . . . around a face parboiled with fat living, and the high, fluting voice, destitute of R's . . . coaxed and flattered and entertained unceasingly.'[107] His scene with Barbara Jefford's Helen was superb, and A. P. Rossiter likened him to Groucho Marx, leering and wisecracking as he arranged the assignation.[108] But for all his accomplishment, he emerged 'as a pathological nanny instead of a nasty old man with a positive pleasure in bedroom administration',[109] and Hope-Wallace likened him to 'a poor imitation of Peter Ustinov imitating an old woman'. As in 1948, Pandarus left early. Here the ensuing action seemed anti-climactic without his vitality and dominating personality.

Rossiter suggested that the play was well-suited to modern dress. Malcolm Pride's visual cues, however, were classical, and received the favourable reviews denied to other aspects of the production. Two sturdy segments of wall with gates were pushed onto the stage to represent Troy's defenses, while draperies and gauzy tent flaps quickly denoted indoor spaces such as Helen's rooms, the Greek council area, or Achilles' domain. Low steps front and back bordered Stratford's main playing area. At the rear, a forest of small shields, standards and masts evoked the Greek camp. Platforms on the walls provided viewing areas and posts for guards with elaborate torches. The costumes were less idiosyncratic than Motley's, with conventional classic armour. Brief tunics were underpinned by tights and escaped the criticism that greeted later, more revealing productions. The women wore long draping costumes and simple hairdos, while the Myrmidons stood out with lank dark hair and huge, scantily clad torsos. Patroclus' striped loincloth and languid poses suggested decadence, but homosexual aspects were not yet emphasized, for in the mid-fifties the British government was enforcing laws criminalizing same-sex relationships. A visually interesting though not coherent or compelling production, it did set Stratford on the path of more frequent revivals.

The most stylish, popular and influential production of the decade was Tyrone Guthrie's for the Old Vic in 1956, which visited America that winter. The costuming underlined a double-edged satirical approach that missed some of the harsher tones and character complexities, and treated the sexual aspects lightly. By the late Edwardian period the incompetencies and hardships of the Crimean and Boer conflicts were often glossed over. Many still considered war heroic and

107 David, p. 391.
108 A. P. Rossiter, 'The Modernity of "Troilus and Cressida"', a talk given at Stratford-upon-Avon, 25 August 1954.
109 Eric Keown, 'At the Play', *Punch*, 21 July 1954, pp. 130–1.

Figure 5. Cassandra visits the Trojan Council in Glen Byam Shaw's production, Shakespeare Memorial Theatre, 1954.

Guthrie wedded satire of this attitude and of German militarism to the satire in Shakespeare's play in a 'vigorous bravura style verging on burlesque'.[110]

Frederick Crooke, the designer, wrote that the play felt too modern for a Greek setting, but did not suit a post-nuclear era when war seemed unthinkable. The early 1900s provided opportunity for comedy of manners touches and appealed to the post-Second World War love of escapist pageantry. He saw a parallel in the death of the Archduke and the theft of Helen as excuses for action.[111] 'Guthrie caught a sense of two societies in conflict, two nations locked in a war of values, and this in a period near enough to be poignant but not conveying the fatal dissonances of a contemporary war.'[112] British audiences probably also brought their own sense of futility, for the run coincided with the abortive invasion of Egypt over control of the Suez Canal.

Costumes distinguished the romantic, more sympathetic Ruritanian Trojans from the battle-weary, hardened Germanic Greeks. The Trojans sported yellow-coated Horse Guards uniforms with dove-grey breeches, high black boots, shiny breastplates and plumed helmets. By contrast, Richard Wordsworth's Ulysses resembled an admiral in navy blue, guarded by sailors, and Ajax stood out in a red general's tunic. The Greeks had spiked German helmets and a few Kaiser Bill moustaches and, like Guthrie's soldiers in *All's Well*, were given extra business with much stamping and heel clicking. Atkinson grumbled that these high spirits undercut the dialogue.[113]

The Trojan civilians could have stepped in from then popular *My Fair Lady*. Paul Rogers' foppish Pandarus, in grey top hat and cutaway, shared binoculars with stylishly attired Rosemary Harris as they watched the returning Trojans in 1.2. Alexander, in jockey's attire, completed this early suggestion of war as sporting event. Helen's gold and white piano recalled Macowan's staging, and she (Wendy Hiller / Coral Browne), leaned against it in a risqué off-the-shoulder gown and a headband with aigrette.[114] An Edwardian opportunist evoking Lillie Langtry, cocktail in one hand and cigarette holder in the other, she flirted with Paris in his gold-braid-trimmed dinner jacket and Pandarus, now in white tie and tails. In this production, clothes made the people.

The list of properties, like Macowan's, was greatly enlarged and emphasized social position and manners. The Greek generals posed for official photos in

---

110 Kaula, p. 272.   111 Quoted in *PP*, May 1956, pp. 196–7.

112 Berry, *On Directing Shakespeare*, p. 17.

113 Brooks Atkinson, 'Mars is Mauled', *NYT*, 27 December, 1956, p. 21.

114 There were some cast changes for the US tour; the first name indicates the London production. Unattributed descriptions are from my notes on a production in New York, January 1957.

front of a period camera. Thersites (Clifford Williams / John Neville) was a correspondent with the expeditionary force. A slight, clever Cockney in glasses and dishevelled tweeds, he wore the waistcoat and tie appropriate to the era, and occasionally took notes as he commented. Large, often drunk Achilles (Charles Gray) and heavy-fisted Ajax (Laurence Hardy / Ernest Hare) delighted in threatening him, but avoided today's heightened physicality.

Stylish scenery suggested completeness, yet was flexible and easily shifted. The war setting included a column, an emblem and a trophy cannon. Heavy curtains (red for Troy, blue for Greece) backed the council scenes.[115] The same curved table, with different coverings, bowed toward the audience for the Trojans and away for the Greeks. Flags, lances, rifles and drums, stacked or held by sentries, completed the stage dressing for military scenes. The food images were given concreteness as the men drank and nibbled while debating. Pre-set trucks were rolled on for the civilian scenes. Helen's apartment had a trellis of poles and vines, with the piano, a table and chairs. Pandarus' more sombre house included a raised bedroom area. At the end, the ravages of war were signalled by smoke, shattered cannon, tattered flags and theatrically elaborate lighting.

Despite frequent farcicality and somewhat flat characterizations necessitated by the satiric emphasis, the production did suggest deeper problems. Ulysses took centre stage to point out the lack of order in shortened speeches, but without distracting business by Nestor or Agamemnon. Paris (Ronald Allen) was drunk in the Helen scene, perhaps tiring of his kept woman. This made his earlier argument for keeping her ring hollow, and lent irony to Hector's decision to continue fighting. Henry Hewes enjoyed the New York run, commenting that for once the Greek generals were 'not a congress of headmasters in togas'. They represented military stupidity, shored up by spit-and-polish guards. Hewes noted Achilles' sadism, Patroclus' decadence and Troilus' youth, which made him vulnerable to disillusionment. He also remarked on Pandarus' lecherous glance at every young boy. Unfortunately, trivial details of Thersites' performance obscured what should have been enlightening comments on the action.[116] Other critics were less kind, seeing the satire as mere surface, rather than coming from the inner bitterness of the play. They found the long speeches unintelligible, although I was not aware of that problem at the Winter Garden. More obvious was a lack of depth and balance that a more serious and focused treatment of the love story could have provided.

115 Wood and Clarke detail the use of these hangings.
116 Hewes, *SR*, 12 January, 1957. Jeremy Brett was replaced by Derek New as Patroclus in the US, and in turn replaced John Neville as Troilus.

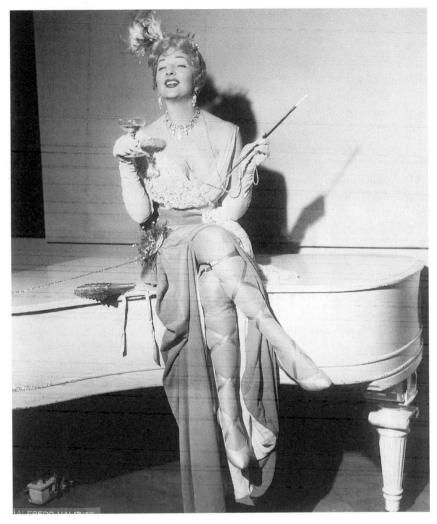

Figure 6. Coral Browne as Helen in Tyrone Guthrie's Old Vic production American Tour, 1957.

Festivals and continuing resurgence

While Shakespeare Memorial Theatre tours made the canon more available to the provinces, the trend grew in North America for dedicated Shakespeare festivals. At Stratford, Ontario, in 1953, Guthrie opened a theatre with the thrust stage he considered essential for Shakespeare. Two years later, Stratford, Connecticut, inaugurated its theatre, which failed in the 1970s despite huge potential audiences. On the west coast a festival started in Ashland, Oregon, in 1938 was expanded greatly after the Second World War. The Folger Shakespeare Library, with its replica stage, provided another venue, as did festivals in Colorado, Georgia, New Jersey, Ohio, Utah, Vermont and elsewhere. While Stratford, Connecticut, staged just one revival of *Troilus and Cressida*, Stratford, Ontario mounted its third in 2003 and Ashland presented its fourth in 2001. The state festivals mentioned above all revived the play at least once, and there have been numerous other performances, including those at professional repertory theatres connected with universities. As Howard Taubman noted when reviewing Stratford, Ontario's first production, *Troilus and Cressida* had become 'very much a festival play for our time. Its bitter disillusionment with heroes, makers of policy, war and love, cuts deeply into the exposed nerves of our disoriented, destructive and troubled world and the debased values by which so much of it conducts its private and public affairs.'[117]

In 1960 Stratford-upon-Avon's new director, Peter Hall, assisted by John Barton, overcame the deficiencies of the Memorial Theatre's earlier productions. His fast-paced, well-spoken, coherent revival in classical costume was in tune with growing disillusionment, and began Stratford's increasing fascination with the play. The production also visited the Edinburgh Festival (the play's first appearance in Scotland), toured, and arrived in London strengthened by additional textual cuts and some cast changes. It became a touchstone for later productions. There was humour, including Paul Hardwick's muscle-bound Ajax with his oversized spear and shield, but the relatively full text was generally not played for laughs as the Old Vic's had been. Taking his cue from the talk of degree, time and value that scholars had repeatedly noticed, Hall focused on the breakdown of order and blurring of standards as the years had passed. Cressida's forgotten vows, Hector's death, and Pandarus' decline were all outcomes of a larger malaise. Military events seemed more important than the title love story, but overarching decay linked all, and made modern parallels more apparent than they are in many productions in contemporary dress.[118]

The set provided a remarkable visual and symbolic context for the interpretation, which was dubbed 'the sand pit *Troilus*'. Leslie Hurry's foot-high, twenty-five-feet-wide octagonal frame, partially filled with white sand, followed the outline of the Memorial Theatre's new forestage and brought the action close to the audience. Max Adrian's Pandarus exploited this contact, while Peter O'Toole's Thersites missed it. The abstract backdrop was perhaps a patched terra cotta wall, perhaps the blood-splotched legacy of seven years of war. A bench for Helen, camp stools, chairs and a portable throne for Priam suggested various locales. Soldiers holding distinctive banners or emblems signalled different territories in the military story. During the duel, ensigns and a few stools

117 Taubman, *NYT*, 30 June 1963.   118 Alan Brien, *Spectator*, 29 July 1960.

around the edge were the only décor, allowing maximum space in the pit for a realistic, sand-kicking fight that was more exciting than the customary chore-ographed combat.[119] Troilus, Cressida and Pandarus sat on a bench or on the rim of the sandpit. Thersites crouched and scrabbled there during his encoun-ters with Ajax, or lurked at the edge as a spectator. Space outside the pit allowed Ulysses and Troilus to overhear Cressida and Diomedes in 5.2, with Thersites well away from them, commenting to the audience and creating the sense of layers of observation.[120] Eight Myrmidons in black cloaks and depersonalizing eye-masking helmets surrounded Hector with spears in 5.9, and the effect was of a doomed animal at bay, his body dragged out like a dead bull's. William Shaw commented years later that the setting symbolized a spiritual wasteland that becomes physical,[121] confirming the lasting impression the production made on many of us who saw it.

Stark white lighting on the sand suggested Mediterranean sun, with appropri-ate darkening for night scenes. Although there were no cannon, the final battle was suffused with the smoke that has become standard for Stratford wars, with shafts of light piercing the murk and glinting off armour. Fighters were obscured and the effect was hellish. Noises added to the sense of confusion out of which Troilus tried ineffectually to make some order. Robert Speaight noted that the final battle involved the entire company and was not the stylized fencing match that sometimes occurs.[122]

Hurry copied clothing and properties from Greek vases: short tunics, leather breastplates, greaves and armlets. The Greeks' costumes looked worn, but their bodies were well-muscled and glistened with oil, an historically correct touch for a Spartan army. The older men had long cloaks fastened over one shoulder, as did Troilus and Achilles when not fighting. Helen and Cressida wore gowns with tight bodices, a bare shoulder and gracefully draping long skirts. The similarity suggested parallels rather than a contrast between them. Pandarus, in toga-like robe and short curls, resembled a classical statue and a servant often held a large fringed parasol to give him luxurious shade. Animal skin rugs on the sand, surrounded by campstools, and trays with goblets and pitchers of wine suggested

119 The same design was adapted to the Aldwych stage, though the relationship to the stalls audience was somewhat altered. My observations are based on notes made at a performance of the 1960 version.

120 G. Wilson Knight was soon to note the eye and its multi-valenced importance in the theatre, and in *Troilus and Cressida* (*Shakespearian Production*, p. 239). Photographs of London and Stratford productions between 1960 and 2000 and a database of details were available as of 2003 at *Designing Shakespeare*.

121 William P. Shaw, '*Troilus and Cressida*; Giving Chaos a Local Habitation and a Name', p. 53.

122 Cited by Shaw, ibid., p. 54.

Figure 7. Achilles, Patroclus and the Greek commanders in Peter Hall and John Barton's 'Sandpit' production, 1960–2.

some comforts during the council scenes without the stark contrast between Greek camp and Trojan city of some productions. Everything harmonized and seemed to have its purpose. Critics wrote of the care with details, from the pouring of wine to the placing of soldiers with spears across the back of the sandpit.

Both Hall and Barton had assisted George Rylands at the Marlowe Society and were comfortable with Elizabethan verse. They devoted extra time to coaching the actors, who handled the complex speeches with a natural ease. Hall was also anxious to create a coherent company who could explore the depths of their roles.[123] Dorothy Tutin's Cressida evoked Marilyn Monroe. Flirtatious, with a sensuous walk and curvaceous body, she was consciously pleased with her ability to attract men. But she also suggested hesitation and thought rather than a casual shift of affections as she turned to Diomedes. Ian Holm replaced Denholm Elliott as Troilus in Edinburgh and more successfully exploited the opportunity for deep

123 Penelope Gilliatt, 'Peter Hall's first Stratford Season', in the SMT souvenir programme, 1960.

emotion. Max Adrian found vulgar joy in his role as pander, giggling and almost dancing with delight in the decadent atmosphere. By the end, however, he was a decrepit physical symbol of the moral collapse of the play's world. O'Toole's muted Thersites was the least successful characterization, insufficiently disgusted at the rot around him. The Stratford production delivered its message without him, however, and in London, when Gordon Gostelow replaced O'Toole, the run was praised for heightened coherence and intensified focus.[124]

While praising Hall and Barton's work, the *Times* critic called *Troilus and Cressida* 'a mighty and permanently modern work for which no satisfactory style of production has yet been found'. Nor did Jack Landau, at Connecticut's American Shakespeare Festival find that style in 1961. Reading the Trojan War as civil strife, he sought a period that might resonate with the audience and enrich the story as the Essex rebellion overtones were supposed to have resonated with Shakespeare's contemporaries. Although he wrote elsewhere 'it is not the look, the sets and costumes, but the acting and the words of Shakespeare that make the total effect', in the programme he explained 'we are trying to . . . use the symbols of American history to make certain ideas in this very complicated, difficult and beautiful play a little more immediate'.[125] On the centenary of the American Civil War, a spate of books and re-enactments familiarized many with details. There were numerous parallels: relatives, like Hector and Ajax, fought on opposite sides; there were turncoats and prisoner exchanges; love blossomed between enemies like Achilles and Polyxena or Cressida and Diomedes; Atlanta burned as Cassandra (the Southern gothic madwoman?) prophesied Troy would. Landau, however, miscalculated the vivid emotional overtones he was unleashing, and the power of the Civil War to overwhelm parts of Shakespeare's play for viewers whose grandfathers were veterans. Like Claire McGlinchee, the audience struggled to match ancient and Civil War counterparts.[126]

Motley provided accurate costumes. Greeks, in Federal blue, invaded the South, their army hampered by poor leadership as the North had been early on. Trojans were in Confederate grey, their women in crinolines. The South was popularly seen in a romantic light, with eager young gentlemen, like the Trojan princes, defending their homeland from Yankee draftees sent to fight on foreign soil.[127] Will Geer, a courtly, white-bearded Priam, resembled Robert

124 'Heroic Acting in a Sandpit – Transparent Clarity', *LT*, 16 October 1962, p. 16. By the London run, Barton and Hall had made extensive cuts, shortening the text by about 700 lines. Maxine Audley succeeded Elizabeth Sellars as Helen.
125 Landau, 'The Key to the Production is The Present', *TA*, August 1961, p. 62; Landau quoted by John Beaufort, '"Troilus and Cressida" Overgrown by Magnolias', *CSM*, 25 July 1961, p. 5.
126 McGlinchee, p. 421.
127 More recently, Ken Burns has unearthed many letters that show Northern troops equally committed to a cause, but Landau was dealing more with popular conceptions than factual details. Drawing on the popularity of Burns' television programs, vivid

E. Lee.[128] Patrick Hines, a coarse, cigar-smoking black-bearded Agamemnon, recalled Ulysses S. Grant. Pandarus was a Kentucky colonel with ribbon tie, satin lapels and cummerbund, or elegant dressing gown. Kim Hunter's Helen was perfectly coiffed, with a cameo above her scooped neckline. Carrie Nye's Cressida looked more demure, with ruching at her neck and conservative travelling attire. Paris, Hector and Troilus were dashing officers, while Thersites was a dirty, insolent lower-class Union volunteer. The production led audiences to hunt for stock types, and Nestor became the cracker-barrel sage in a country store.

Robert O'Hearn's settings recalled period films. The pillared porch of an ante-bellum mansion, with peeling stucco over brick, provided a vantage point for watching the returning Trojans, a meeting place for Priam's council, and a platform for Cassandra's warnings. Pandarus' orchard was suggested by greenery against the stage's lattice background. Symbolic decay became physical with the partial collapse of the pillars in the final battle. The Greek camp, its wooden entrance posts and crosspiece familiar from films, occupied an outdoors setting with overhanging branches. A covered wagon at the rear centre provided a refuge for Thersites, Achilles and Patroclus while the Greek council gathered on period camp chairs.[129]

Reviewers often went to Stratford prepared to scoff. Judith Crist found the effect distracting: was it the end of Tara or Troy?[130] Others, including Beaufort, expressed surprise at how much of Shakespeare's original remained. Landau said he wanted an 'American style', but Stratford often cast for box office appeal rather than Shakespearean experience, mixing stars with novices and a few classically trained actors. Jessica Tandy, in Cassandra's black gown, was focused and dominated her scenes, but many others had a more difficult time. Without the firm direction Hall and Barton provided in England, there was a mélange of approaches and accents, difficulty with the verse and lack of ensemble cohesion. Ulysses, Aeneas and Achilles (Paul Sparer, Richard Waring and Donald Davis) moved and spoke formally, which distanced them from others of similar status, such as Pat Hingle's Hector. Ted van Griethuysen played Troilus with

local associations, and nearby place names like Athens and Sparta, Tom Markus again used the Civil War setting as 'Troy, Georgia' for the Georgia Shakespeare Festival in 1996.

128 The audience recognized other overtones of a lost cause: Geer was still banned from film and television by the House Un-American Activities black list.

129 Photographs are at the New York Public Library, Lincoln Center. My notes from late July, 1961, recall the potential of the settings but remark that many actors were not completely comfortable in their roles.

130 Crist, *NYHT*, 24 July 1961.

Figure 8. Cressida among the Greeks in Jack Landau's American Shakespeare Festival production, Stratford, Connecticut, 1961.

'great ardor and desperate disillusionment', more foolish than tragic. Cressida occasionally struck a sultry note, but generally played a preliminary study for a very romantic Juliet until she suddenly yielded to Diomedes. Some Trojans tried southern accents; others were more clipped.[131] The production lacked the depth and complexity that new attention to women's status might have provided. In an era of growing frankness about sexual matters, Pandarus glossed over the unsavoury parts of his character. *Gone with the Wind* came to the minds of a number of critics whose attention had wandered. 'The play . . . is overlaid by secondary considerations in order to give the whole enterprise an air appropriate to a festival.'[132]

Despite the diverse acting styles and lack of a deeper perspective, the production gained in excitement in the second half. Civil war officers still used swords, so single combats could take place naturally amid cannon fire and rebel yells. But, as Howard Taubman noted, there was a crucial problem. The Southerners tended to treat the war heroically, and this play scorned heroes.[133] More accurately, North and South both celebrated those who had fought on their sides. Lacking Guthrie's satiric note, this attempt to locate the play in a meaningful period context highlighted the disjunction between the romanticized memories and morally important cause of the Civil War and Shakespeare's searing message about the folly of war. Although some critics sensed a feeling of underlying decay in a society too long preoccupied by conflict, the specificity of the chosen period obscured that interpretation.[134]

In 1963, the Birmingham Repertory Theatre was far more successful. A programme note states 'If "Hamlet" was the play for the 1930s, "Troilus" is surely the one for the 1960s.' Director John Harrison focused on its 'mature disillusion' with romantic idealism and inherited values, and its rejection of suffering for a cause, considering it not a tale of Greeks and Trojans, but a morality play.[135] This gave the almost full text production more coherence than mere emphasis

---

131 Beaufort and Crist.

132 'Arthur Pumphrey at the Theatre', *TA*, September 1961, p. 24.

133 Howard Taubman, 'Stratford Puts Troilus and Cressida to 1860s', *NYT*, 24 July 1961. Southern accents also distracted, as did the confusion of two dissimilar wars, in Tom Markus' Civil War period production when it was revived in Colorado in 1997 (Alan Dumas, '*Troilus* Sends Bard Off to Civil War', *Rocky Mountain News*, 18 July 1997, p. 16).

134 My notes repeatedly make references to stock characters from films that actors and actions recall. They also comment that Shakespeare made it easier for the cast in the second half, with more action and less talk.

135 Unlike L. C. Knights, he did not specify morality abstractions or types: Troilus = Faith; Cressida = Inconstancy; Pandarus = Pander, or equate the council scenes with morality debates on metaphysical issues (*TLS*, 2 June 1932, p. 408).

on cynicism would have. Cressida (Jennifer Hilary) was not just a 'wanton tart', but a sort of 'devil to herself'.[136] Derek Jacobi's Troilus pushed emotions close to the breaking point, both as the conventional lover with his values shattered, and as the new leader building from the ground up at the end. He was helped by Cressida's apparent bafflement at her change of heart after her father sent her to Diomedes.[137] Passion was deepened by a psychological element that suggested both actors had fully analysed their characters. Reviewers agreed this intensity made the lovers more central than they often are, and Thersites' humour provided an essential contrast.

The setting represented both barren disillusion and sensuality. Photographs show a twenty-foot-high backcloth painted with flames and an impressionistic line drawing of a semi-nude female figure. Emblems of Troy or Greece could be lowered to signal location. A barbed-wire-entwined football goal suggested characters metaphorically tearing themselves on the thorns of life as well as actually bleeding in the war game. Unfortunately, reviewers found the murder of Hector strangely flat. Achilles led a gang of leather-jacketed motorbike toughs and the attack, with wrench and chains, exemplified contemporary street violence, but failed to horrify. Perhaps audiences were more inured to urban violence than to violation of a military code. The critics also complained of battle scenes hampered by the smallness of the stage and the awkward two-handed swords that jarred with the costumes.[138]

Generally, however, the costumes enhanced the meaning. Arthur Pentlow spoke the Prologue as a Colonel Blimp in officer's uniform, then switched to a dustman's attire and Cyrano nose for Thersites, and commented with detachment on the people whose trash he collected. Ralph Nossek, possibly miscast, was an older and frailer Pandarus than usual, and reminded one critic of 'an ineffectual vicar . . . a startlingly sympathetic character who plainly regrets having to say half the lines he does'.[139] Nestor resembled a verger, and was not played solely for comedy. Roy Patrick's tattooed Ajax added humour with a barbell routine and physically dwarfed Philip Voss' Achilles, who was more serpent than bull. Georgine Anderson was a frolicsome Helen on violet cushions, in sharp contrast to thoughtful Cressida. In a strikingly innovative and pertinent touch, Lesley Nunnerley's Cassandra was not the raving prophetess of tradition, but a modern 'leader of the Trojan peace party, carrying a trophy with the slogan "Let Helen go"'.[140] This obliterated any otherworldly quality but reminded the audience of

---

136 Programme note by J. H. (John Harrison, Artistic Director of the Birmingham Repertory Theatre), 19 February 1963.

137 W. H. W., 'The Best "Rep" Shakespeare in Years', *The Mail*, 2 February 1963.

138 Gordon Chester, 'Triumph at Rep', *Dispatch*, 20 February 1963.

139 Anonymous review, 20 February 1963.

140 J. C. Trewin, *ILN*, 6 April 1963, p. 518.

the unheard pleas for peace and disarmament in the early 1960s. Her positioning as part of the growing contemporary protest movement let her succeed where Macowan's Cassandra had failed in 1938. Harrison also set a precedent by having Thersites crawl on muttering 'wars and lechery' during Pandarus' epilogue, visually linking the two commentators.

That summer Stratford, Ontario presented a generally conservative revival rather than a groundbreaking reinterpretation. Director Michael Langham 'trusts the play, and consequently the play rewards him by emerging, as it should, as a sound, artfully structured play of ideas. Closely argued, daringly set on several levels of observation, a clean, ironic chronicle of errors.'[141] Rather than emphasize modernity through costume and properties, Langham invited the audience 'to take an objective view of its own pathetic delusions and to laugh or cry or mock them'. Viewers quickly grasped universal disillusionment with war, heroes and socially ruinous state policies. William Hutt and Eric Christmas were masterful as Pandarus and Thersites, while Martha Henry's Cressida was 'so fully susceptible to the wanton pleasures of love that from the beginning we knew she was lost'.[142]

The classical costumes included heavily sculpted breastplates, round shields and crested helmets, and an occasional cloak over the warriors' short tunics. Well-coiffed, womanish Pandarus wore a light-coloured crimplene gown with a heavy necklace and carried a flywhisk. Desmond Heeley's sketch for Helen (Diana Maddox) emphasized an empire line, with a flowing skirt and overskirt, in flamboyant orange and red, and a jewelled tiara.[143] Contrast with this blatant sensuousness rather than a visual parallel was suggested by Cressida's light gown, demurely gathered at the shoulders, and plain hairstyle in comparison to Helen's elaborate curls. At the Festival Theatre, costumes and limited properties provided colour and a sense of place on the thrust wooden stage with its plain balcony reached by steps up both sides, and its multiple entrances that include the auditorium aisles.[144]

The Ajax–Hector combat departed from usual staging practice. In occasional amateur productions and the 1999–2000 Oxford presentation, the fight was off-stage, despite the build-up of audience expectations after the delivery of Hector's challenge in 1.3. This is understandable where actors are not competent swordsmen or where formal duels run counter to the production's time period. John Colicos and Tony van Bridge in classical costume could have fought convincingly,

---

141 Gordon Rogoff, *PP*, October 1963.   142 Hewes, *SR*, 17 August 1963.
143 Reproduced in the 1963 souvenir programme; Diana Devlin, *TW*, September 1963, p. 27.
144 My notes from July, 1963, include sketches for a double-wide chaise for Helen and Paris, but few other properties,

Figure 9. Ajax, Thersites, Achilles and Patroclus in Michael Langham's Stratford Festival of Canada production, 1963.

however, and at the Festival Theatre combats are excitingly close to the front rows. Langham made us passive watchers of active spectators. As Taubman recounted, the Greeks and Trojans recreated the flow of the match, straining to see, agitated, and registering disappointment when the unseen duel was broken off.[145] Perhaps this treatment was intended to make the fight between Hector and Achilles (Leo Ciceri) more striking. Taubman likened that to a western film episode, with Achilles losing his sword and shield, and suddenly flashing a bullwhip before he withdrew. Although the lighting and sound effects were generally unobtrusive, there was one very modern theatrical touch at the end: a loudspeaker reminded us of Cassandra's words as the Myrmidons moved in for the kill.

Numerous professional revivals now precluded university-affiliated semi-professional performances from receiving the attention they had earlier, but

145 Taubman, *NYT*, 30 June 1963.

many, including Cambridge, England (1964), Cambridge, Massachusetts (1960, 1968), Ann Arbor, Michigan (1968) and Princeton (1969) made more people familiar with the play in production. Students were again in tune with a work that they had struggled through a decade earlier, for it echoed their growing cynicism about war and the establishment.[146] Public perception was also diverging from the military ethos that still romanticized battlefield action in John Wayne's fashion. Joseph Papp found the mid-sixties an opportune time for *Troilus and Cressida* in New York's Central Park.

Papp wanted his huge audiences from all walks of life to relate to characters and actions, though he did not always use modern costuming to emphasize relevance. In 1965 Theoni Aldredge devised classically styled costumes – tunics with leather armour and greaves for the soldiers, and toga-like bordered cloaks over longer robes for the older men. The identification problem was solved at the vast Delacorte Theatre by giving the Greeks conventionally crested helmets, while the Trojans had spikes on theirs. Ming Cho Lee's set harmonized with the costumes. Column bases, short sculptured blocks, and a low back wall with a molded design provided seating and a sense of locale on the spacious stage. A throne for Priam in 2.2, or an extra couch for Paris and Helen could be moved on quickly, and hangings between taller columns stage left indicated indoor scenes.[147]

Papp's actors emphasized comedy. Amplification made them audible to those of us in the rear, but the size of the theatre and outdoor distractions required broad rather than subtle interpretations. Papp was an early proponent of colour-blind casting, and Roscoe Lee Brown, Al Freeman, Jr and Bill Gunn were Ulysses, Diomedes and Patroclus, respectively. Nestor (Tom Aldredge) was a senile buffoon among the windbag Greek generals, Pandarus (Frank Schofield) was distractingly busy and silly, and Ajax (James Earl Jones) was amusingly clumsy.[148] Richard Watts complained of 'The insect scale of the Greek warriors, the shady activities of old Pandarus and the venomous bile of Thersites'.[149] Helen (Jane White) was ageing and 'no longer a beauty to be fought for',[150] in contrast to young, sensuous and lovely Cressida, whom Troilus let go without protest. This highlighted the issue of extrinsic valuation as the Trojans argued about keeping Helen, and helped explain Diomedes' disgust.

146 *LT* and *FT* praised the Marlowe Society's emphasis on text, not production tricks (10 March 1964) and *Gdn* called attention to the appropriateness of the play during the Cuban missile crisis, when people understood 'gunnery and venery'.
147 My notes from a mid-August production commented on the ease of movement around these many properties because of the size of the stage.
148 Lewis Funke, '"Troilus and Cressida" in Park', *NYT*, 13 August 1965.
149 *New York Post*, 13 August 1965.
150 Herbert Kupferberg, 'Papp's "Troilus" Bold, Inconsistent', *NYHT*, 13 August 1965.

Reviewers who were unhappy about the flat characterizations approved the vigour of the fight scenes. Hector's death, especially, was 'electrifying and moving'. Papp cut roughly four hundred lines, but the production still ran three-and-a-half hours with one interval. Earlier revivals were often done in three acts, but most modern directors have one break, usually, like Papp's, after 3.2. This rounds off the courtship as Troilus and Cressida head for bed, but reduces Shakespeare's ironic juxtaposition of Calchas' quickly approved request for his daughter in 3.3, which reinforces the perception that men are unfeelingly arranging her life.

Despite the emphasis on comedy, Papp's notes show his concern with deeper aspects of character and structure. He recounts Paul Stevens' unsuccessful struggle to find a way of showing motivation for Hector's about-face in 2.2. More important, he articulates growing questions about Troilus. Anticipating later feminist readings, he considers him a cad and Cressida his victim. Troilus (Richard Jordan) argued persuasively for keeping Helen, yet quickly accepted giving up Cressida after sleeping with her. Self-centred, he became preoccupied with her faithfulness when he should have been convincing others to let her stay in Troy. Papp believed that Cressida (Flora Elkins) needed more than speeches about loyalty and saw in Diomedes one who understood obligations better than Troilus. Unlike the Victorian and early twentieth-century critics who so often damned Cressida as the villain, Papp felt this label went to Ulysses, if to anyone, for his detached manipulation of others. He remarked that men in the audience applauded Thersites 'whore' couplet (5.2.112–13) while women remained quiet. His notes mention, incidentally, the difficulty of getting a post–Second World War audience to understand how immoral the 3.2 assignation is, and how shocking it would have been to earlier audiences with different standards of behaviour.[151]

John Barton returned to the play in 1968 as sole director with a controversial RSC production that again toured and transferred to London to conclude the decade's major revivals. The text seemed transformed by emphasis on corruption images and, a month before British stage censorship ended, by heterosexual and homoerotic displays far beyond what a director would have dared a decade earlier.[152] The production also benefited from a rich mix of 'scholarship and theatricality' that became more obvious on repeat viewing.[153]

151 Joseph Papp, 'Directing Troilus and Cressida', *Festival Shakespeare*, pp. 23–71. At about this time Joyce Carol Oates was still calling Cressida 'evil' and 'villainous' (p. 178).

152 Grigely and others would later theorize on how text is not fixed and paradoxically emerges from performance (pp. 108, 118), but as Rutter notes, Barton's work was 'long in advance of any cultural theorization on these issues' (p. 135).

153 Frank Cox, *PP*, August 1969, p. 49.

By now, Jan Kott's *Shakespeare Our Contemporary* was influencing productions from *A Midsummer Night's Dream* to *King Lear*. Its chapter on the modernity of *Troilus and Cressida* highlighted the political overtones of Ulysses' self-serving schemes, and explained Hector's reversal in terms of losing face. 'Face' had been a major issue in Korean truce negotiations and remained important as the escalating Vietnam conflict generated questions about the sense and cost of war. Kott focused on the mockery in the portrayals of the Greek heroes and the parody of courtly romance in the Paris–Helen scene. He saw Cressida, who had grown up during the seven-year siege, as cynical, but aware and afraid of her passions. 'She is our contemporary because of this self-distrust, reserve, and a need for self-analysis.' In several chapters Kott emphasized sexuality and the grotesque, which he deemed crueller than tragedy.[154] Grotesque sexuality characterized Timothy O'Brien's costuming of scab-covered Thersites with a mouldy vest, ragged loincloth, and a mask-like codpiece whose long rope trunk could be pinned up behind or waved obscenely like an oversized phallus. Norman Rodway came closer than earlier performers to matching Chapman's description of Thersites as 'the filthiest Greeke that came to *Troy*'.[155]

No sand pit focused the action, but a large bull's head reminiscent of Spartan sculpture hung on the backcloth, suggesting sex and cuckoldry. With a limited costume budget, Barton decided to emphasize the bodies of well-muscled Greeks and Trojans rather than use costly armour. Brief white costumes, copied from peplums on Greek vases, contrasted with tanned skin, and actors were encouraged to emulate historic hairstyles and poses. The homoerotic element was sharply criticized by many reviewers uncomfortable with modern homosexuality, though it probably was a reasonably accurate representation of life in a Spartan military camp and I felt added important tension. Alan Howard's blond Achilles, with his elegant lounging robe and fringed fan, and John Shrapnel's Patroclus, with his flywhisk, took their cues from archaeological evidence.[156] Other properties were effectively used: a small tree and bench became Pandarus' orchard, a bed centred Helen's quarters, and a few stools and chairs didn't impede the physically active production.[157]

---

154 Kott, pp. 75–83. The English translation had appeared in 1964.
155 Chapman, *The Iliad*, Book II, quoted in Bullough, VI, 120. Other aspects of the description have influenced later portrayals: 'he had a goggle eye: / Starcke-lame he was of eyther foote: his shoulders were contract / Into his breast and crookt withal: his head was sharp compact, / And here and there it had a hayre.' I found Rodway the most exciting of the half dozen performances of the role I had seen to this point.
156 Anne Barton provided much of the information on the choices made for this production in conversation with me during late August, 1968.
157 Gareth Lloyd Evans, one of the severest critics, complained of everything from Agamemnon's straw hat to Troilus' slightness (*SS 22*).

Figure 10. Achilles, Patroclus and Thersites in John Barton's Royal Shakespeare Company Production, 1969.

The heterosexual was subordinated to the homoerotic, with Trojans and Greeks meeting 'like lovers . . . agog for the dark orgasmic flutter of killing or being killed'.[158] Adding to the sexual complexity of Barton's reading was Achilles' veiled entrance on Helen's litter after the duel, wearing a blond wig and arousing momentary expectation in Menelaus. After unveiling, he indulged in sexual byplay with Thersites' codpiece, to Menelaus' acute embarrassment.[159] Thersites' 'Nothing but lechery! All incontinent varlets!' at the end of 5.1 seemed unusually appropriate, and most sexual encounters coarsened to fit his perspective. But Rodway was not the sole choric figure. As in 1960, the cast spoke well and the thoughtful content of many of the lines was expressed clearly.

In rehearsal notes Barton said the play was to some extent an attack on our habit of making general statements to 'smooth over the confusion of life', as Ulysses tended to do. This production, like most modern revivals, did not treat the speech on order as the central philosophical statement but valorized a multiplicity of opinions. Barton added that the characters were better at 'analysis than at upholding any positive course of action', a feature that made *Troilus and Cressida* the most modern of Shakespeare's works. Though Barton refused to take a single

158 Benedict Nightingale, *NS*, 16 August 1968, p. 208.
159 Frank Cox, p. 50. Eve Sedgwick later examined this sort of male homosocial desire in great theoretical detail.

viewpoint, again the deleterious effect of passing years became obvious. But in contrast to the 'ludicrous' basic situation, there were positive beliefs and values, including Aeneas and Nestor's chivalry, Hector's generosity, and the tone of the meeting after the duel, before Achilles broke the mood.[160]

Again the RSC had the depth the many important roles require. Despite Barton's emphasis on the war, the young lovers were unusually effective. Helen Mirren's Cressida realized that her attractiveness and sensuality were leading her into a vulnerable position similar to Helen's. She was not a villain in being false, nor merely a victim wanting sympathy. There was a parallel with Helen (Sheila Allen), who was highly sensual in her scene with Paris, but also had more wit and intelligence than the painted flirt of many productions. Even before feminist re-readings, actresses were beginning to see Cressida and Helen's responses to circumstances as more than mere sensuality. Also remarkable was Michael Williams' Troilus. Although some reviewers disliked the portrayal, I found his one of the most successful conceptions. His argument for keeping Helen was thoughtful rather than purely romantic. Though he was young and overly passionate in his love for Cressida, he exhibited anguished depth instead of the self-centred surface emoting at her loss that often weakens him in 5.2. Clearly he had the strength to become the next Trojan leader, and his final speeches were a logical development in a man who was consistently respected by others. Bloodied, he seemed appropriately vicious with Pandarus at the end. Again Thersites reappeared in 5.11, this time to accompany the epilogue with bangs on his tambourine. Peter Roberts, praising the production, commented: 'it is the very open-endedness of the play and the author's refusal to deal with the play's themes in neat sonata-form that make it a peculiarly accessible play for us today'.[161]

Hunting for direction in the 1970s

The RSC mounted a revival or two per decade, usually with two venues and two seasons for each, throughout the rest of the century. The Company's variety of theatres and treatments, and the fullness and accessibility of their promptbooks, as well as post-1980 production videotapes, provide a comprehensive overview of modern approaches that is supplemented by revivals elsewhere. Several of these revivals in the early 1970s demonstrate what may succeed and what fails when directors are working with weaker companies than Barton's RSC, or do not trust the play. Trinity Repertory Company's 1971 effort, and the New York Shakespeare Festival's in 1973, fell prey to idiosyncratic concepts, while the Bristol Old Vic's straightforward 1972 presentation was a moderate success, as was one in Ashland, Oregon.

160 RSC Programme for *Troilus and Cressida*, 1968–9.
161 Peter Roberts, 'Whores and Cuckolds', *PP*, October 1968, p. 65.

Providence, Rhode Island's Trinity Rep, one of America's better regional companies, developed a house style that emphasized ensemble creativity during rehearsal, physical activity, music by a resident composer, set designs that reconfigured the main theatre to change audience/actor relationships, and eclectic costuming for Shakespeare. This succeeded for *The Tempest*, but failed for *Troilus and Cressida*. Protests against the Vietnam War were rife. A truck half-buried in the stage, camouflage netting and a walkway patrolled by soldiers gave an initial impression of topicality. But added vaudeville turns, blatant homoeroticism that went far beyond a statement on male bonding in wartime, and continual metatheatrical touches distracted.[162]

Boston's senior dramatic critic, Eliot Norton, headlined his scathing review 'Shakespeare by the Boys in the Band' and catalogued things he found wrong. Three old men in female wigs set the tone, singing a new prologue to piano accompaniment. Thersites had apparently parachuted in, dirty long underwear tucked into combat boots. Paris, hair dyed and teased, lolled with an older, sluttish Helen in a frizzy wig. Cassandra wore an Afro, Agamemnon had borrowed Macbeth's kilt, and Ajax strapped on a phallus for his wrestling match with Hector, who wore a bandolier and minimal undershorts throughout.[163] Costuming generally diminished characters, but, I hoped, occasionally had symbolic intent: Achilles' tattered robe matched his moral condition, and Ajax' football pads under a windbreaker gave him false bulk and suggested that the Troy expedition was a long sports rivalry. Production ideas seemed to have come from the same onstage trunk that randomly yielded props, and we were distracted by the struggle to understand many of the choices.

A flurry of action, air raid sirens, a spotlight and horns created no inner tension. Samuel Hirsch, often more sympathetic to experiment than Norton, called it 'madcap', 'irreverent', and a 'nightmare farce'. The last may have been director Adrian Hall's intention. The production was, however, 'bruising' in bad ways: too long and prolix, and 'too permissive of excesses'.[164] Actors were uncomfortable with their lines and substituted shouts, mutters or extra action for clear presentation of the verse. George Martin's Pandarus, in his derby and pinstripes, was a detached master of ceremonies. Only Richard Kneeland, the company's leading actor, was well cast, handling Ulysses' long speeches with intelligence and ease. Hall recognized the topicality of the play, but by weak control produced one of several revivals in the last third of the century

---

162 My notes from an early December performance kept noting a detail of action or property and asking 'why?'

163 Elliot Norton, *Boston Record American*, 1 December 1971.

164 Samuel Hirsch, '"Troilus and Cressida" At Providence's Trinity Square', *Boston Herald Traveler*, 5 December 1971.

that seemed to be mocking it, rather than underlining its mockery of love and war.

Emphasis on political manipulation and parallels to current debates on continuing a war became common, regardless of the style of production. Distrust of politicians further undercut the scheming Greeks. Howard Davies, in his 1972 Bristol Old Vic revival, presented Ulysses as a smooth quasi-diplomat, rational and devious, and Thersites as an editorializing reporter. Noel Purdom noted the play and production's 'brassy' quality, with a Prologue who shrugs off his function of explaining things, and an Epilogue who insults his audience.[165] Sardonic laughter predominated, and Ajax was punned into A-jakes. Reviews praised excellent acting, including Anna Calder-Marshall's Cressida, in a visually coherent production.

During the summer of 1972, Ashland, Oregon, staged its second revival. Where James Sandoe's 1958 production had romantic adaptations of Renaissance costumes, with classical touches that resembled the early *Titus Andronicus* sketch, Jerry Turner's used stylized classical dress on the Elizabethan stage, and presented a more politicized reading of the text. In 1958, Sandoe had drawn attention to Cressida, who exhibited early skepticism and fear that the love would not last. She was genuinely despairing at the news of the exchange, but managed to adopt an ironic tone as she parried the Greek commanders.[166] By contrast, Turner saw the play as a realistic, sneering modern political pamphlet, with the action framed by two clowns, Pandarus and Thersites. Pandarus tried to procure pleasure and ended engulfed in chaos, and Thersites was also swallowed by the war. Turner emphasized that even Hector's death produces no catharsis, and the play solves nothing.[167] Both productions, so differently conceived, demonstrated how the play can fit the mood of the times when carefully controlled.

During the last third of the century New Yorkers had seen a number of fringe revivals by small companies. In December 1973, however, there was a higher-profile production by the New York Shakespeare Festival at the studio theatre in Lincoln Center. David Schweitzer's interpretation resembled Trinity's, though less eclectically costumed and without vaudeville overtones. Reviewers of idiosyncratic productions often neglect individual performances to concentrate on the whole effect. Here, grotesquely inappropriate costuming undercut the main characters. 'Diomedes in a transparent black negligee, Achilles in a bikini with matching green feather boa . . . All the war accoutrements seemed to imply transvestiture, bestiality or something else popularly deemed obscene.

---

165 BOV, Theatre Royal, Bristol, Programme notes, 1972.
166 Mary Elaine Adams, *CSM*, 25 August 1958.
167 Jerry Turner commentary, 1972 OSF souvenir programme.

Thus was war declared obscene.'[168] Photographs of Ron Faber's Nestor, in prosthetic breasts and fez with bull's horns, suggested a bi-sexual cartoon Viking. Agamemnon (Jack Hollander), also barefooted and in shorts, wore an old football helmet with a vulture as a parody crest, presumably indicting the military as scavengers. Ulysses (Leonard Frey) was forced to deliver his speeches in shorts and undershirt. There were numerous sports allusions, including Troilus' flattened baseball shield, to suggest war as game in this camp attempt at a modern idiom. The Greek generals met in a steam room, a feature occasionally repeated more recently.[169] Paul Zalon had created an impressive frieze as a permanent background, then draped a distracting dead horse over the edge of the stage to hammer home the brutality of war.

Critics concurred that gimmicks obscured the play's own mockery. Actors spoke colloquially but monotonously, missing the music and often the sense of the lines.[170] *The New York Times* kept score: ten negative reviews to one positive! Walter Kerr suggested that the production was 'a parody of a Shakespeare burlesque'. Its echo microphone merely garbled words and its visual images were meaningless.[171] Reviewers ignored the extensive doubling. Madeleine LeRoux was Cressida, Helen and Cassandra. Perhaps this emphasized parallels between the first two, or implied a universal woman in many guises, but costume changes, cuts and superficial differentiation among the three made any depth of characterization of Cressida impossible. Other doubling could evoke character comparisons – Patroclus and Paris (Richard Kline), Pandarus and Calchas (William Hickey), and Nestor and Priam (Ron Faber) – or be merely puzzling – Menelaus and Ajax (Richard Masur) or Thersites and Diomedes (Charles Kimbrough, who played the former as a spastic). Extensive cutting enabled the doubling, but meant there was no Andromache pleading with Hector, nor Thersites commenting on the betrayal.

In 1976, Alvin Epstein and the Yale Repertory Theatre staged a more conservative, strongly pro-Trojan revival. Contrary to modern emphasis on the body and sensuality on both sides, sexuality was downplayed among the Trojans. Pandarus (Jeremy Geidt) was the old-fashioned avuncular busybody, arranging the meeting between demure Cressida and shy Troilus without voyeuristic leers or salacious delight, joining their hands sincerely in 3.2, rather than as a sleazy mock marriage the gesture usually becomes. Costumes helped create the idyll threatened by senseless war. Pandarus wore a long quilted robe, and Troilus and

---

168 Comtois, p. 406.
169 That year the San Diego Shakespeare Festival at the Old Globe introduced a steam bath for the Trojan council.
170 John Beaufort, 'Gimmicky Shakespeare at the Newhouse', *CSM*, 5 December 1973.
171 Kerr, *NYT*, 9 December 1973.

Cressida were in white. The most notable change was adding an idealized view of Paris and Helen's 'inheritors' (4.1.64–5). Carmen de Lavallade played a beanbag game with six children. The couch became the centre of domestic bliss, with a happy housewife and loving father.

Walter Kerr noted the unusually sharp contrast between 'sanitized' Troy and the unwashed Greek camp. The Greeks, in dirty, dark clothes, were preoccupied with sex, expressed not only in Thersites' words but also in Achilles' near rape of Patroclus.[172] Cressida (Laurie Heineman) became the helpless victim of a group of boors, though this was not a feminist reading of her character. The contrast between the two sides was underlined by Hector's gracious refusal to continue the duel and his costly sparing of Achilles. Though he added no dialogue, Epstein gave the argument for keeping Helen a moral tone, for the Greeks lacked any redeeming qualities.

There were no triumphs in England in 1976 either, as two potentially major revivals in sharply contrasting styles received mixed reviews. The National Theatre, awaiting the Cottesloe's completion, created a cockpit at the Young Vic for a subdued production. John Barton, assisted by Barry Kyle, staged his third RSC revival, where his familiarity with the play led to a concentration on details rather than a broad sweep of action.

The National's dirt-floored U with its rear platform and hangings could have been used to advantage, but promptbook directions often indicate entrances made randomly from below or off the platform just to get characters onto the floor. Extras occasionally perched on the cockpit walls, blocking sightlines. Vaguely Caroline costumes in muted colours made it hard to distinguish the armies, though several critics, hunting historical parallels, suggested Greek Roundheads against Trojan Cavaliers. An occasional string undershirt and a Greek helmet for the Prologue made no meaningful point.[173]

Elijah Moshinsky's direction was described as 'decorous' and lacking a viewpoint.[174] While RSC performances were generally becoming more physically active, not only in fights and the Helen scene, but also during the discussions, the film and promptbook show this one comparatively static. Characters often stood or sat through entire scenes, though Thersites shifted on the wall during

172 Kerr, 'An Oddly Virginal "Troilus and Cressida"', *NYT*, 18 April 1976, II, 8.

173 Details and sketches of the costumes are available at the NT Archives, as are video-tapes of both NT productions. These and tapes of recent RSC productions at the Shakespeare Centre Library give interesting evidence about the ways promptbook notations and performance practice may diverge, as well as showing differences between the performance that was filmed, critical recall of opening night details and my own notes on performances I saw, generally a few weeks into a run.

174 Michael Coveny, *FT*, 19 June 1976.

some of his observations. The actors usually spoke well, but seemed distant as they discoursed on time, value or order. Michael Billington remarked that little seemed at stake when Hector and Troilus argued.[175] Individual performances stood out. Pandarus (Robert Eddison), in his rose-coloured over-robe and stringy grey hair, was likened to Juliet's Nurse, sly, bustling and enjoying the intrigue.[176] His fussy character dominated the less sharply drawn lovers and helped detach their affair from the bitterness of war and lechery. After the betrayal, reviewers were not sure whether Troilus (Simon Ward) was supposed to be pure, and paired with an inherently bad or mischievous Cressida (Diana Quick), or whether this was 'Romeo and Juliet gone rancid'.[177] Unlike Michael Williams' interpretation, Ward's Troilus was weak and ineffectual until after 5.2, when he suddenly and unbelievably transformed into the new Greek leader.

Ulysses, Hector, and Ajax (Philip Locke, Denis Quilley, and Gawn Granger) gave individually memorable, relatively stylized performances. Ulysses was the necessary outsider, respected but not liked for his superior intellect. Ajax, called a 'cross between a musketeer and a prize bull', showed shallow chivalry stemming from pride as he strutted in his laurel wreath and moustache. Hector, the most successful of the three, had genuine heroic stature, and the audience felt the loss when the helmeted Myrmidons carried him off.[178] Nestor, Menelaus and Agamemnon were satirically presented as flat caricatures of 'garrulous senescence, stupid cuckoldry, and bluff pomposity', but did not give the necessary edge to an argument against senseless war. Nor was Philip Stone's somewhat puritanical Thersites, resembling a 'dismissed under gardener' in his apron, ankle boots and rolled sleeves, sufficiently bitter.[179] The purely satirical casting of small, undernourished Achilles, in golden robe, laurel wreath and chains, might have worked. He seemed an effete bisexual posing as a prizefighter, unworthy of Ulysses' elaborate scheming, which thus was satirized. A featherweight fighting in black velvet trousers and a breastplate, he clearly needed the Myrmidons in his grossly mismatched meeting with Hector. Unfortunately, the lack of a strong unifying concept and ensemble playing vitiated the play's impact in the wake of Vietnam.

The Barton/Kyle revival in Stratford and London presented different problems. A strong title pair, Francesca Annis and Mike Gwilym, balanced Barbara Leigh-Hunt (Helen), Tony Church (Ulysses), Robin Ellis (Achilles), Michael Pennington (Hector) and David Waller (Pandarus). The text was further cut from Barton's earlier Stratford revivals, but running time was unchanged. The season's permanent set, with its balconies, many entrances, downstage trap, and

175 Billington, *Gdn*, 18 June 1976.   176 Irving Wardle, *LT*, 18 June 1976.
177 Frank Marcus, 'In the Ring', *ST*, 20 June 1976, p. 16.
178 Sally Emerson, *PP*, September 1976, p. 32.   179 Eric Shantz, *DT*, 13 June 1976.

flanking walkways, was enhanced with classical properties. Each of the balcony supports, arranged in a semicircle around the stage, had a baulk at the base that could hold military insignia or serve as a seat, and helped produce a focused playing area.

Barton had not altered his basic reading of the text, though the programme's critical quotations now included one on Vietnam parallels.[180] The emphasis was again on war and time's deleterious effects on society and values, with diverse viewpoints admitted. And again, the sensual and homoerotic predominated. There was a shift in style, however. Extra business began with the Prologue's props. Cressida shared grapes with Pandarus and dropped a handkerchief onto Troilus' spear in 1.2. Agamemnon had a frying pan at the Greek council, where people fussed with straw hats and papers, and each speaker rose mechanically, sometimes comically vying for attention. Many actions became stylized. Balletic soldiers replaced natural fighters who made the final scenes so exciting in 1960. This may have suggested the coordinated movements of a hoplite phalanx, but seemed stiff to modern eyes. Roger Warren concluded that Barton knew the text so well he forgot the needs of the audience and allowed small emphases to distract from the broad strokes that had made his earlier productions clear and compelling.[181] Annis found interesting psychological depth in a changeable Cressida, who moved between wit and seriousness. Her costume, however, was now the heavy tiered skirt and stiff patterned bodice of a Minoan snake goddess. As Carol Rutter points out, the designer can shape audience response counter to the actor's conception, and this production was masculine and war-centred, diminishing Cressida despite her strong performance.

Many interpretations stemmed from the 1968 production. Achilles' effeminacy increased. Thersites was again scabby, with a long red tongue dangling obscenely from his codpiece. Feminist criticism had pointed out the commodification of women, however, and Helen was reduced to a captive whore. Led by a golden chain, she seemed forced to utter the lines about disarming Hector that normally provide a revealing contrast to her earlier 3.1 banter.[182] Mike Gwilym played Troilus sincerely and without overstatement, but others indulged in distracting business that undercut important speeches. Even Pennington, who powerfully dominated his scenes, wavered between playing sincerely and parodying heroism, thereby diminishing the impact of Hector's death.

In 1978, a production at Ottawa, Ontario's National Arts Centre picked up the trend of mixing formality and blatant sexuality. Pandarus (Erik Donkin) in

---

180 Souvenir programme, 1976, quoting R. A. Yoder, *SS 25*. Ms Yoder also notes the public 'ceremonial gestures', the contrast between codes of behaviour and the realities of war, and between the extrinsic sense of values Troilus propounds and intrinsic worth.

181 Warren, 'Theory and Practice', p. 174.   182 Ibid., p. 174.

makeup resembling an Attic comic mask, ritually united a rather wooden Troilus (Benedict Campbell) and Cressida (Jennifer Dale). Ulysses (Edward Atienza) looked corpse-like and delivered his long speeches in a beautiful but artificial manner reminiscent of earlier productions. The Bronze Age was suggested by wheeled brass platforms that served as city walls and viewing points, and a copper moon that moved across a scrim backcloth. The most striking scene was Hector's death, when the Myrmidons entered as a phalanx, their shields massed in one surface that reflected the setting sun into his eyes. They broke to encircle and attack as he was temporarily blinded.

Like Barton, director John Wood created sharp contrasts to this formality. Ajax and Hector fought brutally with battleaxes and Thersites (Neil Munro) clowned and interrupted the action with physical comedy. The currently fashionable emphasis on the body, male bonding and fascination with the enemy was explicitly referenced in an opening mime scene. Greeks and Trojans did pushups and engaged in simulated copulation. The Trojan debate about Helen, set in a steam bath, also highlighted the homoerotic. Cassandra burst in as naked men massaged each other.[183] Amidst all this, the love story receded, as it had with Barton and many directors through the 1960s and 1970s.

The decade ended with another Bristol Old Vic production that played at the Theatre Royal and at the Edinburgh Festival. John Warner's Pandarus resembled a turbaned pasha lounging on cushions and sharing an elaborate goblet in a generally conservative production that was praised for attention to the words.[184] Cressida, played for sympathy, lacked wantonness, in sharp contrast to Elizabeth Richardson's sluttish Helen. The two venues highlighted a recurring difficulty: the intimate scenes were better in Bristol, while the fights came into their own on the huge Assembly Hall stage, and allowed the play to build to the end, where black-clad Greeks with square shields and conventional crested helmets battled the more romantic white-garbed Trojans with their round shields and feathered helmets.[185]

Tradition, experiment and a new Cressida

The anguish of the Vietnam era was lessening by the early 1980s. New social and political agendas were sought as contexts for slightly less frequent revivals. The RSC continued to dominate, but Stratford, Ontario, and the Oregon Festival were among a variety of interpreters. More important, a televized version became easily accessible worldwide in 1981, part of a BBC project to film the entire canon. Unlike a radio broadcast in 1935, George Rylands' cut and clarified 1955 black

183 Richard Eder, 'Stage: Canadians Produce "Troilus" – Rarely Done Bard', *NYT*, 26 January 1978.
184 Michael Coveny, *Obs*, 19 August 1979.   185 John Barker, *DT*, 23 August 1979.

and white version for BBC, or their 1966 rendition, this was widely marketed on tape for educational and private use, along with study materials that noted existential aspects and outlined each character's responsibility within the whole.

Jonathan Miller's production, like many plays in the series, was not critically well received, but had the advantage of speed and the camera's ability to provide broad background shots and close-ups of intimate scenes. In 5.2, control of lighting and sound enabled Troilus to see Cressida and Diomedes as shadows within an illuminated tent. Her dialogue and Troilus' reactions were believably separated. In 1.2, Hecuba and Helen were followed in a tracking shot that established the interiors of Troy. Cameras shifted to show the Trojan warriors returning realistically down a street beneath Pandarus' window. The Greek camp scenes moved in and out of a series of dusty tents, and Achilles and Ulysses did the 'time' speeches as an intimate conversation.

Restrictions on what could be shown, at least on American television, dictated more conservative clothing, a reasonably restrained Helen scene, and damping of the homoeroticism. Rather than the blatant sexual displays of recent theatrical productions, there were suggestions: Suzanne Burden's Cressida appeared in a nightgown after the assignation, and Charles Gray's decadent Pandarus slipped in to check the bed. Miller's daring in casting 'The Incredible Orlando' as a cross-dressed Thersites was muted by camera angles that often focused on the face, even during a laundry scene.[186] Anton Lesser's carefully detailed Troilus was more suited to television than it would be to the RSC stage in 1985, and the young lovers became relatively central. Going against Miller's initial intentions, Burden pointed the way to Juliet Stevenson's 1985 reading, becoming understandably angry as Troilus repeated 'true' and realizing that she needed to preserve herself. Although not a definitive production, it raised interesting points and made the play accessible worldwide for repeated viewings and study.

The RSC also revived *Troilus and Cressida* in 1981, at the Aldwych. Wardle's review, titled 'Terry Hands leaves Shakespeare to fend for himself', found no central theme or emphasis on linear development.[187] In 1973 Hands called it the play he would most like to do because 'the examination of values in the play corresponded to cultural reality'.[188] He later spoke of the importance of letting actors find their keys to interpretation. The result was that many characterizations seemed fragmented or overplayed, and exhibited different aspects at will.

---

186 'Orlando' was the cabaret persona of Jack Birkett.
187 Irving Wardle, *LT*, 8 July 1981.
188 Tape provided by Sister Agnes Fleck, and letter of 15 June 2001 quoting notes taken at the 1973 World Centre for Shakespeare Studies summer course. Jeanne Newlin earlier pointed out how each era can adapt the play for its taste because of the range of tones in it ('Modernity').

Farrah's eclectic costumes sent messages that the actors did not always match. Troilus wooed in a classic tunic and modern army boots. Helen (Barbara Kingham) resembled Zsa Zsa Gabor in her feather boa and beaded flapper gown, and suggested nineteen twenties looseness.[189] Ulysses (John Carlisle) looked medieval, while Nestor was a classical tortoise, bent under a huge shield slung on his back. Pandarus (Tony Church) and Ajax (Terry Woods) recalled Barton productions with parasol and flywhisk. One reviewer described Ajax as a mix of Obelix and the Cookie Monster.[190] Colour schemes were becoming conventional by now, and all-enveloping Greek helmets depersonalized the black-clad Myrmidons as they fought the predominately orange-clad Trojans.

Roger Warren found strong and interesting performances offsetting 'excesses and confusions'. David Suchet's Achilles was a high point in interpretations of the role – bare-chested and well-oiled, more sumo wrestler than Greek athlete. At first he seemed quietly threatening and brutal, but in mid-play, with rouged nipples and cheeks, he assumed a nasty bisexuality, then donned armour as a final transformation. Patroclus oiled him fondly and listened closely as Ulysses talked of reputation in 3.3.[191] His salacious Middle Eastern dance, years before men were taking up the Raks Sharki, seemed to hypnotize Hector in 4.5 and again suggested the wartime fascination with enemies that psychologists have recognized.

There was satire in the parade of warriors, who quaffed wine while Paris preened in a mirror. Troilus (James Hazeldine) shambled on, crying and apologetic in 2.2, but rushed into battle at the end as if on a suicide mission.[192] Reviewers noted scenes played for broad comedy or heightened sexuality. Ajax demolished the breakaway boxes littering the camp until Achilles stopped the rampage by grabbing his genitalia. Helen's sigh 'Cupid, Cupid, Cupid' referred longingly to a group of young, feathered, curly headed servants playing darts. They joined Paris in groping Pandarus as he sang, giving his 'Is this the generation of love . . . Is love a generation of vipers?' new and peculiarly bitter meaning. Yet despite this Pandarus was delighted to arrange Troilus and Cressida's assignation.

Cressida (Carol Royle) showed some of the disappointed impatience Papp had mentioned, becoming cold and detached when Troilus accepted the exchange and lectured her on faithfulness. She grabbed luggage and donned a symbolic black coat over her white dress as she left with black-clad Diomedes. Her reactions to the Generals and Diomedes could be read as an outgrowth of this disappointment, but there was no real addition to her interpretation. She had shown the same guile, anger and playfulness from the start. Schulman commented that the Women's

189 Sheridan Morley, *Punch*, July 1981.   190 Benedict Nightingale, *NS*, 1981.
191 Warren, 'Interpretations', p. 149.   192 Michael Coveney, *FT*.

Movement should love her for treating vows as cavalierly as men usually do,[193] but this was not a feminist or defiant reading of the role.

Joe Melia's rather likeable Thersites spoke the Prologue and returned at the end, an observer surprised by nothing. The full Aldwych stage was used for the final battle, with Troy's bronze wall pulled away, and barbed wire rimming the muddy green stage cloth. Here Hands took control and choreographed elaborate movement. The Myrmidons surrounded Hector like a dance ensemble and the overdone battle scenes ran half an hour. At the end, barbed wire entrapped even Pandarus. His final speech, while entangled, visually linked the lecherous and the military, and reminded the audience that his world, too, had been destroyed by war.

John Neville-Andrews' presentation at Washington's Folger Theatre in 1983 and Howard Davies' 1985 revival at the RSC were in sharp contrast to Hands' freewheeling approach. Neville-Andrews gave the play a relatively conservative reading, using his experienced resident company to satirize love and war, but also to arouse sympathy for the lovers, who were more central than they had become at Stratford. Diomedes carefully repaired a net in the earlier scenes for use at the end, gladiator style,[194] business that graphically illustrated war's entangling power. The most unusual touch was the Prologue, shared by a boy and girl who reappeared as silent and sombre witnesses to the immature antics of their elders, again suggesting Paris' 'inheritors'.

Davies gave Stratford and London a landmark interpretation that yielded a coherent history play and foregrounded feminist issues. As Shrimpton noted, Ralph Koltai's set 'was crucial . . . [and] invoked the Crimean War . . . to make us think, simultaneously, of the Charge of the Light Brigade and the brutal reality of the wards at Scutari'.[195] The stage became an interior with balcony, formal staircase, shattered window, tattered hangings and dusty chandelier for 'a dance of death through a bomb-lit Heartbreak House'.[196] It visually attested war's destruction of gracious living. Rearrangement of the same tables and chairs didn't sufficiently distinguish Trojan and Greek locales for some viewers, but the production aimed to portray 'aristocratic foolishness on both sides'. In this setting 'Peter Jeffrey's Ulysses is a well-tuned study of a fading professional officer lamenting war's slide into disorder.'[197]

Two exciting performances captured critical attention. Replacing Nicky Henson on two weeks' notice, Alun Armstrong created a Geordie Thersites who acutely observed all through bull's eye lenses, mingling comedy with corrosive

193 Milton Schulman, *New Standard*.
194 John and Ellen Mahon, *Shakespeare Bulletin*, November–December 1983, p. 22.
195 *SS 39*, p. 203.   196 David Ian Rabey, *PP*, August 1985, p. 15.
197 Rabey, pp. 14–15.

satire. Saucepan on head, he accurately parodied Clive Russell's Ajax, destroying his 'pretensions to the stature of a hero'.[198] More realistic than some, he carried a canvas bag of vegetables as Officers' Club mess orderly, and made disastrous attempts at dusting. His disgust grew in response to hypocrisy and factionalism, and his comments became moral indictments, making him 'less a cynic than the voice of a nonconformist conscience'.[199]

Juliet Stevenson's highly intelligent young Cressida roused sympathy as she preserved herself in a male-dominated world. She gained stature by contrast to Anton Lesser's young, unsure Troilus as well as from details of her own feminist performance. Like Miller, Davies had originally wanted a more traditional androcentric interpretation, with Cressida, the temptress who readily yields to men, as part of a less powerful title couple. Stevenson's reading of the part clashed with Davies' concept, but won out as she reconstructed the character to bring out the oppressive effects of militarism and male sexuality.[200] A few critics felt she rejected the long-standing 'Cressida as whore' without giving a new reading. Most, however, saw a young woman finding warmth and humour and using them as the situation dictated. She sparred a bit tensely with Pandarus in their opening scene, took a gentle lead with Troilus, and was shocked to find him powerless to protect her (4.4). She discovered new wit 'as a desperate form of self-protection' among the Greeks, and showed genuine anguish at her infidelity.

Studies of male group behaviour patterns with women supported increasingly broad interpretations of the kissing scene (4.5). Here gang rape threatened. Cressida was passed roughly from man to man, giving her reason to seek the relative safety of Diomedes' care and explaining her change of heart. Male bonding showed in Ulysses' obvious unhappiness at having a woman enter his world. This and her witty rejection of him explained his insulting description and diminished him, with the result that Cressida 'snatches the moral heart of the play'.[201] Twenty years earlier, Kott had commented on her amazing, many-faceted character, and within the decade Carolyn Asp and Gayle Greene, among others, had examined the theoretical basis where a woman tended to see herself as men rated her. This Cressida was aware of the defenses she created, but also responded within the parameters of her male-dominated society, though as Rutter noted, her costume in 5.2 was not in keeping with the personality Stevenson had established.[202]

Lindsey Duncan shared the deeper reading, playing Helen as 'devalued but dully sensate of her suffering'.[203] Tipsy Paris could be demanding, and her wit

198 Barry Russell, p. 31.   199 Shrimpton, p. 205.
200 See Helms on the problems of playing Cressida from a feminist perspective, pp. 200–3.
201 John Elsom, *PI*, June 1986, pp. 18–19.   202 Rutter, p. 130.
203 David Nice, *PP*, July 1986, p. 26.

Figure 11. Pandarus and Cressida in Howard Davies' Royal Shakespeare Company Production, 1985.

with him and Pandarus was also a form of self-defence. Her scene was incorporated into a boisterous party where Pandarus (Clive Merrison) was debagged by Trojan soldiers. David Nice felt the blatant groping and disorder helped explain why Helen has become what she is ' – not a rotten cause, but a cause made rotten by war'. From 5.4 on Pandarus, now seedy, tried to maintain his world by playing the piano under the balcony as battles swirled around him. The rottenness of war reached a climax when Achilles and his Myrmidons invaded the house, coldly checked their guns and shot Hector from downstage when he disarmed on the balcony.

Although Papp wrote from Cressida's perspective and some productions in the seventies made her actions more understandable, Stevenson created the strongest, most understandable Cressida to date, as the play's balance gradually shifted. The formal verse speeches by Ulysses, Hector and Troilus on order, chivalrous honour and fidelity, have become less central. They express conventional historical male viewpoints that seem out of touch with our disordered world. Geenblatt and Cohen have pointed out that Shakespeare's world was not as orderly as Tillyard maintained. Shakespeare expresses this disorganization when Achilles is roused not by Ulysses' carefully constructed, honour-based scheme, but by the primal need to avenge his lover. Hector's chivalric challenge yields no result, and his boastful dismissal of Andromache's concern and later pursuit of fancy armour make him less unequivocally admirable. Davies' production spoke to the mood of the mid-eighties as women found their voices, and it temporarily broke the tendency of the 1960s and 1970s to make the war and male relationships paramount.

Two idiosyncratic revivals of the sort Muriel Byrne criticized followed in 1987. She had deplored early attempts at director's theatre, where 'the producer . . . treats Shakespeare as a peg on which to hang his own fantastic ideas', instead of trusting the play to good actors.[204] David William utilized Stratford, Ontario's proscenium-stage Avon Theatre for a camp rendition, the least successful of the season's five anti-war plays.[205] Sub-sets of society – drag queens, English bullies in studded leather, and ethnic show-offs – highlighted homoeroticism, brutality and factionalism. Pandarus resembled Carmen Miranda. Ulysses (Nicholas Pennell) was a 'tight-lipped Colonel Blimp', and much of the revival pushed Shakespeare's satire to the breaking point.[206] The A-jakes pun became visual when Ajax entered kicking down an outhouse door, farting and buttoning his trousers. Later he pushed Thersites' head into the latrine. Marilyn French's programme notes mentioned the 'locker room sensibility' of the all-male Greek world. But there was also a suggestion of the British Raj at a time when colonialism was being examined in *The Tempest* and other works. The Trojans in council resembled Indians, while the Greeks were British in tropical khaki shorts.[207] Helen involved the Trojans in a drag orgy, and Thersites illustrated cuckoldry in 2.3 by making a Ken doll rape Barbie.[208] William did emphasize the brutality and futility of war, but Shakespeare's text was often sacrificed to extraneous business. Irving Wardle commented that much of it went 'down the drain' along with Thersites' head.[209]

Matthew Francis' National Youth Theatre production was more specifically politicized. Christ Church Spitalfields became Lebanon, the current hot spot, with sandbags and camouflage netting. Reviewers said the concept and staging often distracted both cast and audience. The extended metaphor of 1.1 was actualized, with Pandarus as 'a mountainous Turkish baker' while others rolled pita dough or sipped coffee.[210] The Trojans were figures of current sympathy – turbaned Arab freedom fighters struggling against US Marines. Ulysses resembled Ollie North conducting a news conference. Acknowledging popular culture,

204 Byrne, p. 11.
205 John F. Burn, 'Winds of Change Blow Through Ontario's Theatre Festival on the Avon', *NYT*, 5 July, 2:29. The other anti-war plays were *Cabaret*, *Mother Courage*, Sherriff's *Journey's End* and Stephen MacDonald's *Not About Heroes*.
206 Bill Marx, 'Battle of the Bard', *Boston Phoenix*, 3 July 1987, 3:8.
207 Mel Gussow, 'Of Shakespeare, Brecht, and Canada's Stratford', *NYT*, 11 June 1987, C19.
208 Bowen, p. 54.   209 LT, 25 July 1987, p. 20; Gussow.
210 Michael Ratcliffe, *Obs*, 27 September 1987.

Francis turned Ajax into Rambo. The media were there, with intrusive cameras, flashing lights and flickering screens that allowed Pandarus and Cressida to watch the returning Trojans on television. Thersites was a Graham Greene burned-out alcoholic, a correspondent in Hawaiian shirt, slurring out his bitter comments. Amid this, Achilles lolled in a Turkish bath.

Past directors often made cuts and rearranged the text to facilitate staging, focus on the military, provide a more dignified ending or increase Thersites' importance. Francis cut and rewrote to emphasize the grimness of war, perhaps with a visual reference to M*A*S*H*, the still-popular Vietnam-era indictment of the Korean conflict. Thersites died in a field hospital, surrounded by limbs. Nurse Cressida surrendered to Diomedes just before a noisy modern battle with convincing carnage.[211] Like Landau's Civil War references, however, these were too emotionally charged. Many of Shakespeare's more general points were submerged by the specifics of current politics, and the title romance again lost significance.

There were several minor German productions of *Troilus and Cressida* at the end of the Second World War, but English-language revivals have outnumbered the Continental since 1950. Translations, however, still have the advantage of being able to modernize language, often clarifying and reshaping troublesome passages or pointing satire.[212] Hans Fischer's 1962 Dresden revival was 'highly popular' as a subversive attack on Communist party rules and government figures. Horst Schulze scored with his 'deconstructive clowning' as Thersites, whose lines were rearranged and foregrounded to heighten his impact. The anti-war statement was heightened by the appliqué of a reproduction of 'Guernica' on the curtain. Hortmann, however, referring to Hans Hollmann's 1970 Hamburg revival, declared that 'debunking the characters to suit programmatic anti-militarism was bound to lead to a diminishing . . . of stature . . . [and] significance'.[213]

In the 1980s, however, there were two landmark German revivals, the 1985 Berliner Ensemble post-modernist interpretation that visited the Edinburgh Festival in 1987, and Dieter Dorn's 1986 ritualized five-hour marathon that was later televized. Elements from both influenced later revivals in Britain. The Munich Kammerspiel is small, and Dorn kept his audience involved. Deciding that 'theatre Greeks' were too stagey and modern uniforms evoked extraneous associations, Jurgen Rose chose 'indeterminate' designs. The costumes were eclectic – battledress trousers, greaves, bandoliers or vaguely heraldic tunics for the fighters, and oriental pearls over rough tribal cloth for Cressida and

211 Claire Armstead, *FT*, 23 September 1987; Robert Hanks, *In*, 30 September 1987.
     Mark Sanderson referred to 'PLO chic' costumes (*Time Out*, 30 September 1987).
212 Dennis Kennedy, 'Shakespeare with his Language', Bulman, pp. 135–7.
213 Hortmann, pp. 377–9, 245.

Pandarus, 'resulting in a powerful blend of incompatibilities'. Rose's stage had irregular raised segments.[214] At the Berlin Theatre festival in 1987, the colour-splotched set overlaid with graffiti reminded audiences of their hated symbol. A rusty shipwreck attested to the length of the war, and the whole seemed 'Hockneyesque'.[215]

With six months of rehearsal at the Kammerspiel, Dorn was able to mix elements of Kabuki, Manouchkine Theatre du Soleil, Kurosawa spectacle and stasis. A percussion band suggested pagan ritual and provided appropriate rhythms for different characters and the production achieved the effect of 'ferocity barely restrained, of a primitive culture in its harsh exoticism'. Michael Wachsmann's translation was uncut and Hortmann felt 'the dramatically irrelevant philosophical reflections and verbal heroics took even [Dorn's] highly competent and long-rehearsed cast to their limits'. Hortmann mentions 'Exotically abrupt movements', ritual gestures, a bowl of water for the Greeks and fire for the Trojans.

Dorn's success lay partially in 'not proclaiming a message'. By 'denying himself this easy road to clarity of meaning . . . [he] constrained himself and his actors to fathom the ambiguities of character and the ambivalence in Shakespeare's treatment of the themes of war, authority, love and fidelity'.[216] Pandarus, devoted to Cressida but suspecting her frailty, 'presented a picture of the frailty of age as moving as it was repellant for its suggestion of folly and vice'. Cressida suggested contradiction with an innocent face and a restless body 'eager for physical knowledge'. She was 'a creature of the moment, both helpless prey to conflicting impulses and playful coquette enjoying her short-lived . . . power'. Hortmann found her a 'shockingly abused victim and a very willing but also tragic slut in the Greek Camp'. Despite the length of the production and its complexities, the control of style made it riveting and evocative.[217]

The Berliner Ensemble, playing in Edinburgh's King's Theatre, gave Britain its first brief taste of a live foreign-language rendition of the play in a style very different from Dorn's, but also benefiting from long rehearsal and strong ensemble playing. Co-directed by Joachim Tenschert and translator Manfred Wekwerth, this revival from East Berlin's Schiffbauerdamm impressed British reviewers by the strength of the company and the skilful use of Manfred Grund's deceptively simple stage set. There was a Brechtian aesthetic in the 'shredded grey arch' with its long white front veil that could be bed, tent, separate chamber, projection screen, shroud or even balcony railing as Pandarus and Cressida reviewed the warriors. The black, grey and white colour scheme was relieved only by a

---

214 Ibid., p. 325.
215 Olivia Fuchs, 'Berlin Theatre Festival, *PP*, July 1987, p. 35.
216 Hortmann, p. 327.   217 Ibid., p. 326; Fuchs, p. 35.

few touches of blue, patently artificial makeup, and an iridescent cheek patch for each warrior.

Thersites was spokesperson for a production that focused on the power of war to destroy not only life, but all that matters in life. Ekkehard Schall, swinging a rat by the tail, was physically able to hold his own and not forced to use words as Adlerian compensation.[218] There was visual satire as he towered over a diminutive Ajax. Corinna Harfouch's Cressida was an awkward, anxious adolescent trying desperately to understand her feelings as she realized she was the object of male fantasy but also merely a commodity in a wartime bargain. In this deeply psychological reading, she wore a 'maidenly veil' with Troilus, but donned a mink stole and gloves as she braced for the exchange.[219] Wekwerth cut Hector's sparing of Achilles and focused on the final brutality in 5.9, when Achilles apparently relented, unarmed Hector gratefully backed into the sheet, and hidden Myrmidons speared him from behind.[220] Hooded figures in black boiler suits shovelled up discarded weapons and dragged Hector off, reminding the audience that they were viewing theatre as well as the waste of war. While the physicality and rough clothes showed a sophisticated society being reduced to savages, formally dressed musicians sat stage left, playing everything from Handel to a twanging tune on a Jew's harp. Each effect was calculated and meticulously rehearsed, and the production made its point even when people could not understand the words.[221]

Stratford and the National dominate the 1990s

Britain's major subsidized companies dominated the 1990s. The RSC mounted three revivals that ran in Stratford, London or on tour for parts of five years, and the National ended the century with a striking production. Sam Mendes chose an eclectic style that mirrored the play's inconsistencies and subtly universalized it for an exciting RSC Swan Theatre production in 1990 that is recognized as another landmark.[222] In his very full critique, Peter Holland comments that Mendes trusted the play, fitted it admirably to the small stage and 'realized [its] multivocality, [and] its refusal to hierarchise the competing tonalities'.[223] Predictably, reviewers had differing reactions. Irving Wardle complained there

218 Graham Bradshaw, 'The essence of ensemble', *TLS*, 4 September 1987, p. 957.
219 Michael Ratcliffe, *Obs*, 23 August 1987; Cordelia Olish, *PI*, October 1987, p. 55; Michael Billington, *Gdn*, 20 August, 1987.
220 Graham Bradshaw.   221 Martin Hoyle, *FT*, 19 August 1987.
222 Poel's performances at Stratford used this small theatre before it burned. It now provides the thrust stage and galleries that approximate Elizabethan intimacy between actor and audience. My recollections are from notes made in August 1990.
223 Holland, pp. 69–70.

was no character the audience could believe in. Gary O'Connor said that Mendes had done 'an enticing repair job' on a play that had presented problems to many directors.[224] The actors were comfortable with the verse and the play's many spokespeople received due emphasis, though Pandarus and Thersites dominated.

Anthony Ward left the thrust stage bare except for a focal circle upstage centre. It became a pool where Cressida and Pandarus dabbled and the returning warriors ritually washed. Later, a grate with lights shining up supported the dead Patroclus, cast an eerie light on the fighting soldiers and was the appropriate site of Achilles' vengeance on Hector. At stage rear, three sets of heavy horizontal slats with entrances between could serve as ladders, and partially obstructed the view of a giant, half-decayed female head that symbolized destructive processes. A few canvas chairs provided seating, but generally characters stood or knelt, exuding energy. Modern touches, such as the table light and coffee mugs during the Greek council, or a boom box playing 'Lover Man, Where Can You Be' while Achilles and Patroclus awaited Hector, contrasted with the looming head that reminded the audience of the story's classical roots, making the set timeless but 'not over clever'.[225]

The costumes were eclectic but not distracting, and facilitated audience recognition of details. Thersites was grotesque in his grubby oversized flasher's mac and leather cap, surgical gloves covering scabby hands and a public school tie holding up his wrinkled pinstripe trousers. Achilles (Ciaran Hinds), with slicked hair, and Patroclus (Patterson Joseph), in chains and zippers, could have frequented a sleazy gay bar, accompanied by Ajax (Richard Ridings), a huge skinhead. Ulysses, Nestor and other Greeks wore boots and black leather trench coats that suggested seven rough years in the field, in contrast to the cleaner Trojans. Pandarus (Norman Rodway) was obviously a roué in nattily striped blazer and white trousers until his final decay. Cassandra (Linda Kerr) wore conventional black while Cressida (Amanda Root), wore white.[226] Greek helmets and Renaissance breastplates bridged the gap between modern garments and the swords used for individual combats, avoiding a disjunction between words and actions. My notes from August 1990 commented that the eclecticism worked because the costume choices were generally in muted colours and logically suited their various characters.

Simon Russell Beale's landmark Thersites, limping and pale faced, with rheumy eyes and red nose, dominated the Greek scenes. He seemed to welcome the beatings that defined his place, though his accent showed him the equal of the

---

224 Wardle, *Independent on Sunday*, 6 May 1990; Gary O'Connor, *PP*, August 1990, p. 29.
225 Christopher Edwards, *Spectator*, 12 May 1990.
226 John Simon described the women's costumes as 'neo-Grecian resort wear' ('London, Part I', *New York*, 2 September 1991, p. 48).

other Greeks, and only disease and deformity made him an outcaste. Disgusted and disgusting, he carefully drooled into the food he prepared for Ajax. His role as licensed jester was denoted by a fool's bauble that he occasionally pulled from a bag,[227] and he functioned as master of ceremonies for the battles.

Cressida, abandoned by her turncoat father, had developed 'cheeky self-protective strategies' that she momentarily forgot in her attraction to Troilus. When neither he nor her father saved her from the Greeks, she was forced to rely on her own skills for self-preservation. Amanda Root made this plain in an interpretation that was less overtly feminist than Stevenson's but more sympathetic. Ralph Fiennes' 'formalized and declamatory Troilus' stood out from the other performances, and the lovers became more balanced and convincing at the Pit, where Patterson Joseph's athletic and vulnerable young man seemed crushed rather than relieved in 5.2.[228] As Holland noted, Fiennes gave no suggestion of sexual excitement, and his distress at loosing Cressida was merely verbal. Sally Dexter's Helen, a Jane Russell sex symbol, contrasted sharply with Cressida. She was carried in on a fluted dish / litter, wrapped in gold – a morsel to be opened by Paris – and bulged from a tight, low-cut red costume with a broad gold collar that might have anchored a slave's chain.[229]

Mendes emphasized the verbal wit. The scenes with Ulysses, especially the council, were unmarred by intrusive clowning, so the language could be appreciated. When humourous actions were added, they made a point, such as Paris' narcissistic preening at the pool in 1.2. Cressida, Pandarus and Helen were allowed to highlight their clever repartee, and the banter contrasted sharply with the tone of 3.1.128–39, lines that are often thrown away.

The intimacy of the Swan made it possible for most of the audience to see small details. Pandarus touched the crest on his blazer pocket when he introduced himself as 'A Prologue armed'. Patroclus looked anguished when Ulysses mentioned Achilles' interest in Polyxena (3.3.193–4). The final fights had a ritual beginning as warriors moved downstage to engage each other when their turns came. But the matches were short, personal and fierce, and only a few feet from the audience, in contrast to often ill-defined or stiffly choreographed skirmishes on larger, more distant stages. I watched some people in the front rows draw back self-protectively.

The RSC returned to the main house in 1996 with a visually opulent but rather predictable production that left reviewers cold. John Gunter's set had an epic

---

227 Beale talked in detail about his role within the broader conception of the play in *Players of Shakespeare 3*, pp. 160–73.
228 *SuT*, 29 September 1991.
229 Martin Hoyle, *FT*, 28 April 1990. Apparently in some performances she was wrapped in gold, in others, shiny black plastic.

quality, with its battered, slightly sculptural metallic wall stage right and rear, upper-level opening to view the troops, and huge gates for Troy.[230] Hangings quickly drawn down a slightly raised platform at stage right or across the main level suggested tents. Emblems on poles enhanced the décor and a cello-shaped shield hung by the proscenium, stage left, indicating Achilles' area. The council scenes started on the platform, and the Trojans had a heavy table, gold chairs and appropriate cups and pitchers. The set enhanced the duel scene (4.5) when the Trojans marched in through the great rear gates to the sound of trumpets. It also allowed effective blocking for 5.2, with Diomedes and Cressida near Calchas' tent on the platform, Troilus and Ulysses overhearing from mid-stage left, and Thersites, intermediary between action and audience, observing from slightly down the stage front steps in the ultimate example of the layers of observation that are an integral aspect of the play.[231]

Although the set suggested a conservative concept, Judge emphasized physicality in keeping with increased critical attention to attitudes toward the body in Shakespeare and with the tradition Barton had established at Stratford. The returning Trojan warriors came up the stage front steps into a changing room where they disarmed and toweled off as Pandarus and Cressida watched the fleshy display from above. Later the stairs led nude Paris and Helen up from their bath, where they were dressed beside the chaise and cushions that, along with a red tent cloth, served as suggestive props for Helen's quarters. The sexual took a further turn as Pandarus, in loose robe, chopines and heavy makeup, shared their bed.

Other costumes and actions also emphasized the sensual. Achilles (Philip Quast) was 'handsome, physically impressive, besotted with his young, fair-haired Patroclus and naively proud of the contours of his own body'. Pandarus showed the longing for Troilus that Carol Cook carefully delineates in her analysis of desire in the play.[232] Joseph Fiennes tolerated this until Cressida was secured, but pushed Pandarus violently out of the final embrace (4.4.13) and kicked him off the platform in the letter scene. Victoria Hamilton was more ardent with Troilus than most Cressidas, and her bare midriff and low-cut harem top proclaimed sexiness as she embraced him. Her revealing dress drew all eyes when she entered the

---

230 See Smallwood, *SS 50*, pp. 211–15 for a detailed review and David Murray, 'All Sweat and Tangas', *FT*, 2 December 1996, p. 17.

231 Barbara Hodgdon has examined the intricacies of 'seeing' in this play at a level one can't perceive during a production, but which illuminates another of the play's amazing complexities. Some critics found the blocking distracting and felt it diminished Thersites, but it came across well when I saw the production a month into the run, when Thersites may have been further up the steps than on opening night.

232 Cook, especially pp. 185–7.

Greek camp, and her conduct, especially with Patroclus, made Ulysses' speech unusually accurate. While not the villainess of old, she was the product of a body-oriented, lustful society. Later, she seemed torn, teasing Diomedes, enjoying him, but occasionally thinking seriously of Troilus. Joseph Fiennes, less distant than his brother, still suggested self-pity more than deeply felt loss as he watched her performance in 5.2.[233]

Physicality also dominated the duel scene. Achilles manifested a taunting fascination with the enemy as he confronted and flashed Hector. Ajax and Hector first wrestled then, despite the putatively chivalric situation, grabbed staves from a can. Hector finally hit Ajax with the can before graciously breaking off. From 5.3 on, there were quantities of 'Stratford smoke', this time red-tinged. Cassandra, present during the entire debate on Helen, re-entered in 5.3 against a glow that forecast the burning of Troy and Hector's sunset. Pandarus (Clive Francis) ended the play scab-covered and weak-voiced, probably an AIDS victim. The departing Trojans brutally kicked him down the platform steps, and he slowly rose, body twisted, to address the audience.

In contrast to the cynical note Thersites (Richard McCabe) gave to the Prologue ('and *that's* the quarrel?'), and the caricaturing of most of the Greeks, there were notable moments when the verse came across seriously and clearly. Ulysses (Philip Voss) spoke of degree and time with a natural understanding, and the Greeks listened, rather than indulging in distracting business. His delivery was in sharp contrast to Fiennes' more declamatory, self-indulgent style. But the result, like Barton's in 1976, was 'embellishing and decorating the parts [rather than] providing an overview of the whole'.[234]

The last of the century's RSC revivals, designed to tour with a reduced cast and a text cut to under three hours, opened at the Pit in 1998, toured, and eventually reached the Swan the following season. Tom Piper's dark wooden doorway and white plastered back wall minimally suggested a battered cottage interior. Reviewers had wondered why no director chose Ireland as context for the deleterious effects of a long struggle. Now they saw a niche to the right representing a Catholic home altar, heard Trojans speaking with slight brogues and saw Helenus in clerical collar. Predictably, the Greeks were British. Benedict Nightingale typed them: Agamemnon was a Scots scoutmaster, Ulysses a Midlands trader, Diomedes an Ulster police chief, Menelaus (who absorbed Nestor's role) 'a struck-off Harley Street abortionist', Achilles an 'upmarket roughneck', Patroclus an androgynous giggler, and Ajax 'a Welsh bandit'.[235] In contrast, brown-suited Priam resembled a middle-class Irishman, accompanied by relatively beefy sons in corduroys. Pandarus had vestiges of dandyism. The

233 Paul Taylor, *In*, 26 July 1996, p. 6.   234 Smallwood, *SS 50*, p. 215.
235 Nightingale, 'Troubled View of the Trojan Wars', *LT*, 7 November 1998, p. 20.

Trojan women's dark print dresses seemed to connote a conservative society in mourning. Cressida (Jayne Ashbourne) wore a cross, and Cassandra clutched a bundle of rags that perhaps represented a lost child. By startling contrast, Helen (Sara Stewart) appeared in 3.1 as the statue in the niche, her blue and white robes a cynical take on the Virgin Mary that blasphemously equated worship of Helen and the central figure in Roman Catholic ritual. To the accompaniment of hymns from several crone-like votaries, she showed pleasure as Paris emerged from beneath her skirts, the opposite of Cressida's numbed reaction to her treatment by the Greeks. The typing and simple furnishings stimulated associations for the audience, although Robert Smallwood in his very full review also mentioned Spain, and several others suggested that the setting might be Bosnia, then engaged in its grinding civil struggle.[236]

Shakespeare mentions classical gods, but focuses on human actions. Michael Boyd, however, reshaped the text to emphasise human responsibility within religious contexts that mixed Christian referents and pagan ritual. The extratextual details, often iconoclastic, produced shock and a moral ending. Thersites (Lloyd Hutchinson), who spoke the Prologue as a slide-illustrated lecture, later commented while photographing sleazy Greek conduct. Directed by Ulysses, Diomedes shot Patroclus to bring Achilles brawling into action. Achilles (Darrell D'Sylva) practiced voodoo with blood and chicken feathers. When he shot Hector (Alistair Petrie) point blank, he ripped out the heart in a scene reminiscent of '*Tis Pity She's a Whore*. The Myrmidons were cut and this presumably provided substitute brutality. Paris' true evaluation of Helen was revealed when he used her as a shield in the final battle. Pandarus had spoken his epilogue at the end of 5.3, and bombs, sirens and shots accompanied the killings. The end involved more rewriting. Helenus conducted Hector's burial. Troilus spoke his final lines accompanied by singing of 'Lord have mercy . . . Christ have mercy on us' while Cressida stood unacknowledged behind him. With Troilus suicidally bent on continuing the fight, the production reverberated as an indictment, within a Christian context, of continuing senseless wars.

Michael Boyd's promptbook often reflected a reductiveness akin to DVD scene titles. He gave them labels such as 'Cressida in Love' (1.2), 'Press Conference' (1.3), 'New, Improved Ajax' (2.3) and 'Chicken Tonight' (5.1). Cressida was less central than in 1985 or 1990. A simple, round-faced country girl, she was interested in William Houston's eager young Troilus. When he failed to protect her from the exchange, however, she mechanically shunned his embrace, packed her bag and left. Smallwood considered her about-face with Diomedes mere baffled desperation.

---

236 Smallwood, *SS 53*.

Some of Boyd's additions were in keeping with the setting and generally domestic style. Priam and Hecuba presided at a family meal during the Trojan council, with Cassandra and Andromache at table. There was one unconventional casting choice: Patroclus was played by Elaine Pyke in male attire. Today, the intent of this transvestism raises questions not addressed by Boyd in the programme, whereas it might have been ignored in Poel's time.[237] Smallwood summed up Boyd's work as 'an odd, quirky production, short on respect for the text . . . long on bright ideas, but curiously watchable and exciting'.

The 1990s also saw outdoor productions at familiar venues, attesting the play's continuing acceptance for more relaxed summer entertainment. At New York's Delacorte in 1995, in contrast to Papp's coherent earlier production, Mark Wing-Davey and costume designer Catherine Zuber produced a hodge-podge of styles, but followed current custom in emphasizing the decadently sexual. Ulysses (Steven Skybell) spoke of order to generals glued to a television set. He got their attention but not the audience's by grabbing the remote and changing channels! Brantley complained that olive drab, medieval armour, Japanese kimonos and 'road warrior' tatters were mixed, as were lances and rifles, Asian and popular American music, all without apparent purpose. Themes were given visual equivalents: a billboard photo of Helen (Tamara Tunie) reminded audiences of the cause; actresses on pedestals during the Trojan council represented the idealization of women. The acting styles were wildly mixed. Thersites (Tim Blake Nelson) used updated obscenities. Pandarus (Stephen Spinella) was straight from Kabuki. Remarkably, Cressida was a success. Elizabeth Marvel showed 'an affectingly uneasy mixture of surface sophistication and adolescent uncertainty . . . [She] adroitly reconciles the character's contradictions by attributing them in part to the intoxication of a young woman just becoming aware of the effects of her sensuality on men.' But unfortunately Wing-Davey incorporated 'elements of all previous productions . . . into one gigantic heap of cultural compost'.[238]

By contrast, in 1998 Alan Strachan showed that the play could succeed in Regent's Park if London weather co-operated. Edwardian costuming contributed to understanding the interpretations. Reviewers welcomed a change from the three-decades-long homoerotic emphasis.[239] Achilles (Daniel Flynn) played down his passion for Patroclus (Damien Matthews). Cressida (Rebecca Johnson), though not interpreted strongly, was touching in her puzzlement when the waffling behaviour that worked with Troilus (Robert Hands) was useless with

---

237 Paul Taylor, *In*, 7 November 1998, and Rutter, p. 141. Pyke also played Polyxena, who was brought in for no apparent reason.
238 Ben Brantley, 'Surfing Through Shakespeare', *NYT*, 18 August 1995, C3.
239 Charles Spencer, 'A Compelling Love is in the Chill Air', *Telegraph*, 15 June 1998.

Diomedes (Harry Burton).[240] Pandarus (Christopher Goodwin), natty in grey suit and monocle, represented outwardly respectable, inwardly sleazy Edwardian society as he set up his niece or, bearing a bottle of champagne, joined Paris and Helen in bed. In keeping with current taste, Strachan's portrayal of pre-First World War society was more risqué and less humourously satirical than Guthrie's, and included the transformation of Pandarus into a pox-riddled wreck at the end. The heroes on both sides were satirized for their blustering arrogance in their fine uniforms (white for Trojans, turquoise for Greeks). Jeffrey Dench's Priam was weighted down with medals; Paris was a conceited little man who would have looked 'at home on a yacht with his rather vulgar Helen'.[241] Although the period costumes lacked the immediacy of modern wartime overtones, audiences were familiar with the visual referents as a result of television's period films, and the chivalric touches could be evaluated within a context where they might still be valid.[242]

The ruined Art Nouveau mansion, reminiscent of the RSC in 1985, effectively masked the natural background.[243] The production was 'intelligent' and clear, though there was disagreement on how effectively it suggested the nasty reality of war, for the fighting was less lively and effective than might have been expected on the large stage.[244] Strachan's programme notes focused on how Shakespeare undercut pride and levelled characters by showing their stupidity and failure to achieve the honour they talked about. Ulysses unfortunately missed the subtle deviousness that can enliven his set speeches and emphasize the contrast between his clever manipulation and Ajax's boorish frontal attacks. Troilus also was less successful than he should have been, emoting rather than playing the range of feelings he has at various junctures of the play.[245]

The century ended with two sharply contrasting productions. The Oxford Stage Company bridged 1999–2000 with a modest effort, and the Royal National Theatre triumphed in 1999 with Trevor Nunn's elaborately staged, powerful rendition. Nunn's casting broke new ground in England.[246] Earlier, gender had been the area of experiment. Yale employed all men, Rockford College all women and Poel had some cross-dressing, all of necessity. In 1977 Ronald Hayman

240 Jeremy Kingston, *LT*, 13 June 1998.
241 Sarah Hemming, 'The Trojan War is Rained Off', *FT*, 7 July 1998.
242 Berry, *Shakespeare and the Awareness of Audience*, pp. 109–10, examines Shakespeare's perception of chivalry's collapse 'into organized posturing'.
243 Jeremy Kingston, *LT*, 13 July 1998, p. 21.
244 Hemming; Nicholas deJongh, 'One Loud Cheer for the Problem Play in the Park', *St*, 16 July 1998.
245 Charles Spencer.
246 Alf Sjoberg's 1967 anti-imperialist Swedish production had light-skinned French and Americans parachuting in against the dark-skinned Trojans (Bowen, p. 49).

presented his unsuccessful, perverse, completely transvestite Roundhouse
revival. In 1993, the Contact-Tara Theatre had emphasized transvestism and
colour in its seven-person cast. Jatinder Verma had a black male as Cressida and
Helen, and a female as Thersites and Diomedes, apparently for shock value.[247]
Some productions, especially in North America, practised colour-blind casting.
Trevor Nunn, however, chose to have black Trojans except, inexplicably, for Pandarus. Even when arguing they had a familial unity lacking in the faction-riddled
all-white Greek camp, Mary Warnock's essay on 'The Morality of War' referred
to the Trojans as 'a clan', but made no mention of them in a colonial context,[248]
although the implication was inescapable.

I found disturbing socio-political overtones unrelated to Shakespeare's text.
Though commerce is a recurring image, Calchas, a black pleading with whites for
his daughter in exchange for a black prisoner, heightened the idea of commerce in
humans. Cressida was subject to the abusive kisses of a group of powerful white
men, and was touched during her exotic dance among them before exiting to her
father's tent with Diomedes. Blonde Helen stood out among the dark-skinned
Trojans, though David Bamber's white Pandarus muted the dynamics of her
scene. She plainly enjoyed her 'white goddess in Africa' status as a special captive.
Did Nunn intend to say 'all men are brothers' when black Hector (Dhobi Oparei)
declared kinship with white Ajax and allowed himself to join in an exotic dance
with Achilles (Raymond Coulthard)? Was Achilles daring in loving Polyxena, or
the white man wanting an available black woman? The production emphasized
differences, but suggested an added theme of miscegenation where Shakespeare
showed parallels.[249]

Trojan exoticism was heightened by their flowing white costumes with African
or Middle Eastern touches. The Greeks wore darker clothing, occasionally with a
Chinese look for servants, but generally in a stylized modern design that included
worn leather coats. Though the costumes were a mix of modern European and
timeless ethnic, both sides had swords, shields and helmets. The Greek helmets
were classic and splendidly crested while the Trojan headgear resembled caps
with cheek pieces and made them seem vulnerable in battle.

Designer Rob Howell spread the stage with red earth, but there resemblance to
the 1976 NT cockpit ended. The Olivier's huge stage was used effectively and its

247 The Company used only seven actors, and made extensive cuts, including most of
    Thersites' part, so that much of the play's complexity was lost. The emphasis was
    strong on life under siege and on racism, and the Prologue was replaced by Queen
    Elizabeth's 1601 decree expelling blackamoors. In the 1980s seminars and papers on
    transvestism in Shakespeare's works began to multiply.
248 NT Souvenir Programme, 1999.
249 My American background and heightened sense of 'political correctness' may have
    skewed my responses. Generally these points were not emphasized by reviewers.

problems overcome. A semicircle of six pivoting pairs of tall panels represented the gates of Troy or served singly as doors to interiors. The aisles of the auditorium provided additional entrances. A brilliantly simple double flap of canvas could be spread at various angles to suggest different tents. This concentrated attention on the area under and in front of the flap, so that intimate scenes were not lost. Fire bowls on tripods, jangling metallic banners, wine, a bowl of fruit, a hookah, a cot and a selection of stools were all the furnishings needed. Swift scene changes added to the dynamism. While torches suggested the Elizabethan method of indicating night scenes, subtle amplification let the actors deal easily with the Olivier's acoustics. The overall effect was of an exotic world, not classic, but not ours.

Nunn not only cut many lines, but rearranged the text extensively. The changes, especially before the interval following 3.2 and after 5.4, may have clarified things for newcomers, but presented a puzzling hopscotch for those of us familiar with the text.[250] Opening the play with Cressida watching the warriors and showing her again in witty repartee between halves of the Greek council scene focused attention on her. The rearrangement introduced the major Greeks and Trojans before beginning the intricacies of Troilus' love or Achilles and Patroclus' relationship. Nunn's treatment of the last act also made this very much the tragedy of Cressida.[251] Sophie Okonedo made her a clever woman, serious about her love, and Pandarus united her to Troilus (Peter de Jersey) without the camp overtone we might have expected from his earlier scenes. Her yielding to Diomedes showed resigned recognition of necessity following Troilus' failure to save her, the indignities with the Greek generals, and her father's pimping in Pandarus' stead. To complete his interpretation, Nunn had Pandarus bring her, heavily made up, to Troilus after the 'Hope of revenge' exhortation (5.11). Troilus spurned them both, and Thersites, sneering about 'wars and lechery', returned the glove she had given Troilus. After Pandarus' epilogue, she was left, as Smallwood wrote, 'lost and bewildered, circling helplessly in the growing darkness . . . Other wars, other spoils of war, other victims of male possessiveness and brutality, were encapsulated in that forlorn and desolate figure.'

Although the weight of the production fell on Cressida, the cast provided strong support, with sensitive readings and no extraneous business to create laughs. Jasper Britton downplayed the humour in Thersites, and scavenged

---

250 The whole cast mimed behind the Prologue, then the play opened with the procession of Trojan warriors in 1.2. The Greek council scene to 1.3.215 followed, with an added brief battle. Finally Troilus and Pandarus met (1.1), with cuts and rearrangements, followed by 1.2.1–176 and the last few lines of the scene. The remainder of the Greek council scene (1.3) followed the Trojan debate (2.2), so Aeneas' entrance with the challenge followed Hector's announcement of it.

251 Smallwood, *SS 53*, pp. 257–9, reviews her performance at length.

Patroclus' corpse. Roger Allan mastered the intricacies of Ulysses' long speeches and paced them so that the ideas came across clearly. Ulysses achieved a stature he had lacked in some of the past two decades' performances, where his cleverness was treated as mere political manipulation. The betrayal scene centred on Diomedes and Cressida before Calchas' tent, with Thersites stage left and Troilus and Ulysses right on the outer wooden rim. Amplification enabled the watchers to whisper yet be heard, letting us believe Cressida and Diomedes were indeed unaware of their presence and we alone shared their reactions.

Nunn and Boyd's work raises anew questions about textual authority. Reviewers have long asked what interpretations or cuts could be introduced without creating something other than Shakespeare's play. Early in the century, prevailing taste and unfamiliarity with the work led many to accept revisions by Poel and other directors, especially at the end, where they wanted a tragic final picture in place of Pandarus' scurrility. The emphasis on homoeroticism, often with added business, in a play whose main stories turn on two heterosexual affairs, became a continuing point of contention in the 1960s. Gradually, as attention has shifted to Cressida, Pandarus and Thersites, Ulysses, Hector and Achilles have lost the prominence they once had. But as Bradshaw asked of the Berliner Ensemble, 'What in the play is too fundamental to be changed, what can be re-interpreted?'[252] Where is the line between interpretation and adaptation? The shift in emphasis on characters by selective cutting to highlight different aspects of Shakespeare's complex text does not create a post-modern 'death of the author' situation, where the only authority is the production at hand. Did Francis at the National Youth Theatre in 1987, or Boyd or Nunn cross the boundary, however? Certainly they retained more original lines than Dryden did, and Nunn rearranged rather than extensively rewriting. None killed off the title characters. But the text no longer retained the authority it had had for many directors, and the tone of the ending in the last two cases was far removed from the cynicism of Pandarus' epilogue spoken without visual reminders from Cressida, whom Shakespeare left with her father and Diomedes.

The new century and old concepts

Today *Troilus and Cressida* remains relevant as Middle Eastern societies break down, political motives are questioned, and Americans are told they will be in Iraq for 'as long as it takes'. The Oxford Stage Company's arrival at the Old Vic in 2000 provided Londoners with a stark modern contrast to Nunn's production. Dominic Dromgoole quoted Kott in his programme and opted for a 'form of concrete, if impoverished, modernity' because of the 'brutal realism at the heart

252 *TLS*, 4 September 1987, p. 957.

of the play'.[253] Anthony Lamble's central scaffolding within the proscenium arch recalled the Glasgow Citizens' setting of 1973, though less complex and with a miniature cityscape background and an occasional piece of canvas to suggest locales.[254] Like Boyd's, this production evoked Ireland invaded by the British. The Greeks had English accents. Agamemnon (David Cardy) 'looks and sounds like the front man for a south London firm of gangsters'. Ulysses (Paul Ritter), sly and grubby, was in command of his long speeches, in contrast to most of the cast, who were less used to verse.[255] The Trojans, with occasional brogues, reminded Marmion of 'an Irish clan of urban street fighters'. Priam resembled 'a worn-out Ulster patriarch' connected to his oxygen tank in a sauna. Troilus was a 'corner boy' and Cressida 'the gutsy girl next door'.[256] Frenzied young Cassandra slipped into the sauna's plunge pool. Pandarus (Darragh Kelly) oozed bonhomie. Except for Pandarus' blue blazer, and a couple of suit jackets, informal and unkempt modern clothing further diminished the Greeks and Trojans, who washed at a distracting standpipe amid the shards and wood piled about the stage.

Dromgoole had made his reputation directing modern works, and modern cultural referents were always present – Ulysses' espresso pot, Pandarus' Karaoke mike, the chains and coshes of football hooliganism, wielded in slow motion in the final scenes. Hector and Ajax fought offstage, and Dromgoole cut the Myrmidons, so Achilles simply downed unarmed Hector, slit his throat and claimed vengeful victory. There was less emphasis on Cressida than feminism demands, though Eileen Walsh made her an interesting and sympathetic, if slightly understated combination of understanding and vulnerability. Matt Lucas' bald Thersites, in his grubby mackintosh, was the most memorable character. He was strong enough to have been the spokesman, but was allowed to improvise gags and make rude gestures, and became a detached, enjoyable scene stealer rather than the disgusted choric observer the production needed. Paul Taylor likened it to Sam Mendes' 1990 revival, but without the penetration or polish.[257]

The Bristol Tobacco Factory Company provides a striking final British example – the small company that often outdoes higher-profile ensembles. Andrew Hilton is known for avoiding gimmicks and for focusing on a full, well-spoken

---

253 Dominic Dromgoole, 'Notes from the Director', Oxford Stage Company Old Vic Programme, 2000.

254 The Glasgow Citizens' was three stories high and resembled a child's attempt at a Trojan horse, with scaffolds, planks, and beaded hangings. The actors, in their mostly modern costumes, made more use of it than Dromgoole's cast did of their centerpiece (photographs in Birmingham Shakespeare Library).

255 Paul Taylor, *Independent Friday Review*, 7 April 2000, p. 20.

256 Patrick Marmion, *Time Out*, 5–12 April 2000, p. 143.

257 My notes are from July 2000, near the end of the run.

text.[258] In the spring of 2003 John Mckay gave life to Ulysses' speeches, and Jamie Ballard mixed humour and sarcasm as Thersites,[259] whose club-footed, scabby figure provided much of the production's unpleasantness. The emphasis, at a time of macho posturing against Iraq, was on men's love of a fight: the bored Greeks were galvanized by Hector's challenge and the scheme to get Achilles back into battle.[260] Again Edwardian costumes forced the audience to draw its own parallels to current events, though there was modern sexual frankness, and the lovers (Lisa Kay and Joseph Mawle) showed true passion. Cressida was, however, merely a pawn in a patriarchal world. Aware of her danger in the sexually charged meeting with the generals, she acted out of necessity. In the scene with Diomedes, her body language showed that 'her heart and head are telling her completely different things'.[261] The head won in a macho military world.

The Trojans and Greeks were cavalry officers, in grey and khaki respectively, satirizing the foolish romanticizing of war in ways modern grunge or military fatigue costumes cannot. Reviewers caught a public school overtone: Achilles (Alisdair Simpson) was the rich boy in cloak and headscarf with his fag Patroclus (Mark Hesketh), and Ajax (Tom Sherman) was 'the school dimwit'. The war was not that far removed from the playing fields. Of a slightly later period, Pandarus (Ian Barritt) suggested the Noel Coward era, a louche 'old fruit who exists through the erotic and heroic life of others'.[262] Not so high-spirited as Guthrie's revival, Hilton's conception did focus on the comic aspects, but the carefully detailed acting strongly suggested the rot underneath. Decay and sensuality were also portrayed by the main scenic device, Andrea Montag's patchy erotic frescoes on the plinths of four large iron pillars (ceiling supports) surrounded by weeds in the central playing space. Keeping their encircling audience in mind, the actors were never static, and both intimate scenes and the final battles gained from their closeness, 'where every blink told'.[263]

North American trends or trendiness

In North America the new century has begun with three major productions. None broke new ground or achieved complete success, but they show the range

258 Peter Wood, *British Theatre Guide*, 2003. Gordon Parsons noted the lack of Blair/Bush look-alikes ('Spin is Nothing New', *Morning Star*, 13 February 2003).

259 Caron Parsons, 'Love and War at the Factory', *BBC Going Out in Bristol*, 10 February 2003 (www.bbc.co.uk/bristol).

260 Wood.

261 Lyn Gardner, '3 stars Tobacco Factory, Bristol', *Gdn*, 13 February 2003.

262 Rhoda Koenig, 'Troilus and Cressida, Tobacco Factory, Bristol', *In*, 17 February 2003; John Peter, *ST*.

263 Jeremy Kingston, 'Heady Mix of Sex and Laughter', *LT*, 10 February 2003.

of current interpretation. Peter Hall revisited the play in New York in 2001. Ashland staged a lively revival that summer, and Stratford Canada mounted it late in their 2003 season.

Four decades after his landmark work at Stratford, Peter Hall again used a fighting pit, now larger, twelve-sided and filled with tan sand, to centre his production. There was less Mediterranean brightness and no evocative canvas backdrop. Designer Douglas Stein added audience seating behind the pit, creating an in-the-round configuration at The American Place's proscenium auditorium. A walkway outside the sandpit rim provided extra playing space and entrances – especially when Trojans came to the Greek camp – used theatre aisles. Action spilled out into the auditorium in the final battles,[264] and audience contact was more intense than it had been in 1960. The furnishings were fewer than in the earlier revival: a few rustic stools, some cushions, and battlefield debris that was removed at the end of the prologue and returned at 5.4.

Martin Pakledinaz followed the trend of costuming the tougher Greeks in dark, worn leather, heavy materials, combat boots and, like others who have bridged the gap between the centuries, classical crested helmets and armour for the battles. Thersites was a ragged, half-naked, scab-covered hanger-on, his feet in strips of cloth and his entire possessions in a pouch where he tucked found treasures such as Achilles' discarded wine goblet. The Trojans were sensual, barefooted, and reminiscent of the Middle East. The men wore skirts over their trousers, and shades of orange and red predominated. Helen stood out in her turquoise gown, not yet sartorially assimilated after seven years. Hall gave Agamemnon and Menelaus steel crowns, and Priam a white robe, so rank was more easily recognized than usual in modern productions. Scott Thomas Zielinski further heightened distinctions by lighting the Greek camp in cool blues and greens, while Troy was suffused with a warm pinkish glow. Audience responses were influenced by this, and further manipulated by the highly theatrical use of spotlights. 'Three overhead follow spots contributed a dynamism to the lighting that small playing places like American Place often lack, . . . constantly highlighting characters . . . and keeping the focus of the scenes under tight artistic control.'[265] Hall directed attention the way a camera does, rather than letting his audience choose a broader focus.

In an interview, he said he wanted to provide a 'corrosively cynical' look at the legendary warriors, as well as at war. Before the play began, the audience saw a couple of corpses amid some rubble and two skeletons face-to-face in a compromising position that linked sex and destruction. Critics, accustomed

---

264 As of this writing, Kastan's very full description of the production is still available at
   the Theatre for a New Audience web site (www.tfana.org/2001/Troilus).
265 Kastan (at tfana.org).

to fast-moving productions that emphasize social decay and the horror of war, were less startled and impressed than they would have been forty years earlier. There was also a perception that Hall, though drawing on past experience, was overly flexible and willing to accommodate actors' suggestions, when his mostly American cast could have benefited from the tighter control he had exercised earlier. Michael Sommers called it 'a whirling weathervane of a play that screams for bold direction to point it one way or another'. Instead, there were 'numerous meaningless shifts of tone and inconstant characterizations'. Achilles (Idris Elba) seemed stoned to one reviewer, and a drunken brawler to another. He made the homoerotic less obvious than it often is. Thersites (Andrew Weems) was an excessively excited commentator, foaming at the mouth as he spat out invective. Troilus and Cressida (Joey Kern, Tricia Paolucci) were popular culture types – the surfer dude and valley girl,[266] (conceptions often reserved for Paris and Helen). Although it was difficult for her to overcome the initial impression, Paolucci did become defiant in the Greek camp, and her switch to Diomedes had a psychological base, springing more from the way men had treated her in the past than from mere casualness.[267]

Tony Church (Pandarus) was Ulysses in 1976, and Pandarus in 1981 and 1990 at Stratford, while Cindy Katz (Helen and the richly clad knight) had played Cressida in Yale Rep's 1990 production. But roughly half the cast lacked professional experience with Shakespeare, and Hall concentrated on the verse. Without the longer rehearsals and the ongoing ensemble that he had enjoyed at Stratford, however, the result was merely careful, and turgid speaking prevented lively characterization. Sommers found that even Pandarus, wreathed in scarves, was not humourous.

Across the continent Ashland mounted an active, almost full-text revival that pleased audiences and was closely attuned to current social and political malaise. Where Richard E. T. White's 1984 production had used classical ruins in the Angus Bowmer Theatre to indicate 'a sick, broken, burnt-out landscape . . . where survival is the only objective', this time the Elizabethan stage provided Kenneth Albers with a visually less evocative playing place.[268] Susan Mickey's costumes suggested the classical, rather than copying ancient costumes exactly. The young men were in laced segments of dark leather that 'exposed lots of flesh, but at the same time . . . got in the way of body language'.[269] Older men had longer gowns over their tunics, and Helen and Cressida were similarly and attractively clad in

---

266 Michael Sommers, 'Shakespeare's Tough Nut Stays in Shell', *The Star Ledger*, 19 April 2001, p. 63.
267 The tfana web site provides many keys to the interpretations.
268 Richard E. T. White's Programme Notes, OSF, 1984.
269 Edward Brubaker, unpublished commentary.

Figure 12. Ajax and Thersites in Kenneth Albers' Oregon Shakespeare Festival Production, 2001.

flowing white. There weren't the contrasts of colour or style that often make a statement about Greeks and Trojans, or aid the audience in battle scenes, and Brubaker found that 'one had to hesitate to figure out who was who'.

Over the years Ashland has developed a company that is comfortable with verse, speaking quickly and clearly, and able to animate the long discussions in

1.3, 2.2, and 3.3. The missing element in this production was the wit. Although Albers mentioned farce in his programme notes, the focus was on the brutality of war and its effects on all, from young Cressida to the older Greek leaders. One key to the interpretation was 'emulation' (to the Elizabethans 'bitter rivalry') that helped debase war and love.[270] Thersites (James Newcombe), 'more nimble with his game leg and caustic tongue than any warrior, savagely deconstructed the combat',[271] but lacked the masochism that made Simon Russell Beale's response to maltreatment so interesting. The brutality continued as the sex-starved Greeks grabbed and groped Cressida, and her repartee lacked any flirtatiousness in the face of such degradation. Her father, silently placed onstage by Albers, could do nothing to help, and her turn to Diomedes as protector was totally understandable. Feminism was not an issue so much as survival in a generally debased world.

Richard Monette directed Stratford, Ontario's third production in the late summer of 2003. Almost a century after Fry's first English revival, Monette's work clearly attests the changes theatre and society have undergone. Where the earliest productions presented the play relatively straightforwardly, this was described as 'an intrusive production in terms of lighting, music, voice-overs – [with] audience response highly manipulated'.[272] Gay Pride marches, plays and media shows focusing on same-sex relationships, sometimes satirically, sometimes seriously, and arguments about an Episcopal bishop made homosexuality a well-discussed topic in the summer of 2003. Burgeoning queer theory studies have placed the text's references to Achilles and Patroclus and a few hints from Pandarus in a wider context. As a result, the blatantly camp displays Monette staged in 2.3 and 3.1 failed to shock as Barton's focus on homoeroticism had in 1968, and at the same time seemed pointlessly overdone. Furthermore, feminist readings of Cressida over the past decades made this production seem reactionary. M. J. Kidnie noted a misogynism and 'regressive' treatment of women that recalled pre-First World War attitudes rather than 'modern sexualities.'

The first visual impression was one of 'a refreshing and intelligent con-servatism' as actors moved easily in Ann Curtis' classical costumes on a terra-cotta-coloured stage with four broad steps at the rear and a few easily moved benches. A shield on the panelled background signified the Greek council, cush-ions and a rug sufficed for Helen, Paris and their group, and an effective small black tent downstage left served Achilles. Curtis found the Greeks more serious. 'Even their conversations are measured', and 'dark, rich colours . . . reflect that'.

---

270 Hilary Tate, 'War and Lechery', *Prologue*, *The OSF Members' Magazine*, Spring 2001.
271 Steven Winn, 'Troilus Triumphs in Ashland; Cynical Comedy is Best of Opening trio at Summer Shakespeare Festival', *San Francisco Chronicle*, 19 June 2001, E1.
272 Margaret Jean Kidnie, unpublished comments, September–October 2003.

The Trojans, who at first took the war less seriously, wore predominately gold, red and orange.[273] The acting went counter to Curtis' conception of Cressida in 3.2, brought to Troilus 'completely veiled . . . "gift wrapped" with a sense of sacrifice'. Claire Jullien played her part with a 'glad eye and knowing enthusiasm for love and gossip'.[274] Kidnie found her playing 'morally slight' in a production that seemed to make its central point 'This love will undo us all' (3.1.94), which was repeated with emphasis by Pandarus at the end of the Helen scene, just before the interval.

Taylor felt that Wayne Belt's smarmy and impatient Agamemnon and Peter Donaldson's 'calmer and wiser' Ulysses both demonstrated the Greeks' problem by not providing effective leadership. Other reviewers were less sympathetic. The straight Greeks were exaggeratedly masculine back-slappers and the production was 'big on the externals and not so hot on the intellectual values underneath'.[275] Ouzounian accused Monette of cashing in on the trend to emphasize the homo-erotic, so that the heterosexual affairs central to the love and war plots were overwhelmed by the 'campy theme park entertainment'. David Shelley's Patro-clus' full monty for Agamemnon and the audience in 2.3, and Pandarus' seduction of 'a manservant with a feather fan between the legs and a coin in the palm' in 3.1 were salient examples.

Theatrical traditions developed in the past four decades were abundant here. Pandarus (Bernard Hopkins) 'would, in a less politically correct climate, be called a raging queen' in blond wig, androgynous gown and pearl necklace, a voyeur who 'enjoys the sheer sexual intensity'.[276] Ajax (Jeffrey Renn) was the muscle-bound dolt, Achilles (Jamie Robinson) 'a kohl-eyed sybarite' and Paris and Helen (Tim Campbell and Linda Prystawska) were 'blond airheads'. Troilus (David Snelgrove) tended to overact, and his gasping, weeping grief at Cressida's betrayal continued until Hector armed in 5.3.

Alan Somerset's programme essay called attention to shifting values in the play, as Ajax is elevated above Achilles, Helen is seen from different perspectives, and even in the first act there are subtle hints that Troilus and Cressida's love is not ideal. R. A. Foakes years ago described the play as comedy in Acts 1–3 and 'unpleasantness' in 4 and 5. Monette echoed this, characterizing it as a 'comic

---

273 Quoted from an interview with Ann Curtis by Sharon Malvin in the SFC Pro-gramme. A large number of small military costume sketches in the season's souvenir programme illustrate this contrast.

274 Kate Taylor, 'Trojan gallop falters at the last hurdles', *Toronto Globe and Mail*, 15 August 2003, R2.

275 Richard Ouzounian, 'Queer eye for Shakespeare's Greeks', *Toronto Star*, 17 August 2003.

276 Martin F. Kuhn, 'Sex, Violence and Shakespeare', *Detroit Free Press*, 24 August 2003.

love story until the end of the first act, when it turns into satire and darkness', but making no connection between Shakespeare's portrayal of war and its social consequences and the current Middle East situation. Like other users of classical costume, he left it to the audience to find the reverberations. After the blatant displays that included Paris and Helen coupling on pillows, there was difficulty in switching from the comic and high-pitched sexuality to the quieter meeting of Troilus and Cressida in 3.2 and the later darker tone he mentions.

Thersites (Stephen Ouimette) was not the centre that he has often been recently. Kidnie felt that 'Sex and disease [shaped] our take on the action, not cynicism and wit'. Taylor commented that 'creepy' Thersites occasionally provided 'the note of menacing cynicism that this production could use in many other places', but Kidnie and others felt it became Pandarus' show. A 'weepy' Andromache, a weak Cassandra, and a Helen played merely as a 'giddy and shrieking' sex partner helped make the women less consequential. More important, Cressida was young and cute, but relied on her uncle and avoided eye contact as she faced the others. At first afraid of the kissing, she began to like it, and Ulysses seemed to read her correctly. She showed some guilt in leaving Troilus, but apparently fancied Diomedes, rather than turning to him of necessity.[277]

The action encompasses only a few days, and Pandarus' sudden transformation into a decrepit wreck in many productions seems symbolic rather than realistic. As in Nunn's production, here Pandarus' decline was forecast by a 'really gross cough' as Cressida left with Diomedes. By the letter scene, he had lost his wig and shoes, and was suffering from a rheum that he tried to hide with his hand. At the end his eyes were stuck shut and scabs splotched his head. The emphasis on sex took an even more brutal turn when he exited to Nine Inch Nails' rendition of 'Closer to God'. The contrast to Boyd's 1998 chant could not have been sharper. Here the audience heard not a plea for mercy but the repeated 'I want to f . . . you like an animal', and a final voice-over: ''tis but the chance of war'.

In contrast to the pioneering directors, Monette had all the resources of an established Shakespeare festival, with its variety of theatres, large professional cast, guaranteed run in repertory, and extensive sound and lighting resources. Fry, Poel, Atkins and others used the lighting and sound equipment available to them, but not in the cinematic way Hall in 2001 or Monette did. Where they might have chosen one aspect, such as cynicism, as a focus, they did not interpret or emphasize the bitterness to the degree that is currently regarded as essential in a more open, destabilized society.

Debates about ongoing wars for dubious ends, distrust of politicians who manipulate public opinion, concern over AIDS and other diseases, frankness about sex, and even the emphasis on commercialism that is reflected in the play's

277 Kidnie notes.

imagery all give us points of contact with the text that make the modern director's task easier. On the other hand, shortened attention spans, especially the ability to listen to long speeches, pose great problems for actors who must try to make Ulysses' and the others' arguments fresh and coherent. Subtlety is often lost on people accustomed to being bombarded or controlled by the loud sounds and quickly shifting images of modern media. The temptation is to compensate by presenting a difficult and complex play like *Troilus and Cressida* with numerous cuts and ever more distracting physical activity, voiceovers and other sound effects and special lighting.

Both of these aspects were revealed in Steven Barkhimer's treatment for the open air Publick Theatre in Brighton, Boston Massachusetts in the summer of 2004. 'I've cut it liberally' but kept the 'complexity and ambivalence of [its] exploration of war and the human relationships that play out within it'. The war 'started on an awful pretext but now . . . must continue or [they'll] lose face'. The parallels between Iraq and Troy seemed so obvious to Barkhimer that there was no need for 'heavy-handed underlining'. Instead of Dick Cheney look-alikes, characters appeared as classical Greeks. Nor was there an attempt at elaborate staging to try to evoke the recent film, *Troy*.[278] *Troilus and Cressida* has become a staple of well-established companies with substantial backing like the RSC, and more modest operations in converted factories and at outdoor summer festivals. Most important, directors like Hilton who trust the play, and have the actors to cope with a number and range of good roles that would have been anathema to the old star actor-managers, have proven this an exciting work accessible to a wide modern audience.

278 Louise Kennedy, 'Moral Ambiguity? A Questionable War? How Very Modern', *Boston Sunday Globe*, 4 July 2004, p. N4.

TROILUS AND CRESSIDA

LIST OF CHARACTERS

PROLOGUE, *an armed man*

Trojans

PRIAM, *King of Troy*
HECTOR
DEIPHOBUS
HELENUS, *a priest*   } *Priam's sons*
PARIS, *Helen's lover*
TROILUS
MARGARELON, *a bastard son of Priam*
CASSANDRA, *Priam's daughter, a prophetess*
ANDROMACHE, *Hector's wife*
AENEAS   } *Trojan commanders*
ANTENOR
PANDARUS, *a lord, Cressida's uncle*
CRESSIDA, *his niece, Calchas' daughter*
CALCHAS, *Cressida's father, a priest who has joined the Greeks*
ALEXANDER, *Cressida's servant*
SERVANTS *of Troilus and Paris*
SOLDIERS
ATTENDANTS

Greeks

HELEN, *Menelaus' wife, now living with Paris in Troy*
AGAMEMNON, *the General*
MENELAUS, *his brother and Helen's husband*
NESTOR
ULYSSES
ACHILLES   } *Greek commanders*
DIOMEDES
AJAX
PATROCLUS, *Achilles' friend*
THERSITES
MYRMIDONS, *soldiers of Achilles*
SERVANTS *of Diomedes*
SOLDIERS
ATTENDANTS
TRUMPETER

TROILUS AND CRESSIDA

Prologue

[Enter the PROLOGUE *in armour]*

The Prologue, added in the Folio, concentrates on the war in formal Latinized verse and omits any reference to the eponymous lovers. Poel suggested it was satirical, based on Marston and Jonson (Programme notes, 1912). Some productions, including Guthrie's (1956–7) and Landau's (1961) have omitted it. More frequently, lines 12–19 are cut, with their reference to 'the fresh and yet unbruised Greeks', a description at odds with modern portrayals of a war-weary group. The talk of gates and ships, verbal scene-painting for Shakespeare's non-illusionistic stage, is often regarded as too much detail for today's non-historical minds. Ekkehard Schall, with the Berliner Ensemble in Edinburgh, 'pretends to half forget the play's most famous names', a double satire on the old actor's memory and the familiarity of the Troy story (G. Taylor, p. 299). In 1976, 'Instead of guiding us into the arguments and conditions . . . [Barton's] Prologue declaims the opening speech and obliterates its points.' (David Zane Mairowitz, *PP*, October, 1976, p. 20.)

Fry took his cue from line 23 and presented a figure with classical helmet, breastplate and spear in dim light. At curtain up, he 'raised one hand to appeal to the audience' (James O'Donnell Bennett, London, 1 June 1907). Poel presented him in full Renaissance armour. The speaker can easily double another role, as Arthur Pentlow did at Birmingham in 1963, when 'as a modern colonel, [he] explains the war, using a blackboard in an academic take-off' (W.H.W., 'The best "Rep" Shakespeare for years', *Birmingham Mail*, 2 February, 1963), then changed into Thersites' dustman costume. In SMT 1960, Paul Hardwick was a 'fine spoken' Prologue who 'hit each line', then became the broadly comic Ajax 'from a sleazy gym' (William Shaw, *TS*, 11 May 1981, p. 54). Alexander doubled the lines and his part without much change in appearance at the Old Vic in 1923 and again for Papp (NYSF 1965). Thersites has been the most frequent choice if a principal character takes the part (London Mask 1938; RSC 1996, 1998; Hall 2001). The formal verse gives another dimension to his choric status. Gordon Crosse found him 'inappropriate' in 1938, for the language did not suit the 'weak, sniveling, bad-blooded hanger-on of the army' (Notebook XVII). In 1981, at the RSC, 'Joe Melia, a rather pleasant Thersites', tried to make the speech caustic (Warren, *SS 35*, p. 149), but omission of 'the ringing names . . . undercut the heroics' (Robert Cushman, *Obs*, 8 July 1981). In 1998 Boyd staged a lecture with slides of the First World War carnage by an 'old style cameraman' in 'yellowing tatters' (Benedict Nightingale, 'Troubled View of Trojan Wars', *LT*, 7 November 1998, p. 20). Ulysses was comfortable with the formal language for Dromgoole (OX 1999–2000). Mendes' 'decision to have Pandarus as Prologue was a tidy one, economically linking the beginning, the middle and the end . . . together, making the diseased Pandarus of the epilogue a distorted image of the dapper figure at the start' (Holland, *English Shakespeares*, p. 70).

There have been additions or substitutions of lines or characters: TR's three cross-dressed old men with their 'heavy-handed . . . vaudeville-type song parodying the golden apple story' (Hirsch, *Herald Traveler*, 5 December 1971), John Neville-Andrews' boy and girl sharing the lines (FTG 1983), or Wood's preliminary mime of exercise and sex (NAO, 1978) show the range. In Manchester 1993, Jatinder Verma, forecasting a focus on discrimination, replaced Shakespeare's expository Prologue with a reading of Queen Elizabeth's 1601 proclamation banning blackamoors from England. In 2001 Peter Hall had Andrew Weems preface the Prologue by reading, from a battered paperback, the quarto address to the reader proclaiming this a new play (Kastan).

In Utah, Libby Appel began with a dumb show by Cassandra, Thersites and Pandarus. Pandarus toyed with a decaying corpse in armour, 'the emblem of rotting reality beneath a veneer of chivalry'. Cassandra (Theresa Pugh) spoke the prologue, then remained on Cedar City's Elizabethan stage balcony as a choric figure for much of the action, her classical dress resembling a Fate among the Elizabethan costumes (Aggeler, p. 230). Harvard-Radcliffe (1985) provided a visually striking frieze of characters silhouetted against an orange-lit background, resembling an Attic amphora, and the NYTh used a 'sandalwood smell that evoked the Middle East' in 1987 (Michael Ratcliff, *Obs*, 27 September 1987).

The text suggests one actor standing to deliver his thirty lines. From Poel on there have often been additions of people or business. Poel's promptbooks call for a series of groupings not keyed to the words being spoken: first Troilus, Cressida, Pandarus and their servants; then the Greek commanders, followed by Thersites with Ajax, and Achilles with Patroclus; then Trojan warriors and finally a tableau of Paris, Helen and a servant. Anthony Quayle (SMT 1948 promptbook) created a comedic domestic atmosphere for his gentle production, raising a quick curtain to reveal a bustling street scene with water-carriers, Trojan soldiers, flower women and other civilians. Pandarus pushed his way through, a boy chased a ball, and Paul Hardwick, in armour, finally turned to the audience and spoke as activity slowed. Action resumed when the boy bumped a soldier and a civilian as he chased his ball. A few extras remained in the background through 1.1 and 1.2. Glen Byam Shaw (SMT 1954) was more formal, with guards opening the gates to Trojan warriors and servants, and a sentinel at his post. At the end, Troilus was left alone to begin 1.1 (promptbook).

Davies (RSC 1985) signaled Pandarus' detachment from the war. Seated at a small table, stage left, in a creamy suit, he read his newspaper while two soldiers worked over a cannon fodder body stage right and the Prologue spoke to the accompaniment of bugle, drum and piano music (F. Shirley notes). In 1999, Nunn choreographed an elaborate sequence behind the

PROLOGUE In Troy there lies the scene: from isles of Greece
       The princes orgulous, their high blood chafed,
       Have to the port of Athens sent their ships,
       Fraught with the ministers and instruments
       Of cruel war. Sixty and nine that wore   5
       Their crownets regal from th'Athenian bay
       Put forth toward Phrygia, and their vow is made
       To ransack Troy, within whose strong immures
       The ravished Helen, Menelaus' queen,
       With wanton Paris sleeps – and that's the quarrel.   10
       To Tenedos they come,
       And the deep-drawing barks do there disgorge
       Their warlike freightage; now on Dardan plains
       The fresh and yet unbruisèd Greeks do pitch
       Their brave pavilions. Priam's six-gated city,   15
       Dardan and Timbria, Helias, Chetas, Troien,
       And Antenorides with massy staples
       And corresponsive and fulfilling bolts
       Spar up the sons of Troy.
       Now expectation, tickling skittish spirits   20
       On one and other side, Trojan and Greek,
       Sets all on hazard. And hither am I come,

speaker on the huge Olivier stage. A phalanx marched by at line 11, and the six large sets of panels slammed shut one by one as each gate was named. The entire cast paraded behind the Prologue, then stood while he finished. A brief battle led into Nunn's first scene, where Cressida and Pandarus watched the returning warriors (NT promptbook). In New York, in 2001, Hall's ragged Thersites, smoking a cigarette, entered with a body that he casually dumped onto the two other corpses the audience had been staring at, symbolizing the waste of war (Kastan).

OSD   Yale's 1916 Prologue rushed on breathlessly. Pentlow entered with stuffy dignity to gave the BR a lecture in 1963. The Prologue appeared in the 'penthouse' (balcony) of Payne's Elizabethan set (SMT 1936). Paul Hardwick (SMT 1960) had a huge spear and shoulder-high shield, adding a slightly comic effect that carried over to the Ajax scenes (F. Shirley notes). Barton and Kyle (RSC 1976) gave the Prologue business, avoiding the effect of a set speech. He popped up from the stage trap with a bag and two swords, took a helmet from the bag, blew off dust and began to speak (promptbook). Miller used a voiceover while the camera panned for the BBC in 1981. In Hall, 2001, Thersites donned a battered armoured jacket and spiked helmet from the stage detritus and posed mock-heroically in the spotlight (Kastan).

14–15   Barton had Geek (bull) and Trojan (sphinx) emblems carried on and set up stage right and left in 1968. Aeneas and Margarelon entered with three Trojan soldiers to salute the Trojan emblem (promptbook).

> A prologue armed, but not in confidence
> Of author's pen or actor's voice, but suited
> In like conditions as our argument,   25
> To tell you, fair beholders, that our play
> Leaps o'er the vaunt and firstlings of those broils,
> Beginning in the middle, starting thence away,
> To what may be digested in a play.
> Like, or find fault, do as your pleasures are,   30
> Now good or bad, 'tis but the chance of war.   [*Exit*]

23   Pandarus touched the crest or medal on his blazer pocket in a clever redefining of 'armed' in
        Mendes' mainly modern dress production (RSC 1990). During his speech, Barton / Kyle's
        Prologue had donned the helmet, and at 'prologue armed' held the swords to his head like horns,
        bent his legs and snarled animalistically (promptbook). Finally he returned the props to his bag,
        closed one side of the trap while Thersites entered to close the other side, and they exited stage
        left and right.

31   Poel used a drum, as 1.3 followed (1912). Birch led into the civilian scenes with Byrd and Farnaby
        (1922). Fry lowered his curtain, then raised it on the Greeks (1907).

ACT I, SCENE I

[**1.1**] *Enter* PANDARUS *and* TROILUS

Producers who felt the war-focused Prologue should lead into a military scene moved 1.3 to this spot and continued the heightened verse tone with the formal Greek discussions (Fry, Poel, Woolley). The Old Vic, 1923, retained Shakespeare's scene order, with its quick shift to introduce the love story. Some interpreters of Troilus' role have emphasized his self-absorption and impatience in love, and consequent distaste for the war (84–7, 106–7) to contrast ironically with his argument for continuing it in 2.2. At The Players, Jerome Lawlor made Troilus a 'matinee idol' (Stephen Rathburn, *NYS*, 7 June 1932), 'mooning like a musical comedy tenor' (Percy Hammond, 8 June 1932), and set himself up more than most as 'silly and self-centred'. At the Tobacco Factory Troilus always 'tried very hard to hide his innocence' in public (John Peter, *The Sunday Times*, 16 February 2003).

Directorial cuts have helped shape the ways Troilus and Pandarus' characters are perceived. Many of Troilus' love-lorn lines (9–12, 32–7, 51b–56) have been omitted by producers ranging from Quayle and Guthrie to Barton in 1968, when he was establishing Michael Williams' stronger portrayal. Between a quarter and a third of the lines are often selectively omitted, including part of Pandarus' long baking metaphor. Political correctness has led to recent cutting of 72b. Troilus' declaration that he is 'mad / In Cressid's love' is always retained, as is Pandarus' praise for his niece, which parallels his praise of Troilus to Cressida in 1.2. Pandarus' expository lines are also usually retained, including his unwitting forecast of Cressida's going to the Greeks to join her father (75–7).

Although this is often imagined as a street scene, the same locale as 1.2, there is usually a bench, a chair or two, or some architectural feature such as the sandpit (SMT 1960) where they can sit. Pandarus' costume and actions frequently set the tone for the remainder of his performance. Hiram Sherman was 'too Pickwickian', and 'too attractive given his function' in Landau's Civil War version (John Beaufort, ' "Troilus and Cressida" Overgrown by Magnolias', *CSM*, 25 July 1961; Judith Crist, *NYHT*, 21 July 1961). Gordon Crosse compared Randle Ayrton, 'delightfully comic in all his silly fussiness' at the SMT in 1936 to Max Adrian in Macowan's revival. Adrian was 'less amusing', but 'attuned to the modern surroundings, [a] suave, affected, elderly roué and society butterfly' (Notebook xvii; see also Notebook xv, p. 144). *The Stage* noted Adrian's 'well-bred air of worldly wisdom' (19 September 1938). At Stratford, Ontario, William Hutt established him as a 'fribble, yet not too affected', 'not completely ridiculous' with his air of

TROILUS Call here my varlet – I'll unarm again.
Why should I war without the walls of Troy
That find such cruel battle here within?

'talcum and eau-de-cologne' (Alan Pryce Jones, *TA*, 1963). The Berliner Ensemble made him younger than usual, dark-haired but emaciated. In NT 1999 David Bamber was a 'hand-flapping, mincing, dressing-gowned old queen . . . with his red fez and fly whisk' among Nunn's black Trojans (Smallwood, *SS* 53, p. 257).

Barton's emphasis on the homoerotic in 1968–9 led David Waller to an elaborate sequence occupying 1–75. He sat on a bench, put his legs over Troilus' right leg, and by 23 had his hand busily exploring until Troilus pushed it away and stood. By 44, Troilus had moved astride the sitting Pandarus, rubbing him with his leg and stroking his hair, and they gradually worked their way along the bench, thus entwined, until shortly before Pandarus' exit (promptbook and F. Shirley notes). In 1976, Barton and Kyle were less explicit. Troilus pretended to hit Pandarus at 44, and tickled him at 69. It was a sharp contrast to the mere glances Pandarus had directed at young men in Guthrie's 1956 reading. There Paul Rogers was a meticulously attired if effete gentleman, while more recently Pandarus has often appeared as an aging, camp queen. Clive Francis carried this to the extreme for Judge (RSC 1996). Smallwood found his 'curled black wig, heavy makeup and lower-class accent' 'overdone'. Francis played him as impressed by Troilus' rank (*SS 50*, p. 212). In 2003 SFC the epicene tradition continued, with ample Bernard Hopkins in curled blond wig, makeup, earrings and pearl necklace, carrying a yellow fan he used to probe men's costumes (M. J. Kidnie). By contrast Clive Merrison had been 'the Edwardian bachelor uncle', interested in 'fun, games and a bit on the side' (John Elsom, *PI*, June 1986, p. 18), or a 'whimpering and ambiguous dandy' (Michael Ratcliff, *Obs*, 18 September 1986, p. 21), dressed in a light suit.

The style of the Trojan civilian world has been created in both illusionistic and more realistic settings. Macowan's programme described the locale for 1.1 and 1.2 as 'a hotel terrace' and photographs show a railing and minimalist modern furniture. In 1954, the gates closed on Stratford's departing Trojan army and a few stylized trees were lowered to create Pandarus' orchard. In Davies' realistically detailed ruined mansion (RSC 1985), Pandarus remained at his small table with his hat, cane and paper as light streamed through the large window stage right.

1 Payne had Alexander and two servants help Troilus out of his Elizabethan armour in 1936. In Quayle's production (SMT 1948), the activity faded as the boy looked over the wall and soldiers slowly marched out, leaving Pandarus to sit on a bench while Troilus stood. Barton and Kyle (RSC 1976) had a slot in the stage where Troilus could dramatically seem to plunge his sword into the ground.

2ff Pandarus clapped for the servant at the RSC in 1968. In Papp's production, Troilus doffed his armour unaided, and dropped it by line 5, and Deiphobus and Margarelon casually entered

Each Trojan that is master of his heart,
Let him to field. Troilus, alas, hath none.   5
PANDARUS Will this gear ne'er be mended?
TROILUS The Greeks are strong and skilful to their strength,
　　　　Fierce to their skill and to their fierceness valiant,
　　　　But I am weaker than a woman's tear,
　　　　Tamer than sleep, fonder than ignorance,   10
　　　　Less valiant than the virgin in the night,
　　　　And skilless as unpractised infancy.
PANDARUS Well, I have told you enough of this. For my part, I'll not
　　meddle nor make no farther: he that will have a cake out of the
　　wheat must tarry the grinding.   15
TROILUS Have I not tarried?
PANDARUS Ay, the grinding, but you must tarry the bolting.
TROILUS Have I not tarried?
PANDARUS Ay, the bolting, but you must tarry the leavening.
TROILUS Still have I tarried.   20
PANDARUS Ay, to the leavening; but here's yet in the word hereafter
　　the kneading, the making of the cake, the heating of the oven, and
　　the baking; nay, you must stay the cooling too or you may chance
　　burn your lips.
TROILUS Patience herself, what goddess e'er she be,   25
　　　　Doth lesser blench at suff'rance than I do:
　　　　At Priam's royal table do I sit
　　　　And when fair Cressid comes into my thoughts –
　　　　So traitor! 'When she comes!' When is she thence?
PANDARUS Well, she looked yesternight fairer than ever I saw her look, 30
　　or any woman else.
TROILUS I was about to tell thee – when my heart,
　　　　As wedgèd with a sigh, would rive in twain
　　　　Lest Hector or my father should perceive me,
　　　　I have, as when the sun doth light a storm,   35

and carried it off later in the conversation (F. Shirley notes). In Davies' late-nineteenth-century conception, officers' club ambience was created by details. Anton Lesser took off a sword and gun belt, poured water into a bowl and washed his face, then poured and drank a glass of wine while beginning the conversation. He lit a cigarette at 35. Pandarus remained in his chair, but put down his paper until 44 (promptbook). In 1990, Mendes placed Pandarus (Rodway) in a chair while Troilus went to the wooden circle on the stage floor and laid his helmet and sword there, establishing it as a special spot. In OX 1999–2000, with modern military fatigue costumes, Troilus took off a bulletproof vest (F. Shirley notes).

Buried this sigh in wrinkle of a smile.
But sorrow that is couched in seeming gladness
Is like that mirth fate turns to sudden sadness.

PANDARUS An her hair were not somewhat darker than Helen's –
well go to, there were no more comparison between the women;   40
but for my part she is my kinswoman, I would not, as they term
it, praise her, but I would somebody had heard her talk yesterday
as I did. I will not dispraise your sister Cassandra's wit but –

TROILUS O Pandarus! I tell thee Pandarus,
When I do tell thee there my hopes lie drowned   45
Reply not in how many fathoms deep
They lie indrenched. I tell thee I am mad
In Cressid's love, thou answer'st she is fair,
Pour'st in the open ulcer of my heart
Her eyes, her hair, her cheek, her gait, her voice,   50
Handlest in thy discourse – O that her hand,
In whose comparison all whites are ink
Writing their own reproach, to whose soft seizure
The cygnet's down is harsh and spirit of sense
Hard as the palm of ploughman – this thou tell'st me,   55
As true thou tell'st me, when I say I love her.
But saying thus, instead of oil and balm
Thou lay'st in every gash that love hath given me
The knife that made it.

PANDARUS I speak no more than truth.   60

TROILUS Thou dost not speak so much.

PANDARUS Faith, I'll not meddle in it – let her be as she is; if she be
fair 'tis the better for her; an she be not, she has the mends in her
own hands.

TROILUS Good Pandarus, how now Pandarus!   65

PANDARUS I have had my labour for my travail, ill-thought on of her
and ill-thought on of you, gone between and between, but small
thanks for my labour.

TROILUS What, art thou angry Pandarus, what, with me?

61ff   Judge had Joseph Fiennes lay his head in Clive Francis' lap, exciting the queen (RSC 1996). Like
many others, Richard Monette made comparisons to *Romeo and Juliet* (SFC 2003 Programme
notes), and Troilus' massaged Pandarus' back during his persuasion, as Juliet had rubbed her
nurse's. Pandarus interpolated a request to rub 'a' t' other side' (Kidnie; *R & J* 2.5.50). Davies let
the discussion between Lesser and Merrison grow heated and Troilus snatched the paper, which
Pandarus grabbed back when he picked up hat, shawl and cane to exit at 82 (1985 promptbook).

PANDARUS Because she's kin to me, therefore she's not so fair as Helen;   70
    an she were not kin to me she would be as fair o'Friday as Helen
    is on Sunday. But what care I? I care not an she were a blackamoor,
    'tis all one to me –
TROILUS Say I she is not fair?
PANDARUS I do not care whether you do or no. She's a fool to stay be-   75
    hind her father – let her to the Greeks and so I'll tell her the next
    time I see her; for my part, I'll meddle nor make no more i' th'matter.
TROILUS Pandarus –
PANDARUS Not I.
TROILUS Sweet Pandarus –   80
PANDARUS Pray you speak no more to me; I will leave all as I found
    it and there an end.   *Exit*

                    Sound alarum

TROILUS Peace, you ungracious clamours, peace, rude sounds!
    Fools on both sides, Helen must needs be fair
    When with your blood you daily paint her thus.   85
    I cannot fight upon this argument,
    It is too starved a subject for my sword.
    But Pandarus – O gods how do you plague me!
    I cannot come to Cressid but by Pandar
    And he's as tetchy to be wooed to woo   90
    As she is stubborn, chaste against all suit.
    Tell me Apollo, for thy Daphne's love,
    What Cressid is, what Pandar, and what we:
    Her bed is India, there she lies, a pearl;
    Between our Ilium and where she resides   95

83ff Troilus summarizes the situation in soliloquy until Aeneas enters at 98 and ends his reverie.
Productions have retained most of the soliloquy, though Poel (1912) and Barton (1968) cut the last
lines and Nunn moved the first five lines to become 1–5 of his third scene.

89SD Quayle (1948) muted the sense of warfare by having music before Aeneas' entry, while Shaw
(1954) emphasized the atmosphere of an armed city when soldiers opened the large gates to
admit Aeneas, who turned to look out when the alarum sounded (107SD). In 1968 Barton used
'Stratford smoke' to accompany the entry from battle with two soldier attendants. Aeneas put
down his arms naturalistically and took a towel and a drink from the soldiers as he greeted
Troilus (F. Shirley notes). In 1985 Lesser moved up the stairs when Pandarus exited, and looked
out the landing window. He came back down during the end of his soliloquy, making room for
Aeneas' entry from the staircase landing. For the soliloquy Mendes (RSC 1990) placed Troilus in
the dramatic striped shadow the metal bars cast, and Aeneas slapped him on the shoulder as he
entered, establishing manly camaraderie.

Let it be called the wild and wand'ring flood,
Ourself the merchant and this sailing Pandar
Our doubtful hope, our convoy and our bark.

Alarum. Enter AENEAS

AENEAS How now, Prince Troilus! Wherefore not afield?
TROILUS Because not there; this woman's answer sorts,   100
       For womanish it is to be from thence.
       What news, Aeneas, from the field today?
AENEAS That Paris is returnèd home and hurt.
TROILUS By whom, Aeneas?
AENEAS Troilus, by Menelaus.   105
TROILUS Let Paris bleed – 'tis but a scar to scorn,
       Paris is gored with Menelaus' horn.
              Alarum
AENEAS Hark what good sport is out of town today!
TROILUS Better at home if 'would I might' were 'may'.
       But to the sport abroad – are you bound thither?   110
AENEAS In all swift haste.
TROILUS Come, go we then together.

                                              Exeunt

108SD   Emphasising the 'war as sport' attitude of the Trojans early in the play with physical contact,
       Barton's Aeneas and Troilus mock fought as they heard the alarum. They used sword and shield
       in 1968, and wrestled in 1976. Where the servant remains onstage, or where Troilus has laid
       down his weapons, he can rearm as he agrees to join Aeneas in the battle (SMT 1954; RSC 1976).
       Judge (RSC 1996) had them descend via the stage-front stairs where they emerged with the other
       warriors in 1.2

[**1.2**] *Enter* CRESSIDA *and her man* [ALEXANDER]

The scene often continues 1.1, with Pandarus returning to the location he left earlier. Alexander's description of Hector's angry behaviour after being struck down in battle by Ajax (4b–14a; 29–31) is usually kept. Most productions cut the description of Ajax (17–26). In earlier productions, some of Cressida's repartee with Pandarus was considered too suggestive to play.

The scene introduces Cressida, who does not appear again until she meets Troilus in 3.2. Directors have used this scene to show her wit, forecast loose behaviour, suggest youth fascinated by self-discovery, or hint at depth of feeling in a difficult situation. 'Struggling to remove the paradox of Cressida's submission to Diomedes . . . some producers have presented her as an artful bitch from her first appearance. This was taken to extremes in . . . 1956 when Cressida was having an erotic liason with his manservant before she seduces Troilus.' (Tylee, p. 67.) Poel called for a 'frivolous coquette' (Speaight, *William Poel*, p. 196). At Stratford in 1936 Pamela Brown was coy, with a 'prettily affected innocence . . . She didn't care about the men she beguiles.' (Alexander W. Williams, 'Shakespeare at Stratford', *Boston Herald*, 23 August 1936.) People other than Tylee called Rosemary Harris an 'obvious, oversexed trollop' or a 'bewitching minx' in Guthrie's production (F.G.B., *PP*, May 1956, p. 22; *TA*, March 1957, p. 18). Papp deemed her banter in response to Pandarus' risqué remarks 'a defense' – talk instead of action. She is 'titillated but not ready to yield' (pp. 25–7). She annoys Pandarus by pretending lack of interest in Troilus, only to reveal her love in soliloquy.

Costume is important. If Cressida appears demure, especially in contrast to Helen in 3.1, then Troilus' eventual shock at her switch to Diomedes becomes more believable. If, like Rosemary Harris, or Madeline Le Roux (NYSF 1973), she always uses sensuous movements to emphasize her sexuality, or if her costume is closer to Helen's and signals flirtatiousness, then Troilus is criticized as a blind romantic idealist in his opinion of her. Smallwood found Victoria Hamilton's Cressida from the start 'pert and sexy, her clothes all chosen to give maximum emphasis to her femininity (*SS 50*, p. 214). Juliet Stevenson dressed conservatively, in good Victorian summer taste, complete with straw hat, in keeping with the thoughtful character she established, until she was traded to the Greeks, still in her nightgown (see Rutter).

In earlier productions, except for Harris' 1956 flirtations, the scene was physically decorous, but Barton's 1968 promptbook calls for many contacts that began as Alexander brushed

CRESSIDA Who were those went by?
ALEXANDER   Queen Hecuba and Helen.
CRESSIDA And whither go they?
ALEXANDER   Up to the eastern tower,
        Whose height commands as subject all the vale,
        To see the battle. Hector, whose patience
        Is as a virtue fixed, today was moved: 5
        He chid Andromache and struck his armourer
        And, like as there were husbandry in war,
        Before the sun rose he was harnessed light
        And to the field goes he, where every flower
        Did as a prophet weep what it foresaw   10
        In Hector's wrath.
CRESSIDA   What was his cause of anger?
ALEXANDER The noise goes, this: there is among the Greeks
        A lord of Trojan blood, nephew to Hector,
        They call him Ajax.
CRESSIDA   Good, and what of him?
ALEXANDER They say he is a very man *per se* and stands alone.   15

Cressida's hair, then sat with her, his arm around her by the time Pandarus entered. After the warriors had processed off, Cressida lay on her back in Pandarus' lap until he tried to mount her, when she threw him off and sat on his stomach (215–30) until just before Troilus' boy entered and Pandarus pushed her off. At the Bristol Old Vic in 1979, a production photograph shows Cressida and Pandarus lounging together on cushions, drinking from jewelled goblets. By contrast, Juliet Stevenson sat stiffly beside Pandarus, then served him tea. For all his emphasis on the body, Judge (RSC 1996) merely had Cressida put her arm around Pandarus (149) and kiss him at 224. She and Alexander had sat familiarly together on the bench at first, but without the close contact Barton orchestrated.

OSD Alexander swept the dirt on the Olivier stage in 1999; in the 1976 NT production he laid a rug on the ground for Cressida beside Pandarus' chair. Cressida came down the stairs of the mansion in RSC 1985 as he spread a rug and placed a tray with a samovar and china near the foot of the stairs. The circle opened to reveal a shallow pool in the Swan's thrust stage in 1990. Occasionally Hecuba and Helen walk across upstage (NY 1932; SMT 1936 and 1954, where they had waiting women; BBC TV 1981, where the camera closed in on them). Poel cut mention of Hecuba and had Helenus accompany Helen. Dromgoole placed them at the rear under the stage-centre scaffold and on its steps to wait for the warriors (OX 2000 – F. Shirley notes). More often Cressida and Alexander merely look offstage. In Quayle's production Alexander dashed past the flower seller and others to check (SMT 1948 promptbook). Boyd (RSC 1998), with his cuts for touring, had Andromache accompany Cressida, taking Alexander's line. Pandarus called her by name before she left at 42.

CRESSIDA So do all men, unless they are drunk, sick, or have no legs.

ALEXANDER This man, lady, hath robbed many beasts of their particular additions: he is as valiant as the lion, churlish as the bear, slow as the elephant, a man into whom nature hath so crowded humours that his valour is crushed into folly, his folly sauced with discretion. 20 There is no man hath a virtue that he hath not a glimpse of, nor any man an attaint but he carries some stain of it. He is melancholy without cause and merry against the hair; he hath the joints of everything, but everything so out of joint that he is a gouty Briareus, many hands and no use, or purblind Argus, all eyes and no 25 sight.

CRESSIDA But how should this man that makes me smile make Hector angry?

ALEXANDER They say he yesterday coped Hector in the battle and struck him down, the disdain and shame whereof hath ever since 30 kept Hector fasting and waking.

CRESSIDA Who comes here?

ALEXANDER Madam, your uncle Pandarus.

Enter PANDARUS

CRESSIDA Hector's a gallant man.

ALEXANDER As may be in the world, lady. 35

PANDARUS What's that, what's that?

CRESSIDA Good morrow, uncle Pandarus.

PANDARUS Good morrow, cousin Cressid, what do you talk of? Good morrow, Alexander. How do you, cousin? When were you at Ilium?

CRESSIDA This morning, uncle. 40

PANDARUS What were you talking of when I came? Was Hector armed and gone ere ye came to Ilium? Helen was not up, was she?

CRESSIDA Hector was gone but Helen was not up.

PANDARUS Even so. Hector was stirring early.

CRESSIDA That were we talking of, and of his anger. 45

PANDARUS Was he angry?

CRESSIDA So he says here.

35SD Max Adrian and Dorothy Tutin perched on the edge of the sandpit while Alexander (Clive Swift) sat in the sand, holding the parasol over them (SMT 1960). Rodway (RSC 1990) joined Cressida as she dabbled in the pool that had been revealed under the onstage circle, carefully removing his shoes, rolling his neatly creased white trousers, and putting his feet in the pool by 44 (F. Shirley notes). His servant sat in the chair he had occupied in 1.1. At the Yale Rep 1990 and NT 1999, Pandarus carried his own parasol as he bustled in.

PANDARUS True, he was so – I know the cause too: he'll lay about him
    today I can tell them that [*He dismisses Alexander*], and there's
    Troilus will not come far behind him, let them take heed of Troilus,   50
    I can tell them that too.
CRESSIDA What, is he angry too?
PANDARUS Who, Troilus? Troilus is the better man of the two.
CRESSIDA O Jupiter! There's no comparison.
PANDARUS What, not between Troilus and Hector? Do you know a   55
    man if you see him?
CRESSIDA Ay, if I ever saw him before and knew him.
PANDARUS Well, I say Troilus is Troilus.
CRESSIDA Then you say as I say, for I am sure he is not Hector.
PANDARUS No, nor Hector is not Troilus in some degrees.   60
CRESSIDA 'Tis just to each of them: he is himself.
PANDARUS Himself? Alas, poor Troilus! I would he were.
CRESSIDA So he is.
PANDARUS Condition I had gone barefoot to India.
CRESSIDA He is not Hector.   65
PANDARUS Himself? No, he's not himself – would 'a were himself!
    Well the gods are above, time must friend or end; well, Troilus,
    well, I would my heart were in her body. No, Hector is not a better
    man than Troilus.
CRESSIDA Excuse me –   70
PANDARUS He is elder –
CRESSIDA Pardon me, pardon me –
PANDARUS Th'other's not come to't – you shall tell me another tale
    when th'other's come to't; Hector shall not have his wit this year.
CRESSIDA He shall not need it if he have his own.   75
PANDARUS Nor his qualities –
CRESSIDA No matter.
PANDARUS Nor his beauty.
CRESSIDA 'Twould not become him, his own's better.
PANDARUS You have no judgement, niece. Helen herself swore th'other   80
    day that Troilus, for a brown favour – for so 'tis I must confess –
    not brown neither –
CRESSIDA No, but brown.
PANDARUS Faith, to say truth, brown and not brown.
CRESSIDA To say the truth, true and not true.   85

---

48   Pandarus had a cane and made slashing motions at 'he'll lay about him' (SMT 1948) while
    Cressida pulled a mirror from a bag and only half-listened to him. In 1981 they finger duelled at
    times during the interchange. In 1985 Merrison motioned Alexander to bring a wicker chair,
    where he sat for tea.

PANDARUS She praised his complexion above Paris'.

CRESSIDA Why Paris hath colour enough.

PANDARUS So he has.

CRESSIDA Then Troilus should have too much: if she praised him above, his complexion is higher than his; he having colour enough and the other higher is too flaming a praise for a good complexion. I had as lief Helen's golden tongue had commended Troilus for a copper nose. 90

PANDARUS I swear to you I think Helen loves him better than Paris.

CRESSIDA Then she's a merry Greek indeed. 95

PANDARUS Nay, I am sure she does: she came to him th'other day into the compassed window – and you know he has not past three or four hairs on his chin –

CRESSIDA Indeed a tapster's arithmetic may soon bring his particulars therein to a total. 100

PANDARUS Why he is very young and yet will he within three pound lift as much as his brother Hector.

CRESSIDA Is he so young a man and so old a lifter?

PANDARUS But to prove to you that Helen loves him, she came and puts me her white hand to his cloven chin – 105

CRESSIDA Juno have mercy! How came it cloven?

PANDARUS Why you know 'tis dimpled; I think his smiling becomes him better than any man in all Phrygia.

CRESSIDA O, he smiles valiantly.

PANDARUS Does he not? 110

CRESSIDA O yes, an 'twere a cloud in autumn.

PANDARUS Why go to then, but to prove to you that Helen loves Troilus –

CRESSIDA Troilus will stand to the proof if you'll prove it so.

PANDARUS Troilus? Why he esteems her no more than I esteem an addle egg. 115

CRESSIDA If you love an addle egg as well as you love an idle head, you would eat chickens i'the shell.

PANDARUS I cannot choose but laugh to think how she tickled his chin – indeed she has a marvellous white hand I must needs confess – 120

CRESSIDA Without the rack.

PANDARUS And she takes upon her to spy a white hair on his chin –

CRESSIDA Alas, poor chin! Many a wart is richer.

PANDARUS But there was such laughing! Queen Hecuba laughed that her eyes ran o'er – 125

CRESSIDA With millstones.

PANDARUS And Cassandra laughed –

CRESSIDA But there was a more temperate fire under the pot of her eyes – did her eyes run o'er too?

PANDARUS And Hector laughed.   130
CRESSIDA At what was all this laughing?
PANDARUS Marry, at the white hair that Helen spied on Troilus' chin.
CRESSIDA An't had been a green hair, I should have laughed too.
PANDARUS They laughed not so much at the hair as at his pretty answer.
CRESSIDA What was his answer?   135
PANDARUS Quoth she, 'Here's but two and fifty hairs on your chin and
    one of them is white.'
CRESSIDA This is her question.
PANDARUS That's true, make no question of that. 'Two and fifty hairs',
    quoth he, 'and one white – that white hair is my father and all   140
    the rest are his sons.' 'Jupiter!' quoth she, 'which of these hairs is
    Paris my husband?' 'The forked one', quoth he, 'pluck't out and
    give it him.' But there was such laughing, and Helen so blushed
    and Paris so chafed and all the rest so laughed, that it passed.
CRESSIDA So let it now, for it has been a great while going by.   145
PANDARUS Well, cousin, I told you a thing yesterday – think on't.
CRESSIDA So I do.
PANDARUS I'll be sworn 'tis true, he will weep you an 'twere a man
    born in April.
CRESSIDA And I'll spring up in his tears an 'twere a nettle against May.   150
                          Sound a retreat
PANDARUS Hark, they are coming from the field. Shall we stand up
    here and see them as they pass toward Ilium, good niece? Do,
    sweet niece Cressida.
CRESSIDA At your pleasure.
PANDARUS Here, here, here's an excellent place, here we may see most   155
    bravely. I'll tell you them all by their names as they pass by, but
    mark Troilus above the rest.

155ff Moshinsky had Alexander fold the blanket where he and Cressida had sat on the dirt by
       Pandarus' downstage chair, in preparation for the soldiers, who marched at a distance across the
       back of the cockpit, single file, to trumpet fanfare (NT 1976). The positioning of Cressida and
       Pandarus on a balcony toward the rear of the Swan stage in 1990 made their commentary less an
       intermediation than it often is, and attention focused on the warriors and 'The ceremony aquired
       the importance invested in it by the participants, an importance that Pandarus could not really
       dent.' (Holland, *English Shakespeares*, pp. 70–1.) Cressida fanned herself in excitement or to
       tease Pandarus as they watched the locker room from a side opening high in the wall in 1996
       (Smallwood, *SS 50*, p. 214).
157SD The parade of the Trojans in military costumes gives directors an opportunity to add business
       beyond the simple 'enter' sd that editors usually emend with 'and pass over the stage' for each
       warrior. Occasionally the heroes are imagined (Old Vic 1956; RSC 1985) and the audience must

Enter AENEAS [*and passes over the stage*]

CRESSIDA Speak not so loud.
PANDARUS That's Aeneas, is not that a brave man? He's one of the flowers
    of Troy, I can tell you, but mark Troilus, you shall see anon.   160
CRESSIDA Who's that?

rely on Pandarus' obviously biased comments. Boyd cut the entire march-past in 1998
(150SD-209).

    The added business occasionally became mildly satirical. Hands had a servant hold a mirror so
Paris could preen (RSC 1981), and Mendes repeated this satire in RSC 1990 by allowing Paris to
wash, pause to admire his reflection, and slick back his hair. The warriors all washed in the pool
Pandarus and Cressida had vacated when they went to a side gallery to watch. Antenor and
Hector ritually cleansed their bloody swords, then all exited up the Swan theatre aisles. In another
touch of humour, Mendes had Helenus forget his sword and return for it (F. Shirley notes). Dorn
had also had a washing ritual in Munich, 1986. The most elaborate addition was Judge's locker
room in 1996. Servants carried on benches with stacks of folded white towels, took the weapons
and body armour as the warriors emerged up the stage front steps, and handed each a towel. The
warriors rubbed their bodies and finally left as a group, attendants carrying benches and used
towels, while Pandarus and Cressida descended from their observation spot in the right wall. The
most detached treatment was the videotaped march-past Pandarus and Cressida watched on their
grainy television (NYTh 1987). In early productions they merely marched across, with Pandarus
and Cressida at a distance on the same level, even where an 'Elizabethan' balcony might have
been used. Gradually other business was added. Payne (SMT 1936) brought on 'four supers and
three girls' to greet the soldiers and their attendants on the crowded stage, and Helenus blessed
the group (promptbook). In SMT 1954 Cressida and Pandarus discussed them from a sentry's
platform on the left wall, well above the soldiers' more naturalistic return. The warriors were met
by servants, and Aeneas and Hector handed over their classical helmets with large brushes;
Hector left while Antenor and Aeneas chatted before leaving, giving Pandarus and Cressida ample
time for comment (production photos and promptbook). In 1976 RSC Cressida and Pandarus, on
the stage right balcony, watched and munched from the bag of grapes she had earlier shared
with Alexander. 'It is Shakespeare's relaxed means of introducing them, but Barton . . . has them
parade by like frozen models in . . . the first of many military fashion shows.' (David Zane
Mairowitz, *PP*, October 1976, p. 20.) Barton's named warriors carried large spears while the
lesser soldiers had short swords. In 1999 Nunn brought the warriors down the Olivier Theatre
centre aisle, wearing flowing white costumes with shields and minimal helmets, while attendants
carried in fire bowls that were set on tripods. As Pandarus and Cressida strolled around the stage
and mentioned them, each turned, raised a sword or knelt very formally, then paraded off
(production film). Dorn had also had a fire bowl as a ritual centre for the Trojans in Munich in
1986. In the 2003 SFC production, tambourines and drums accompanied the procession, with
cheers as each warrior entered and came downstage to acknowledge the crowd (Kidnie).

Enter ANTENOR [*and passes over the stage*]

PANDARUS That's Antenor. He has a shrewd wit, I can tell you, and he's
a man good enough, he's one o'the soundest judgements in Troy
whosoever, and a proper man of person. When comes Troilus? I'll
show you Troilus anon – if he see me, you shall see him nod at me.   165
CRESSIDA Will he give you the nod?
PANDARUS You shall see.
CRESSIDA If he do, the rich shall have more.

Enter HECTOR [*and passes over the stage*]

PANDARUS That's Hector, that, that, look you that, there's a fellow!
Go thy way Hector! There's a brave man, niece. O brave Hector!   170
Look how he looks: there's a countenance, is't not a brave man?
CRESSIDA O, a brave man.
PANDARUS Is 'a not? It does a man's heart good, look you what hacks
are on his helmet, look you yonder, do you see? Look you there,
there's no jesting, there's laying on, take't off who will, as they   175
say; there be hacks!
CRESSIDA Be those with swords?
PANDARUS Swords, anything, he cares not an the devil come to him,
it's all one; by God's lid, it does one's heart good. Yonder comes
Paris, yonder comes Paris.   180

Enter PARIS [*and passes over the stage*]

Look ye yonder, niece, is't not a gallant man too, is't not? Why
this is brave now. Who said he came hurt home today? He's not
hurt – why this will do Helen's heart good now, ha! Would I could
see Troilus now! You shall see Troilus anon.
CRESSIDA Who's that?   185

Enter HELENUS [*and passes over the stage*]

PANDARUS That's Helenus. I marvel where Troilus is. That's Helenus.
I think he went not forth today. That's Helenus.
CRESSIDA Can Helenus fight, uncle?
PANDARUS Helenus? No – yes, he'll fight indifferent well. I marvel
where Troilus is – hark, do you not hear the people cry 'Troilus'?   190
Helenus is a priest.
CRESSIDA What sneaking fellow comes yonder?

Enter TROILUS [*and passes over the stage*]

PANDARUS Where? Yonder? – that's Deiphobus. 'Tis Troilus! There's
a man, niece. Hem! Brave Troilus, the prince of chivalry!
CRESSIDA Peace, for shame, peace!   195

PANDARUS Mark him, note him, O brave Troilus! Look well upon
him niece: look you how his sword is bloodied and his helm
more hacked than Hector's, and how he looks and how he goes.
O admirable youth, he ne'er saw three and twenty. Go thy way
Troilus, go thy way! Had I a sister were a grace or a daughter a   200
goddess, he should take his choice. O admirable man! Paris? Paris
is dirt to him, and I warrant Helen to change would give an eye
to boot.

Enter common soldiers [and pass over the stage]

CRESSIDA Here comes more.

PANDARUS Asses, fools, dolts – chaff and bran, chaff and bran! Porridge   205
after meat! I could live and die i'th'eyes of Troilus. Ne'er look,
ne'er look, the eagles are gone: crows and daws, crows and daws!
I had rather be such a man as Troilus than Agamemnon and all
Greece.

CRESSIDA There is amongst the Greeks Achilles, a better man than   210
Troilus.

PANDARUS Achilles? A drayman, a porter, a very camel!

CRESSIDA Well well.

PANDARUS 'Well well?' Why, have you any discretion, have you any
eyes? Do you know what a man is? Is not birth, beauty, good shape,   215
discourse, manhood, learning, gentleness, virtue, youth, liberality,
and such like, the spice and salt that season a man?

CRESSIDA Ay, a minced man, and then to be baked with no date in the
pie, for then the man's date is out.

PANDARUS You are such a woman – a man knows not at what ward   220
you lie.

CRESSIDA Upon my back to defend my belly, upon my wit to defend
my wiles, upon my secrecy to defend mine honesty, my mask to

196ff   Generally the warriors don't acknowledge Pandarus and Cressida, and her 'Speak not so loud'
suggests avoiding notice (158). But in SMT 1936 Troilus saluted them and in 1976 RSC Troilus
pointed his spear toward the balcony and she dropped a handkerchief on it. In SMT 1948,
Pandarus and Cressida were wearing flowers, and he threw them to Troilus (promptbook).

210   There is a lag as the heroes leave and Pandarus and Cressida come back to the main stage if their
vantage point has been a balcony. In RSC 1976 Troilus' boy entered and looked up, and Pandarus
and Cressida came down, still with the grapes, during the next four lines.

218   Papp had Cressida emphasize the baking metaphor to echo 1.1, while Barton cut the lines (NYC
1965; RSC 1969). 'Meg Davies demonstrated lying on her back on a low daybed, evoking a harem
girl.' (BOV, 1979, in Edinburgh – unattributed review.)

defend my beauty, and you to defend all these; and at all these
wards I lie, at a thousand watches.   225
PANDARUS Say one of your watches.
CRESSIDA Nay, I'll watch you for that, and that's one of the chiefest of
them too. If I cannot ward what I would not have hit, I can watch
you for telling how I took the blow, unless it swell past hiding and
then it's past watching.   230

Enter [Troilus'] BOY

PANDARUS You are such another!
BOY Sir, my lord would instantly speak with you.
PANDARUS Where?
BOY At your own house, there he unarms him.
PANDARUS Good boy, tell him I come.   235

[Exit Boy]

I doubt he be hurt. Fare ye well, good niece.
CRESSIDA Adieu, uncle.
PANDARUS I'll be with you, niece, by and by.
CRESSIDA To bring, uncle?
PANDARUS Ay, a token from Troilus.   240
CRESSIDA By the same token, you are a bawd.

Exit Pandarus

Words, vows, gifts, tears, and love's full sacrifice
He offers in another's enterprise,
But more in Troilus thousandfold I see
Than in the glass of Pandar's praise may be.   245
Yet hold I off. Women are angels, wooing:
Things won are done, joy's soul lies in the doing;

230SD The entrance of Troilus' boy breaks off the banter that has come close to the bone in the 'ward'
       interchange (220–30), lines that were cut in some early productions.
241SD Pandarus kissed the boy on the mouth, and they exited together (SFC 2003, Kidnie).
242–55 The actress playing Cressida has appeared calculating or wondering as she declares her intention
       of hiding her feelings in the closing soliloquy. Although directors have selectively trimmed the
       scene (Barton in 1969 excised almost a fifth of it, and Guthrie in 1956 removed almost a third) the
       formal couplets are spoken in their entirety, forming the last impression of Cressida until the
       assignation, when she has yielded to temptation. Nunn placed the speech later, just before the
       Trojan debate on Helen (NT 1999 promptbook). Stevenson remained seated on the rug in 1985,
       speaking seriously. Moshinsky (NT 1976) had Cressida use the couplets in all their formality as a
       series of aphorisms. Schweitzer and Madeline Le Roux decided on 'sensuous movements to
       emphasize her sensuality and desire' (NYSF 1973).

That she belov'd knows nought that knows not this:
Men prize the thing ungained more than it is;
That she was never yet that ever knew   250
Love got so sweet as when desire did sue.
Therefore this maxim out of love I teach:
Achievement is command, ungained beseech.
Then though my heart's content firm love doth bear,
Nothing of that shall from mine eyes appear.   *Exit*   255

ACT I, SCENE 3

[1.3] *Sennet. Enter* AGAMEMNON, NESTOR, ULYSSES, DIOMEDES, MENELAUS, *with others*

Directors often use trumpets (sennet) or other martial music to emphasize the change of mood as Shakespeare finally introduces the Greeks. The longest scene of the play has been described as 'stuffier than war-office England' (F.G.B., *PP*, May 1956, p. 22). In an interview in 2001 Peter Hall noted the 'mendacity of the political leaders' that the scene suggests (James Shapiro, 'Nurturing an English Flame in America'). Ulysses' set speeches on degree and Grecian problems and his later scheme to deal with Hector's challenge take up almost half the lines. In 1936, Wolfit held the stage with a mix of 'cynicism and eloquence' and 'time-serving diplomacy', while Nestor's occasional speeches were 'an argument for treating the play as sheer burlesque' (*Birmingham Mail*, 25 April 1936).

English Renaissance audiences were accustomed to long, closely reasoned, highly imaged oral presentations (A. C. Sprague lecture, October 1950), but most modern audiences and reviewers find the language hard to follow and the length intolerable. Many of Poel's cuts have become traditional except in the few full-text productions. Cuts begin with Agamemnon's rhetorical 'tortive' opening, where only lines 11–12 and 17b–21 are universally kept. Nestor's verbiage may include the Boreas allusion, but his words are usually shortened from 37, and only essential details are retained. Barton tried a fuller version at Stratford in 1968, but the 1969 London promptbook reveals that he later almost matched Guthrie's cutting of half the first movement of the scene. Davies and Boyd, among others, excised Ulysses' flattering opening, getting quickly to his analysis at line 75. Boyd gave the Greeks a microphone to make what remained a public debate. The speech on 'degree' was long said to express Shakespeare's philosophy, in contrast to Thersites' and Pandarus' warped perspectives, and fit a yearning for order throughout the 1930s in England and Germany (Hortmann). That opinion has lost credence as more recent productions emphasize a balance of viewpoints. Even when it was considered central, the statement was usually mercilessly slashed, losing much of the planet imagery. The salient lines – 75–84, 101b–110a and 128–136 – were always kept, with whatever else the director decided to retain to add substance. In a Boston 2004 production that cut a quarter of the text, much of the paring was done here to 'make it a little more lean and muscular and a little more summer-night friendly' (Steven Barkhimer, *Boston Globe*, 4 July 2004, N4).

Brooks Atkinson remarked that The Players 'cut much of the metaphysics of Ulysses on the cause of war' but there was still 'more talk about the springs of action than action' (*NYT*, 5 and 7 June 1932). In 1946 David Read's Ulysses emphasized the 'integrity of the intellect' in his 'cold austerity' (*LT*, 29 June 1946). Richard David noted that 'The solemn absurdity of the council of war came nearer home with Ulysses in an admiral's frock coat and Menelaus as a be-monocled staff officer' in Guthrie's 1956 production (*SS 10*, p. 130), and revealed the incompetence of the Greek leadership. In Davies, 1985, 'The image of aristocratic ineffectuality in the face of social collapse was a pointed allusion to Margaret Thatcher's Britain' (Bowen, p. 55), with Ulysses the wily politician in winged collar and frock coat manipulating the uniformed officers. In some modern dress, grunge versions, like TR 1971 or the NYSF in 1973, the satire has become more vicious and obvious. Ulysses and the others have only underwear, making their speeches seem more ridiculously pompous and overdone, and letting the ragged Thersites become their visual equal in expressing a Greek viewpoint. Despite the Edwardian costuming in Regents Park in 1998, Ulysses came across as a 'bellowing pedant and schoolmaster' (Nicholas deJongh, *Standard*, 19 June 1998). Hall's 2001 Greeks were 'like some shabby medieval motorcycle gang' (Bruce Webster, 'Shakespeare Staged in a Sandbox Where Nobody Plays Nice', *NYT*, 16 April 2001, p. E5). Barton and Hall (1960) retained the humour as Ulysses described Patroclus miming the generals for Achilles' amusement. Judge (RSC 1996) and Dromgoole (OX 1999–2000) had Ulysses mimic Achilles' voice.

The Quarto and Folio give only entrances and exits and directions for a couple of trumpet calls, but directors have added many movements beyond Agamemnon's line to Aeneas: 'let me touch your hand' at 305. Over the years various devices been used to create an illusion of liveliness or naturalism. Poel (1912) had hung a curtain between the stage pillars, and opened it to reveal a limelit tableau, with the Greeks in their ruffs, doublets and hose, smoking clay pipes. Payne also opened curtains to reveal men sitting around a table on stools (SMT 1936). Each rose to speak, as they would for Barton in 1968, then returned to their places. By contrast, Guthrie's Greeks had gilt banquet chairs around a heavy table, but a number of them stood (F. Shirley notes).

The steam rooms at the NYSF in 1973 and at the NAO in 1978 levelled all from king to 'others' and created an incongruous air of informality for the formal speeches. Hall (2001) treated the speeches ritualistically, with each speaker taking the sceptre from its central tripod as he rose to speak (Kastan). Barton's Greeks had risen from stools to speak at a lectern in 1968. Added actions sometimes became distracting. In 1976, Barton and Kyle's Greeks wandered on, Agamemnon inexplicably with a frying pan. Straw hats and flywhisks gave Agamemnon, Nestor and Menelaus props that often upstaged a speaker, while a gong on a tripod called people to order. Nestor is often a figure of fun, coughing, spitting and palsied, as Patroclus portrayed him (1.3.173–6) (F. Shirley notes). In 1981 Hands let him upstage Ulysses by noisily eating fruit. He left his wheelchair 'with huge effort' on two sticks to gimp among the supply boxes scattered on the stage carpet, a 'shaggy black bedspread that passes for a set' (Sheridan Morley, 'War Games', *Punch*, 15 July 1981, p. 104).

AGAMEMNON Princes,
>What grief hath set the jaundice on your cheeks?
>The ample proposition that hope makes
>In all designs begun on earth below
>Fails in the promised largeness: checks and disasters   5

The relationship of Ulysses to the others reached the ultimate in distancing at NYTh in 1987 when he appeared in a badly coloured television news interview, recalling military figures dissecting American problems in the Middle East (Elaine Armstead, *FT*, 23 September, 1987; Robert Hanks, *In*, 30 September 1987).

OSD   The Greek camp is often denoted by a cloth pulled across the stage to suggest a tent (SMT 1948, 1954; RSC 1996; NT 1999; OX 1999), or by campstools or chairs (SMT 1960; RSC 1968–9; NT 1976; Hall 2001). In 1960 the leather stools were around a large irregularly shaped hide, with Nestor and Agamemnon facing upstage so Ulysses (Eric Porter) could face the audience. Ajax stood stage left with his huge spear and shield (production photo). In 1999 the NT Greeks sat heavily in leather greatcoats in a semi-circle facing outward. A table may add formality to contrast with the ensuing Achilles scene. In Macowan's modern rendering, Guthrie's Edwardian version, with its 'toy soldier pomp and chivalry among the fluttering flags' (*PP*, 1956) and Davies' Crimean period production, the tables were large with seats for everyone. In Landau (ASF 1961) and Mendes (RSC 1990) they were just large enough for a few papers, and most characters stood or sat informally nearby. Occasionally a model of 'six-gated Troy' (SMT 1948; NYSF 1965), or plans, a map, or papers make the conference seem a more carefully planned strategic session (SMT 1954; RSC 1976, 1985, 1990). Davies' promptbook called for a clerk typing notes at a small table stage left of the large council table with its leather straight chairs. The ruined Crimean mansion had become an officers' club with slightly anachronistic gramophone, typewriter, and ticker tape, and a bar where men wandered to pour themselves drinks. In 1938 decanters, glasses and a soda siphon enhanced Macowan's revival, while in 1960 Barton and Hall had a tray with goblets and a wine jug on the hide. Dromgoole (2000) gave the more sophisticated Ulysses an espresso pot, and he and Nestor shared coffee while the others had rolls and wine around a battered card table (F. Shirley notes). Kastan remarked that Agamemnon's position at the council table subtly dictates interrelationships. For Payne (SMT 1936), he sat at the centre, Ulysses to his right. At Stratford, Connecticut, Landau used two uprights with a crosspiece to suggest the entrance to the Civil War-era camp, where Agamemnon sat in the centre camp chair in front of a light-dappled cyclorama (F. Shirley notes). Guthrie switched to red lighting in 1956, while Hall used icy blue in 2001. Usually extras stand guard or pour wine. Fry had sentinels pacing back and forth by the curtains representing the tent opening during the entire scene (James O'Donnell Bennett, 'A Play by Shakespeare, for the First Time Since Shakespeare Lived', London, 1 June 1907). Barton carefully spaced his six soldiers behind the officers so their spear tips crossed (production photos, SMT 1960; RSC 1968). Hands added the sound of a harmonica, recalling First World War films (Wardle, *LT*, 8 July 1981).

Grow in the veins of actions highest reared,
As knots, by the conflux of meeting sap,
Infects the sound pine and diverts his grain,
Tortive and errant, from his course of growth.
Nor, princes, is it matter new to us   10
That we come short of our suppose so far
That after seven years' siege yet Troy walls stand,
Sith every action that hath gone before
Whereof we have record, trial did draw
Bias and thwart, not answering the aim   15
And that unbodied figure of the thought
That gave't surmisèd shape. Why then, you princes,
Do you with cheeks abashed behold our works
And call them shames, which are indeed nought else
But the protractive trials of great Jove   20
To find persistive constancy in men,
The fineness of which metal is not found
In Fortune's love? For then the bold and coward,
The wise and fool, the artist and unread,
The hard and soft, seem all affined and kin;   25
But in the wind and tempest of her frown,
Distinction, with a broad and powerful fan
Puffing at all, winnows the light away,
And what hath mass or matter by itself
Lies rich in virtue and unmingled.   30
NESTOR With due observance of thy god-like seat,
Great Agamemnon, Nestor shall apply
Thy latest words. In the reproof of chance
Lies the true proof of men: the sea being smooth,
How many shallow bauble boats dare sail   35
Upon her patient breast, making their way
With those of nobler bulk.
But let the ruffian Boreas once enrage
The gentle Thetis, and anon behold
The strong-ribbed bark through liquid mountains cut,   40
Bounding between the two moist elements
Like Perseus' horse. Where's then the saucy boat
Whose weak untimbered sides but even now
Co-rivalled greatness? Either to harbour fled
Or made a toast for Neptune. Even so   45
Doth valour's show and valour's worth divide
In storms of fortune; for in her ray and brightness
The herd hath more annoyance by the breese
Than by the tiger; but when the splitting wind

Makes flexible the knees of knotted oaks   50
And flies flee under shade, why then the thing of courage,
As roused with rage, with rage doth sympathise,
And with an accent tuned in self-same key
Retires to chiding fortune.

ULYSSES   Agamemnon,
Thou great commander, nerve and bone of Greece,   55
Heart of our numbers, soul and only spirit
In whom the tempers and the minds of all
Should be shut up, hear what Ulysses speaks.
Besides th'applause and approbation
The which [*To Agamemnon*] most mighty for thy place and
     sway,   60
And thou [*To Nestor*] most reverend for thy stretched-out
     life,
I give to both your speeches, which were such
As Agamemnon and the hand of Greece
Should hold up high in brass, and such again
As venerable Nestor, hatched in silver,   65
Should, with a bond of air strong as the axle-tree
On which heaven rides, knit all the Greekish ears
To his experienced tongue, yet let it please both
Thou great, and wise, to hear Ulysses speak.

AGAMEMNON Speak, prince of Ithaca, and be't of less expect   70
That matter needless, of importless burden,
Divide thy lips, than we are confident
When rank Thersites opes his mastic jaws
We shall hear music, wit, and oracle.

ULYSSES Troy, yet upon his basis, had been down   75
And the great Hector's sword had lacked a master,
But for these instances:
The specialty of rule hath been neglected,

---

54   Ulysses often became impatient as Agamemnon and Nestor talked. Robert Speaight showed a
     'spirit of disintegrating contempt', mixing meanness and eloquence (Desmond MacCarthy, *NS*, 1
     October 1938, p. 491). Ulysses stood or sat restlessly for Barton and Kyle (RSC 1976). In
     Connecticut, he was 'impatient with war games' played by Agamemnon's 'egomaniac'
     commanders (Judith Crist, *NYHT*, 24 July 1961). Hall, 2001, had him seem to interrupt Nestor, then
     sooth resentment with flattery of both men (Kastan). 'John Carlisle delivered [Ulysses' speeches]
     with a booming authority that conveys no idea of the sly politician' in Hands' RSC production
     (Wardle, *LT*, 8 July 1981). 'Robin Midgely's direction made the scene work without Nestor comedy'
     during Ulysses' long speeches at the Marlowe Society in 1964 (*LT*, 10 March 1964).

And look how many Grecian tents do stand
Hollow upon this plain, so many hollow factions.   80
When that the general is not like the hive
To whom the foragers shall all repair,
What honey is expected? Degree being vizarded,
Th'unworthiest shows as fairly in the mask.
The heavens themselves, the planets and this centre   85
Observe degree, priority, and place,
Insisture, course, proportion, season, form,
Office, and custom in all line of order.
And therefore is the glorious planet Sol
In noble eminence enthroned and sphered   90
Amidst the other, whose med'cinable eye
Corrects the influence of evil planets
And posts like the commandment of a king
Sans check to good and bad; but when the planets
In evil mixture to disorder wander,   95
What plagues and what portents, what mutiny,
What raging of the sea, shaking of earth,
Commotion in the winds, frights, changes, horrors,
Divert and crack, rend and deracinate,
The unity and married calm of states   100
Quite from their fixure! O, when degree is shaked,
Which is the ladder of all high designs,
The enterprise is sick. How could communities,
Degrees in schools and brotherhoods in cities,
Peaceful commerce from dividable shores,   105
The primogenity and due of birth,
Prerogative of age, crowns, sceptres, laurels,
But by degree stand in authentic place?
Take but degree away, untune that string,
And hark what discord follows: each thing meets   110
In mere oppugnancy; the bounded waters
Should lift their bosoms higher than the shores
And make a sop of all this solid globe;
Strength should be lord of imbecility,
And the rude son should strike his father dead;   115
Force should be right, or rather, right and wrong,
Between whose endless jar justice resides,
Should lose their names, and so should justice too;
Then everything include itself in power,
Power into will, will into appetite,   120
And appetite, an universal wolf,
So doubly seconded with will and power

Must make perforce an universal prey
And last eat up himself.
Great Agamemnon,   125
This chaos, when degree is suffocate,
Follows the choking;
And this neglection of degree it is
That by a pace goes backward with a purpose
It hath to climb. The general's disdained   130
By him one step below, he by the next,
That next by him beneath – so every step,
Exampled by the first pace that is sick
Of his superior, grows to an envious fever
Of pale and bloodless emulation;   135
And 'tis this fever that keeps Troy on foot,
Not her own sinews. To end a tale of length,
Troy in our weakness stands, not in her strength.
NESTOR Most wisely hath Ulysses here discovered
The fever whereof all our power is sick.   140
AGAMEMNON The nature of the sickness found, Ulysses,
What is the remedy?
ULYSSES The great Achilles, whom opinion crowns
The sinew and the forehand of our host,
Having his ear full of his airy fame,   145
Grows dainty of his worth and in his tent
Lies mocking our designs; with him Patroclus
Upon a lazy bed the livelong day
Breaks scurril jests,
And with ridiculous and silly action –   150
Which, slanderer, he imitation calls –
He pageants us: sometime, great Agamemnon,
Thy topless deputation he puts on,
And like a strutting player, whose conceit
Lies in his hamstring and doth think it rich   155
To hear the wooden dialogue and sound
'Twixt his stretched footing and the scaffoldage –
Such to-be-pitied and o'er-wrested seeming

143   In productions that have Achilles' area indicated in multiple staging, rather than effecting a scene
change after 1.3, Ulysses tends to look toward Achilles' tent or chair. Barton and Kyle imagined
Agamemnon's tent offstage down right with Achilles' across from it, offstage left, and Ulysses
walked left (RSC 1976). At this point Hall's 2001 Ulysses handed around copies of photographs of
Achilles' behaviour that he carried in a battered leather folder. He wore glasses, and behaved
'like a skilled courtroom lawyer' (Kastan).

He acts thy greatness in; and when he speaks
'Tis like a chime a-mending, with terms unsquared,   160
Which, from the tongue of roaring Typhon dropped,
Would seem hyperboles. At this fusty stuff
The large Achilles, on his pressed bed lolling,
From his deep chest laughs out a loud applause,
Cries 'Excellent! 'Tis Agamemnon right;   165
Now play me Nestor: hem, and stroke thy beard
As he being dressed to some oration.'
That's done as near as the extremest ends
Of parallels, as like as Vulcan and his wife;
Yet god Achilles still cries 'Excellent!   170
'Tis Nestor right. Now play him me, Patroclus,
Arming to answer in a night alarm.'
And then, forsooth, the faint defects of age
Must be the scene of mirth, to cough and spit
And with a palsy fumbling on his gorget   175
Shake in and out the rivet; and at this sport
Sir Valour dies, cries 'O enough, Patroclus,
Or give me ribs of steel! I shall split all
In pleasure of my spleen.' And in this fashion
All our abilities, gifts, natures, shapes,   180
Severals and generals of grace exact,
Achievements, plots, orders, preventions,
Excitements to the field, or speech for truce,
Success or loss, what is or is not, serves
As stuff for these two to make paradoxes.   185
NESTOR And in the imitation of these twain,
Who as Ulysses says opinion crowns
With an imperial voice, many are infect:
Ajax is grown self-willed and bears his head
In such a rein, in full as proud a place,   190
As broad Achilles, keeps his tent like him,
Makes factious feasts, rails on our state of war
Bold as an oracle, and sets Thersites,
A slave whose gall coins slanders like a mint,
To match us in comparisons with dirt,   195
To weaken and discredit our exposure
How rank soever rounded in with danger.
ULYSSES They tax our policy and call it cowardice,
Count wisdom as no member of the war,
Forestall prescience, and esteem no act   200
But that of hand; the still and mental parts
That do contrive how many hands shall strike

When fitness calls them on, and know by measure
Of their observant toil the enemy's weight –
Why this hath not a finger's dignity;   205
They call this bed-work, mapp'ry, closet-war,
So that the ram that batters down the wall,
For the great swing and rudeness of his poise,
They place before his hand that made the engine
Or those that with the fineness of their souls   210
By reason guide his execution.
NESTOR Let this be granted, and Achilles' horse
Makes many Thetis' sons.

Tucket

AGAMEMNON What trumpet? Look, Menelaus.
MENELAUS From Troy.   215

Enter AENEAS [with trumpeter]

AGAMEMNON What would you 'fore our tent?
AENEAS Is this great Agamemnon's tent, I pray you?

213SD Shakespeare introduces a tucket, a trumpet call that rouses Greeks and audience alike when
Aeneas brings Hector's challenge, with its promise of single combat (see Shirley, pp. 71–82 for
conventional trumpet signals). This segment of the scene is generally done with almost no
cutting. Nunn broke 1.3 here, and soldiers crossed the stage in a fight, which led into 1.1, as Troilus
threw down his arms. Nunn followed that by the opening segment of 1.2 and the last lines after
the march past. He inserted 2.2, when Hector announced the challenge, before completing 1.3
where it was delivered.

233SD Greek responses to Aeneas' entrance have been quick and courteous (SMT 1936) or slow (NT
1976). There was much heel clicking in Guthrie (1956), while at the trumpet Barton's Nestor and
Agamemnon sat and put their feet up on stools, suggesting disdain (RSC 1976 promptbook).
Shaw (SMT 1954) had the Greeks slowly drift forward by adjusting their campstools each time
they sat after speaking. They were poised to group curiously around Aeneas on the forestage
when he entered. In Central Park Papp had the whole exchange between Agamemnon and
Aeneas to 257a played as broad comedy. Barton accompanied Aeneas' entrance by the usual
smoke and an emblem bearer in 1968, and the lectern was the focal point for delivering the
challenge. In Hands' RSC 1981 production, Aeneas was 'incredulous' 'amid the debris of ammo
boxes and primitive dinner preparations in [the] grubby camp' (Wardle, *LT*, 8 July 1981). In sharp
contrast, Davies' 1985 promptbook delineates late Victorian military practice. Two guards
followed Aeneas down the mansion steps from the landing entrance. He was met by Menelaus at
the foot of the steps, and handed over his identification papers. In London Davies enhanced the
official approach when Aeneas gave a copy of Hector's challenge to Menelaus and another to the
note-taker before repeating the words. In 1990 Mendes brought a Trojan party down the Swan

AGAMEMNON Even this.
AENEAS May one that is a herald and a prince
    Do a fair message to his kingly ears?   220
AGAMEMNON With surety stronger than Achilles' arm
    'Fore all the Greekish heads which with one voice
    Call Agamemnon head and general.
AENEAS Fair leave and large security. How may
    A stranger to those most imperial looks   225
    Know them from eyes of other mortals?
AGAMEMNON   How?
AENEAS Ay,
    I ask that I might waken reverence,
    And bid the cheek be ready with a blush
    Modest as morning when she coldly eyes   230
    The youthful Phoebus.
    Which is that god in office guiding men,
    Which is the high and mighty Agamemnon?
AGAMEMNON This Trojan scorns us, or the men of Troy
    Are ceremonious courtiers.   235
AENEAS Courtiers as free, as debonair, unarmed,
    As bending angels: that's their fame in peace.
    But when they would seem soldiers, they have galls,
    Good arms, strong joints, true swords, and – great Jove's
        accord –
    Nothing so full of heart. But peace, Aeneas,   240
    Peace, Trojan, lay thy finger on thy lips!
    The worthiness of praise distains his worth
    If that the praised himself bring the praise forth;
    But what the repining enemy commends,
    That breath fame blows; that praise, sole pure, transcends.   245
AGAMEMNON Sir, you of Troy, call you yourself Aeneas?
AENEAS Ay, Greek, that is my name.
AGAMEMNON What's your affair I pray you?
AENEAS Sir, pardon, 'tis for Agamemnon's ears.
AGAMEMNON He hears naught privately that comes from Troy.   250
AENEAS Nor I from Troy come not to whisper with him;

Theatre aisles as if marching in from a distance.

246ff   When Papp and Mendes' Agamemnons finally spoke Aeneas' name, they enunciated A-nee-ass
    deliberately, maintaining the upper hand. There was humour in Mendes
    staging: 'In a . . . moth-eaten cardigan worn over an antique Roman breastplate [he]
    had to rifle through the debris of screwed-up briefing papers and scummy coffee mugs
    on the general's map table to find his nameplate and shake it under Aeneas' nose.' (Rutter 118.)

I bring a trumpet to awake his ear,
To set his sense on the attentive bent,
And then to speak.
AGAMEMNON   Speak frankly as the wind,
It is not Agamemnon's sleeping hour.   255
That thou shalt know, Trojan, he is awake,
He tells thee so himself.
AENEAS   Trumpet, blow loud,
Send thy brass voice through all these lazy tents
And every Greek of mettle let him know
What Troy means fairly shall be spoke aloud.   260
                    Sound trumpet
We have, great Agamemnon, here in Troy
A prince called Hector – Priam is his father –
Who in this dull and long-continued truce
Is resty grown; he bade me take a trumpet
And to this purpose speak: kings, princes, lords,   265
If there be one among the fair'st of Greece
That holds his honour higher than his ease,
That seeks his praise more than he fears his peril,
That knows his valour and knows not his fear,
That loves his mistress more than in confession   270
With truant vows to her own lips he loves,
And dare avow her beauty and her worth
In other arms than hers, to him this challenge:
Hector in view of Trojans and of Greeks
Shall make it good or do his best to do it,   275
He hath a lady wiser, fairer, truer,
Than ever Greek did couple in his arms,
And will tomorrow with his trumpet call
Midway between your tents and walls of Troy
To rouse a Grecian that is true in love.   280
If any come, Hector shall honour him;
If none, he'll say in Troy when he retires

265ff   'Hector's challenge . . . exactly suits the conventions of the tiltyard' (Yoder, p. 13) and has been
found at odds with some modern dress productions, making the satiric intent obvious, though it
has its counterparts in modern culture's carefully arranged challenge meetings between rival
gangs. Aeneas has sometimes recited the challenge and sometimes read it as a formal
proclamation. There is always a copy for Ajax to demand in the next scene. In 1976 Barton and
Kyle had elaborate business as Ulysses got the paper eventually, and Nestor slowly read it over
after Aeneas had left at 310.

The Grecian dames are sunburnt and not worth
The splinter of a lance. Even so much.
AGAMEMNON This shall be told our lovers, Lord Aeneas.   285
If none of them have soul in such a kind,
We left them all at home; but we are soldiers,
And may that soldier a mere recreant prove
That means not, hath not, or is not in love.
If then one is, or hath, or means to be,   290
That one meets Hector; if none else, I am he.
NESTOR Tell him of Nestor, one that was a man
When Hector's grandsire sucked; he is old now
But if there be not in our Grecian host
One noble man that hath one spark of fire   295
To answer for his love, tell him from me
I'll hide my silver beard in a gold beaver
And in my vambrace put my withered brawns,
And, meeting him, tell him that my lady
Was fairer than his grandam and as chaste   300
As may be in the world; his youth in flood,
I'll prove this truth with my three drops of blood.
AENEAS Now heavens forbid such scarcity of youth!
ULYSSES Amen.
AGAMEMNON Fair Lord Aeneas, let me touch your hand;   305
To our pavilion shall I lead you first.
Achilles shall have word of this intent,
So shall each lord of Greece from tent to tent.
Yourself shall feast with us before you go,
And find the welcome of a noble foe.   310
                  Exeunt [all but] Ulysses and Nestor
ULYSSES Nestor!
NESTOR What says Ulysses?
ULYSSES I have a young conception in my brain:
Be you my time to bring it to some shape.
NESTOR What is't?   315

311ff   Nestor turns back and he and Ulysses often come downstage, Nestor bringing a stool or chair to
sit on. In 1956, he had a shooting stick. In 1985 RSC they remained at the large table, Nestor in a
chair and Ulysses on the edge of the table. Poel closed the curtains hung from the stage pillars to
set up his next scene. Often directors speed along at this point. Poel, Payne, Guthrie, Landau,
Barton (1969), Davies and Nunn are among those who radically shortened Nestor's long speech
and Ulysses' reply, cutting mercantile images (337b–367), and focusing on the proposed lottery
and Nestor's approval. Barton ended the scene with a bullroar (1968 promptbook).

ULYSSES This 'tis:
        Blunt wedges rive hard knots; the seeded pride
        That hath to this maturity blown up
        In rank Achilles must or now be cropped
        Or, shedding, breed a nursery of like evil   320
        To overbulk us all.
NESTOR Well, and how?
ULYSSES This challenge that the gallant Hector sends,
        However it is spread in general name,
        Relates in purpose only to Achilles.   325
NESTOR True, the purpose is perspicuous as substance
        Whose grossness little characters sum up,
        And in the publication make no strain
        But that Achilles, were his brain as barren
        As banks of Libya – though Apollo knows   330
        'Tis dry enough – will with great speed of judgement,
        Ay with celerity, find Hector's purpose
        Pointing on him.
ULYSSES And wake him to the answer, think you?
NESTOR Yes, 'tis most meet. Who may you else oppose   335
        That can from Hector bring his honour off
        If not Achilles? Though't be a sportful combat,
        Yet in the trial much opinion dwells,
        For here the Trojans taste our dear'st repute
        With their fin'st palate; and trust to me, Ulysses,   340
        Our imputation shall be oddly poised
        In this vile action; for the success,
        Although particular, shall give a scantling
        Of good or bad unto the general.
        And in such indexes, although small pricks   345
        To their subsequent volumes, there is seen
        The baby figure of the giant mass
        Of things to come at large. It is supposed
        He that meets Hector issues from our choice,
        And choice, being mutual act of all our souls,   350
        Makes merit her election and doth boil
        As 'twere from forth us all a man distilled
        Out of our virtues, who, miscarrying,
        What heart receives from hence a conquering part
        To steel a strong opinion to themselves?   355
ULYSSES Give pardon to my speech: therefore 'tis meet
        Achilles meet not Hector; let us like merchants
        First show foul wares and think perchance they'll sell:
        If not,

The lustre of the better shall exceed 360
By showing the worse first. Do not consent
That ever Hector and Achilles meet;
For both our honour and our shame in this
Are dogg'd with two strange followers.
NESTOR I see them not with my old eyes – what are they? 365
ULYSSES What glory our Achilles shares from Hector,
Were he not proud, we all should share with him.
But he already is too insolent,
And it were better parch in Afric sun
Than in the pride and salt scorn of his eyes 370
Should he 'scape Hector fair; if he were foiled
Why then we do our main opinion crush
In taint of our best man. No, make a lott'ry
And by device let blockish Ajax draw
The sort to fight with Hector; among ourselves 375
Give him allowance for the better man,
For that will physic the great Myrmidon,
Who broils in loud applause, and make him fall
His crest that prouder than blue Iris bends.
If the dull brainless Ajax come safe off, 380
We'll dress him up in voices; if he fail,
Yet go we under our opinion still
That we have better men. But hit or miss,
Our project's life this shape of sense assumes:
Ajax employed plucks down Achilles' plumes. 385
NESTOR Now Ulysses, I begin to relish thy advice
And I will give a taste thereof forthwith
To Agamemnon – go we to him straight.
Two curs shall tame each other, pride alone
Must tar the mastiffs on as 'twere a bone. 390

Exeunt

ACT 2, SCENE I

[2.1] *Enter* AJAX *and* THERSITES

Where 1.3 is transposed to the opening scene, Shakespeare's sharp contrast between the formal commanders and undisciplined Achilles and his group is lost. Thersites' position as Ajax's retainer or fool has been less clear when he is a reporter or mess orderly (Macowan 1938; Guthrie 1956; Davies 1985; Boyd 1998). Fry played him as a 'comic Duke of Gloucester' ('The Great Queen Street'), and Skinner and Beale also gave him a hunched back. He seemed very contemporary in 1938, 'one of those clench-fisted youths who march to Trafalgar Square o' Sundays' or, with 'a deplorable suit and a fag never out of his mouth . . . like a Hyde Park orator in a Sean O'Casey play' (*Illustrated Sporting and Dramatic News*, 30 September 1938; James Agate). His red tie suggested leftist leanings (Kastan). At Stratford Connecticut, Donald Herron was an insolent Yankee draftee ('as under an impress', lines 88–9), 'rasp-tongued, saw-toothed' and with a hint of Vermont accent (John Beaufort, '"Troilus and Cressida" Overgrown by Magnolias', *CSM*, 25 July 1961). Played for 'comic depravity' by E. Harmon (1922 Marlowe Society), he was likened to a 'rotten cheese', the 'quotidian of filth' (anonymous review). Four decades later, Pentlow 'looks like a Beckett tramp', 'spits acid' and has 'mental maggots' (anonymous review of Birmingham Rep, 20 February 1963). 'The Incredible Orlando' played him as a shaven-headed transvestite, sometimes stripped to the waist (BBC 1981). In Barton's later productions he became an exaggerated embodiment of decay and disease, scantily clad in rags, with scabs and a grotesquely sexual appendage. Peter Hall kept the scabs and rags in 2001. Adrian Hall gave him a rope to use as a tail or flail (TR 1971). In 1990 Beale, totally covered except for his face, at first planned to wear white butler's gloves, then decided to hide boils with surgical gloves. He projected his disease into thoughts on Agamemnon (2.1.2–7; Beale, p. 166). Gary O'Connor described Beale's 'defective "r's", his flasher's mac and vulturine stoop' (*PP*, August 1990, p. 29).

When he is a camp follower, casually attached first to Ajax then Achilles, he often carries a bag. Beale added a fool's bauble to his possessions (RSC 1990) and Nunn provided a voodoo doll (NT 1999). Sally Emerson complained that 'Philip Stone's unimpassioned Thersites helps subdue the production [NT 1976] into a jumble of words' (*PP*, September 1976). By contrast, Alun Armstrong (RSC 1985) was 'a marvelously unwholesome comic creation, funnier and more realistic but no less memorable than John Nettles' ashen scarecrow' in the Barton / Kyle 1976 production (David Ian Rabey, *PP*, August 1985, pp. 14–15). 'Lloyd Hutchinson . . . makes a truly revolting Thersites . . . looking like some lost vaudevillian from a Beckett play . . . [with] his vile little stand-up routines with their disquieting sexual innuendo.' (*FT* on RSC 1998, quoted by Kastan.) Except for the Berliner Ensemble's Ekkehard Schall, who was as large as Ajax, Thersites tends to be small.

Ajax is generally big, and adds oafish comedy to the grotesque humour of Thersites' insults. He may want to read the challenge Thersites holds, or, occasionally, be an illiterate wanting it read for him. Tattoos or a laurel wreath occasionally signify the modern tough or the over-proud classical warrior. Dromgoole made him a culturally charged symbol – the football hooligan – in sleeveless tee shirt and heavy boots, with spider and lynx tattoos on his neck (OX 1999–2000, F. Shirley notes). In OSF 2001 he was bull-necked and shaven-headed, and bore a resemblance to Jesse 'The Body' Ventura. He has taken pride in his physical condition, working out with barbells, or brandishing an overly large sword and shield (BR 1963; SMT 1960), or he has been pure bulk. Clive Russell's Ajax was 'a thick braggart who obviously couldn't fight his way out of a paper bag' (Russell, p. 37). Rollo Balman portrayed 'not a mulish and boastful professional soldier' that E.A.B. (Baughan?) considered appropriate, but 'a drunken buffoon', 'a potbellied . . . Falstaff' ('Mr William Poel's Production at King's Hall', 11 December 1912). Charles Coburn was 'a drunken blockhead smoking a pipe' at The Players (Percy Hammond, *NYHT*, 8 June 1932), though he looked like a conquistador in Spanish helmet and ruff. Occasionally the comedy has been overdone. Howard Taubman commented that Ajax 'doesn't have to stutter and snigger' and resemble 'Curly in "The Three Stooges" ' as he did for Landau (*NYT*, 24 July 1961). At Guthrie's Old Vic in 1956, Ernest Hare was 'a red-faced, blustering Colonel Blimp', teaming with Charles Gray's out-of-training 'pugilist' Achilles against 'sad sack Thersites' (*TA*, March 1957, p. 18), and the attacks, as in Papp's 1965 NYSF production, became 'pure bullying'. Comic rampages occurred in Terry Hands' RSC production and in William's at SFC in 1987.

The short scene, often with one to two dozen scattered lines of invective cut, was occasionally played in front of a curtain as scenery was shifted or a tableau set for 2.2 (Poel 1912; Payne 1936; Macowan 1938), but generally Achilles and Patroclus are given a locale that is repeated in 2.3 and 3.3, and 2.1 is occasionally combined with 2.3. Deck chairs, a settee or a cot to lounge on, and the suggestion of a tent, whether the rich embroidery of Yale 1916, the scrap of canvas of OX 1999, Judge's large white hanging pulled across a third of Stratford's main stage in 1996, or the effective small black structure of SFC 2003 (Kidnie), provide visual suggestion of their detachment from the other Greeks. Achilles knows the details of Hector's challenge, though he dismisses it and Ajax goes off to play into Ulysses' scheme (109–17). In productions that emphasized the homoerotic, Achilles and Patroclus began to sketch their relationship by holding hands (RSC 1976) or, for Nunn, standing close. Achilles is often in a dressing gown, to contrast with his appearance when he arms. Suchet's bare, oiled chest helped him combine 'masculine brutality and feminine grace', while Alan Howard's long blond curls and fan suggested a more indolent self-indulgence (RSC 1981, 1968). At SFC 1987, Patroclus was a 'California beach bum in bathrobe and sunglasses' (John F. Burn, 'Winds of Change Blow Through Ontario Theatre Festival on the Avon', *NYT*, 5 July 1987, 2:29).

AJAX Thersites!

THERSITES Agamemnon, how if he had boils – full, all over, generally?

AJAX Thersites!

THERSITES And those boils did run – say so – did not the general run
    then, were not that a botchy core?   5

AJAX Dog!

THERSITES Then would come some matter from him, I see none now.

AJAX Thou bitch-wolf's son, canst thou not hear? Feel then.

                          Strikes him

THERSITES The plague of Greece upon thee, thou mongrel, beef-witted
    lord.   10

AJAX Speak then, thou whinid'st leaven, speak! I will beat thee into
    handsomeness.

THERSITES I shall sooner rail thee into wit and holiness, but I think thy
    horse will sooner con an oration than thou learn a prayer without
    book. Thou canst strike, canst thou? – a red murrain o'thy jade's   15
    tricks.

OSD   At the NYTh Ajax and Thersites entered together and squabbled over the remains of a
       McDonald's dinner (Clair Armstead, *FT*, 23 September 1987). Simon Russell Beale carefully
       prepared a plate for Ajax, then drooled a gobbet of spit into it (Peter Holland, *SS 44*, p. 173).
       Quayle had Thersites root in a dustbin and take something out (SMT, 1948). In Cambridge, MA he
       scrawled the names of the generals on the walls as graffiti while he complained (HSSR 1968), and
       in Berliner Ensemble he found a bit of discarded armour in 'a play of scavengers and detritus'
       (Martin Hoyle, *FT*, 19 August 1987).

8ff   Q and F stage directions only specify one blow, probably with a bare hand, but the dialogue
       suggests more between 8SD and 47SD. Ajax may wield a stick (Payne, SMT 1936) or a board
       (Hands, RSC 1981). By 1948 promptbooks began to call for increased physicality. Quayle had
       Thersites fall and scramble away, keeping the dustbin between him and Ajax until Achilles
       entered (SMT promptbook). In 1954 Shaw added kicks and later even Patroclus slapped him.
       Barton and Hall provided a cat-o' nine-tails to send Peter O'Toole scurrying and Patroclus used a
       switch. As Eric Christmas crouched and ducked on the steps surrounding the Stratford, Canada,
       festival stage in 1963, the audience felt the threats a few feet away (F. Shirley notes). By 1968
       Barton's Ajax wielded a stool, and a proof sequence of photos from 1969 shows Thersites forced
       over it, then pushed to the ground. In 1976, audiences could compare the NT's restrained shoves
       and slaps with Barton and Kyle's carefully choreographed RSC bullying that began with a
       takedown kick, followed by a foot on prostrate Thersites' rump and a knee in his back by 19. As
       he recovered, he was doubled over by an elbow to the stomach (35), then bear-hugged and
       dropped as Achilles entered (promptbook). One of Moshinsky's best touches at NT was having
       Ajax wrest the proclamation at 26, then study it uncomprehendingly. In 2001 the Oregon staging
       resembled a TV wrestling match.

AJAX Toadstool, learn me the proclamation.

THERSITES Dost thou think I have no sense thou strik'st me thus?

AJAX The proclamation!

THERSITES Thou art proclaimed fool I think.   20

AJAX Do not, porcupine, do not, my fingers itch –

THERSITES I would thou didst itch from head to foot and I had the
     scratching of thee: I would make thee the loathsomest scab in
     Greece. When thou art forth in the incursions, thou strik'st as
     slow as another.   25

AJAX I say, the proclamation!

THERSITES Thou grumblest and railest every hour on Achilles,
     and thou art as full of envy at his greatness as Cerberus is at
     Proserpina's beauty – ay, that thou bark'st at him.

AJAX Mistress Thersites –   30

THERSITES Thou shouldst strike him.

AJAX Cobloaf!

THERSITES He would pun thee into shivers with his fist as a sailor
     breaks a biscuit.

AJAX [*Beating him*] You whoreson cur –   35

THERSITES Do, do –

AJAX Thou stool for a witch.

THERSITES Ay do, do, thou sodden-witted lord, thou hast no more
     brain than I have in mine elbows: an asinico may tutor thee. Thou
     scurvy valiant ass, thou art here but to thrash Trojans, and thou 40
     art bought and sold among those of any wit like a barbarian slave.
     If thou use to beat me I will begin at thy heel and tell what thou
     art by inches, thou thing of no bowels, thou.

AJAX You dog!

THERSITES You scurvy lord!   45

AJAX [*Beating him*] You cur!

THERSITES Mars his idiot, do rudeness, do camel, do do!

Enter ACHILLES *and* PATROCLUS

ACHILLES Why how now, Ajax, wherefore do ye thus?
     How now, Thersites, what's the matter, man?

---

34 In 1985 Ajax began a series of moves, grabbing Alun Armstrong by the head, smacking him twice
    to drop him, then standing over him and hitting him with his glove as Achilles and Patroclus
    entered. Other soldiers, who were in the officers' club with billiard cues, pipes and drinks,
    listening to circus-like piano music, watched with amusement as a defenseless lower rank was
    bullied (production film). Mendes (RSC 1990) made the treatment sadistic, with Beale pushed
    over a stool for his beating, then thrown to the floor and pummelled until Achilles arrived and he
    could scurry awkwardly out of reach up the stage rear slats (F. Shirley notes).

THERSITES You see him there, do you?   50
ACHILLES Ay, what's the matter?
THERSITES Nay look upon him.
ACHILLES So I do – what's the matter?
THERSITES Nay but regard him well.
ACHILLES Well, why so I do.   55
THERSITES But yet you look not well upon him, for whosomever you
    take him to be, he is Ajax.
ACHILLES I know that, fool.
THERSITES Ay, but that fool knows not himself.
AJAX Therefore I beat thee.   60
THERSITES Lo, lo, lo, lo, what modicums of wit he utters: his evasions
    have ears thus long. I have bobbed his brain more than he has beat
    my bones. I will buy nine sparrows for a penny, and his pia mater
    is not worth the ninth part of a sparrow. This lord, Achilles, Ajax,
    who wears his wit in his belly and his guts in his head, I'll tell you   65
    what I say of him.
ACHILLES What?
THERSITES I say, this Ajax –
    [*Ajax threatens to beat him and Achilles intervenes*]
ACHILLES Nay good Ajax.
THERSITES Has not so much wit –   70
ACHILLES [*To Ajax*] Nay I must hold you.
THERSITES As will stop the eye of Helen's needle, for whom he comes
    to fight.
ACHILLES Peace, fool.
THERSITES I would have peace and quietness, but the fool will not –   75
    he there, that he, look you there.
AJAX O thou damned cur, I shall –
ACHILLES Will you set your wit to a fool's?
THERSITES No I warrant you, the fool's will shame it.
PATROCLUS Good words, Thersites.   80
ACHILLES What's the quarrel?
AJAX I bade the vile owl go learn me the tenor of the proclamation,
    and he rails upon me.
THERSITES I serve thee not.
AJAX Well go to, go to.   85

71ff Achilles and Patroclus held Ajax and took the stick from him, giving it to Thersites at 80 (SMT
    1936). At this point, Thersites often moved behind Achilles for protection. In RSC 1981 Ajax had
    been breaking up the packing cases that littered Hands' set, and was about to hit Thersites with a
    huge board from one of them when Suchet's Achilles grabbed his genetalia. Terry Wood's Ajax
    squeaked (Smallwood, *SS 35*, p. 149).

THERSITES I serve here voluntary.

ACHILLES Your last service was sufferance – 'twas not voluntary; no
man is beaten voluntary. Ajax was here the voluntary and you as
under an impress.

THERSITES E'en so; a great deal of your wit too lies in your sinews, 90
or else there be liars. Hector shall have a great catch if he knock
out either of your brains: 'a were as good crack a fusty nut with
no kernel.

ACHILLES What, with me too, Thersites?

THERSITES There's Ulysses and old Nestor, whose wit was mouldy ere 95
your grandsires had nails on their toes, yoke you like draught-oxen
and make you plough up the wars.

ACHILLES What, what?

THERSITES Yes good sooth: to, Achilles! to, Ajax! to –

AJAX I shall cut out your tongue. 100

THERSITES 'Tis no matter, I shall speak as much as thou afterwards.

PATROCLUS No more words Thersites, peace!

THERSITES I will hold my peace when Achilles' brach bids me, shall I?

ACHILLES There's for you Patroclus.

THERSITES I will see you hanged like clotpolls ere I come any more 105
to your tents. I will keep where there is wit stirring and leave the
faction of fools. *Exit*

PATROCLUS A good riddance.

ACHILLES Marry this, sir, is proclaimed through all our host:
    That Hector by the fifth hour of the sun 110
    Will with a trumpet 'twixt our tents and Troy
    Tomorrow morning call some knight to arms
    That hath a stomach, and such a one that dare
    Maintain – I know not what – 'tis trash. Farewell.

AJAX Farewell – who shall answer him? 115

ACHILLES I know not, 'tis put to lottery; otherwise he knew his man.
                [Exeunt Achilles and Patroclus]

AJAX O, meaning you! I will go learn more of it. *Exit*

91ff Finally Barton's Achilles joined the abuse, pulling Thersites up by the hair and throwing him to the
      ground (1969 photo sequence and promptbook).

104 Achilles grabbed a soda siphon from the officers' club bar and sprayed Thersites, who 'flung off
      his orderly's white jacket in disgust' as he left (RSC, 1985).

109ff Ajax finally hears the proclamation. Mendes had Achilles point out the words with his finger as he
      read (RSC 1990).

ACT 2, SCENE 2

[2.2] Enter PRIAM, HECTOR, TROILUS, PARIS, and HELENUS

The Trojan council has often included Deiphobus and attendants. Priam has a letter or scroll with Nestor's message, 'Deliver Helen . . .' and sometimes passes it around. Priam shows his respect for his eldest son by asking Hector's opinion first, launching the argument for ending the war (Kastan). The actor playing Hector has the difficult job of making his reversal believable as he ultimately yields to family feeling and their 'joint and several dignities' (Papp, p. 204).

When Greeks and Trojans have worn distinctive uniforms, the two councils have contrasted sharply visually as well as in manner. Guthrie's elegant Trojan guardsmen posed gracefully, compared to the stiffer Germanic Greeks. Mendes' dirty Greeks in their heavy coats impressed Holland as too different from the clean Trojans in white (*SS 44*, p. 175), a contrast even more apparent in Epstein's Yale 1976 production. Hall's rosy lighting in 2001 manipulated audience response, as did his icy blue in 1.3. The younger, more sensual Trojans were barefooted, 'in fresh, glowing eastern costumes in contrast to the Greek warriors worn biker styles' (Kastan). Strachan's pre-First World War warriors were 'like arrested schoolboys' 'and one is reminded of the attitudes that prevailed before the officers and men discovered the horrors of war' (Charles Spencer, *Telegraph*, 15 June 1998).

Often about a quarter of the lines are cut, including knottier passages such as Troilus' 28b–32a or Hector's 58–60. The excisions may include the images of mercantilism or food like 69–72a or disorder (176b–82) that are part of the play's undertone. Cassandra's shrieked warnings in mid-scene are almost always kept in their entirety, though Poel, Boyd and Nunn excised some of the preliminaries (97–9) as part of a number of short cuts. The final arguments and Hector's long summary speech (163–93) generally remain comparatively intact.

Directors occasionally add distracting scenic devices. Priam's oxygen equipment in a sauna (OX 1999) or a steam bath (San Diego Globe 1976, tfana.org) undercut council dignity. At Ottawa, John Wood's 'Trojans hold a war council in a kind of sauna; various naked men are seductively massaged by other men. The eruption of Cassandra, shouting warnings, into the gay steaminess becomes purely silly.' (Richard Eder, *NYT*, 26 January 1978.) Davies expanded the scene naturalistically to show the end of a formal Victorian dinner. The women (Cressida, Helen, Andromache and Cassandra) excused themselves, leaving the men to their brandy and cigars,

PRIAM After so many hours, lives, speeches spent,
      Thus once again says Nestor from the Greeks:
      'Deliver Helen, and all damage else,
      As honour, loss of time, travail, expense,
      Wounds, friends, and what else dear that is consumed   5
      In hot digestion of this cormorant war,
      Shall be struck off.' Hector, what say you to't?

and the Greek letter was passed down the table from Priam to Hector at the foot before the discussion (RSC 1985 Promptbook). Helen was a silent witness to the argument in the 1981 BBC production, recognizable because she had been focused on at the beginning of 1.2, while lurking Cassandra was merely an unknown until she shrieked out. The film of Judge's 1996 production shows Cassandra sitting silently at the foot of the long table on the stage right platform. All the women remained in Boyd's simple Irish family dinner (RSC 1998).

OSD   The locale is assumed to be a room in Priam's palace, though visualized in a wide variety of ways. Poel opened tableau curtains on Trojans in flamboyant Elizabethan masque costumes smoking their pipes (1912 promptbook). Macowan had them in white mess jackets, smoking and pouring port from a decanter, with Robert Conradt, a relatively young and lively Priam, in a smoking jacket (London Mask 1938). Distinctive properties have signified Troy where there isn't the solid scenic structure of Quayle's (SMT 1948) or Landau's (ASF 1961) productions. In Hall's first sandpit (SMT 1960), photographs show a larger square rug in the centre replacing the irregular Greek hide, and an attendant passing a tray with elaborate goblets. Four attendants bore on Priam and his large staff of office in an elaborate high gold throne or litter. He sat, three steps above the others, for the council. In 1976 Barton and Kyle used standards with appropriate symbols that reappeared later: horse for Troilus, goat for Paris, griffon for Helenus, and lion for Hector, which were placed in holes in the baulks that surrounded the playing area (promptbook). Nunn conceived of it as a night scene, with six torches ringed around the back of the Olivier stage. Dorn had Priam propped against a totem pole in his ritualistic 1986 version (Olivia Fuchs, *PP*, July 1987, p. 35).

1   In RSC 1976 the Trojans knelt and touched an urn on a carpet in centre stage, then sat on the baulks near the front of the stage. Nunn had them ritualistically kiss Priam's hand. Priam's rank may be emphasized by a seat at the centre of the table or at the head (RSC 1985; SMT 1948), a throne (NYSF 1965) or a larger chair (SMT 1938; NT 1976). In SMT 1954 he was carefully arranged in his robes, stage front left, with the arguing princes across mid-stage, and nine torch or emblem bearers spread across the back and up the wall platforms. If frail, he may be carried in (SMT 1954, 1960) or wheeled on (OX 1999). In 1956 Job Stewart's Priam was bald, with mutton-chop whiskers, but spry and erect. Hector, Deiphobus and Aeneas were behind the Old Vic table, with its fruit bowls and wine, while Troilus and Paris stood near Priam (F. Shirley notes). Priam's lines here are few and to the point, and not cut, while Troilus, Hector and Paris' speeches are generally pruned. (Stefan Bachman in Salzburg in 1998 did cut Priam.) Miller made him speak in an old man's high thin voice (BBC 1981).

HECTOR Though no man lesser fears the Greeks than I
As far as toucheth my particular,
Yet, dread Priam,   10
There is no lady of more softer bowels,
More spongy to suck in the sense of fear,
More ready to cry out 'Who knows what follows?'
Than Hector is. The wound of peace is surety,
Surety secure, but modest doubt is called   15
The beacon of the wise, the tent that searches
To th'bottom of the worst. Let Helen go.
Since the first sword was drawn about this question
Every tithe soul 'mongst many thousand dismes
Hath been as dear as Helen, I mean of ours;   20
If we have lost so many tenths of ours
To guard a thing not ours, nor worth to us
(Had it our name) the value of one ten,
What merit's in that reason which denies
The yielding of her up?
TROILUS   Fie, fie, my brother,   25
Weigh you the worth and honour of a king
So great as our dread father in a scale
Of common ounces? Will you with counters sum
The past-proportion of his infinite,
And buckle in a waist most fathomless   30
With spans and inches so diminutive
As fears and reasons? Fie, for godly shame.
HELENUS No marvel, though you bite so sharp at reasons,
You are so empty of them. Should not our father
Bear the great sway of his affairs with reasons   35
Because your speech hath none that tell him so?
TROILUS You are for dreams and slumbers, brother priest,
You fur your gloves with reason. Here are your reasons:
You know an enemy intends you harm,
You know a sword employed is perilous,   40
And reason flies the object of all harm:
Who marvels then, when Helenus beholds
A Grecian and his sword, if he do set
The very wings of reason to his heels

37ff   Troilus banged the table and began to line up wine glasses as he made his points and by line 72
added the wine jug (SMT 1948). At SFC 2003 he slowly built a pyramid of cups as he made points,
then knocked them down at 92, presumably illustrating how everything collapses without honour
(Kidnie).

And fly like chidden Mercury from Jove,   45
Or like a star disorbed? Nay, if we talk of reason
Let's shut our gates and sleep: manhood and honour
Should have hare hearts would they but fat their thoughts
With this crammed reason. Reason and respect
Make livers pale and lustihood deject.   50
HECTOR Brother, she is not worth what she doth cost
The keeping.
TROILUS   What's aught but as 'tis valued?
HECTOR But value dwells not in particular will;
It holds his estimate and dignity
As well wherein 'tis precious of itself   55
As in the prizer. 'Tis mad idolatry
To make the service greater than the god,
And the will dotes that is inclineable
To what infectiously itself affects,
Without some image of th'affected merit.   60
TROILUS I take today a wife, and my election
Is led on in the conduct of my will,
My will enkindled by mine eyes and ears,
Two traded pilots 'twixt the dangerous shores
Of will and judgement: how may I avoid,   65
Although my will distaste what it elected,
The wife I chose? There can be no evasion
To blench from this and to stand firm by honour.
We turn not back the silks upon the merchant
When we have soiled them, nor the remainder viands   70
We do not throw in unrespective sieve
Because we now are full. It was thought meet
Paris should do some vengeance on the Greeks;
Your breath with full consent bellied his sails;
The seas and winds, old wranglers, took a truce   75
And did him service; he touched the ports desired
And for an old aunt whom the Greeks held captive
He brought a Grecian queen, whose youth and freshness
Wrinkles Apollo's and makes stale the morning.
Why keep we her? The Grecians keep our aunt.   80
Is she worth keeping? Why, she is a pearl
Whose price hath launched above a thousand ships
And turned crowned kings to merchants.
If you'll avouch 'twas wisdom Paris went
(As you must needs for you all cried 'Go, go'),   85
If you'll confess he brought home worthy prize
(As you must needs for you all clapped your hands

And cried 'Inestimable!'), why do you now
The issue of your proper wisdoms rate,
And do a deed that never Fortune did: 90
Beggar the estimation which you prized
Richer than sea and land? O theft most base,
That we have stol'n what we do fear to keep;
But thieves unworthy of a thing so stol'n,
That in their country did them that disgrace   95
We fear to warrant in our native place.
CASSANDRA *[Within]* Cry, Trojans, cry!

97ff   At SFC 2003 'a lighting shift to oranges and reds, accompanied by the faint sound of howling wind
powerfully manipulate and shape an audience's responses to the action' (Kidnie). In 1990
Mendes had all but Paris rise at the first scream, and he stood as Cassandra entered and began to
circle on the small Swan stage, 'a shrunken wraith' 'dotty in neglect' (Martin Hoyle, *FT*, 28 April
1990). Judge's 1996 promptbook lists elaborate movements. She uttered a strangled cry, rose
from the table, circling on her knees at 101, then stood and worked her way upstage, feeling along
the metal wall, returned to Priam and finally sat before Hector's speech. In 1999 Nunn had her go
first to Hector, then to all the others in turn. At Stratford, Connecticut, Jessica Tandy appeared on
the mansion porch, slightly above the Trojans, 'majestic in black, suggesting 'O'Neill's Lavinia
Manon' (Beaufort, *CSM*, 26 July 1961, p. 5). At first the men laughed, then fell silent at RSC 1976.
Although usually she is close to the men, Trewin felt that she was 'appropriately distanced' on
Payne's Elizabethan stage (SMT 1936), when she appeared on the balcony, the men in a line with
Priam in the centre, in the small space below (*Going to Shakespeare*, p. 181). She also appeared
effectively at a window at the back of Strachan's Edwardian set in Regent's Park, wearing green
rather than the usual black (Jeremy Kingston, *LT*, 13 June 1998). She started at the upper level of
Quayle's elaborate Troy setting, then reappeared on the main stage, pushing Helenus aside and
circling the table, pointing to Paris at 110 (SMT 1948 promptbook). Davies brought her down from
the mansion balcony with attendants (RSC 1985). In 2001 Hall had her cry out unexpectedly from
a right hand gallery above the audience before Vivienne Benesch made her way to centre stage
(tfana.org/2001). She shows her agitation in various ways. At Yale 1916, she was 'red-haired and
raging' (H.T.P., *BET*, 19 June 1916). In OX 1999 she stumbled into the sauna plunge pool. At BR
Harrison gave her 'rucksacked followers', making her 'plainly an archetypal ban-the-bomber'
(W.H.W., *Birmingham Mail*, 2 February 1963), though Trewin suggested her protest 'probably did
not get beyond the palace gates'. In Boyd's 1998 RSC production, 'Something was even made of
the problematic role of Cassandra, Catherine Walker presenting a black-shawled little Irish girl
nursing a bundle . . . speaking her prophecies with a quiet intensity that was so much more
effective than the usual screaming.' (Smallwood, *SS 53*, p. 261.) Bachman made her a musician
with a huge Alpenhorn, yodeling, 'very exotic and eerie' (Benedict Nightingale, *LT*, 26 August
1998, p. 28).

PRIAM   What noise, what shriek is this?
TROILUS 'Tis our mad sister, I do know her voice.
CASSANDRA [*Within*] Cry, Trojans!
HECTOR It is Cassandra.   100

       Enter CASSANDRA *raving, with her hair about her ears*

CASSANDRA Cry, Trojans, cry, lend me ten thousand eyes
     And I will fill them with prophetic tears.
HECTOR Peace, sister, peace.
CASSANDRA Virgins and boys, mid-age and wrinkled eld,
     Soft infancy that nothing canst but cry,   105
     Add to my clamours: let us pay betimes
     A moiety of that mass of moan to come.
     Cry, Trojans, cry, practise your eyes with tears!
     Troy must not be, nor goodly Ilium stand –
     Our firebrand brother Paris burns us all.   110
     Cry, Trojans, cry, a Helen and a woe!
     Cry, cry! Troy burns – or else let Helen go!   *Exit*
HECTOR Now youthful Troilus, do not these high strains
     Of divination in our sister work
     Some touches of remorse, or is your blood   115
     So madly hot that no discourse of reason,
     Nor fear of bad success in a bad cause
     Can qualify the same?
TROILUS   Why brother Hector,
     We may not think the justness of each act
     Such and no other than event doth form it,   120
     Nor once deject the courage of our minds
     Because Cassandra's mad; her brain-sick raptures
     Cannot distaste the goodness of a quarrel,
     Which hath our several honours all engaged
     To make it gracious. For my private part,   125
     I am no more touched than all Priam's sons,
     And Jove forbid there should be done amongst us
     Such things as might offend the weakest spleen
     To fight for and maintain.
PARIS Else might the world convince of levity   130
     As well my undertakings as your counsels.

111f   Deiphobus and Hector eventually pulled her away at the Old Vic (1956); Antenor, Paris and Troilus
      led her offstage for Barton (1968); first Helenus then Hector tried to assist her at the National
      (1976). Her attendants escorted her back up the stairs in RSC 1985.
113   Paris poured wine after Cassandra left (SMT 1948).

But I attest the gods, your full consent
Gave wings to my propension and cut off
All fears attending on so dire a project.
For what alas can these my single arms,   135
What propugnation is in one man's valour
To stand the push and enmity of those
This quarrel would excite? Yet I protest
Were I alone to pass the difficulties,
And had as ample power as I have will,   140
Paris should ne'er retract what he hath done
Nor faint in the pursuit.

PRIAM   Paris, you speak
Like one besotted on your sweet delights:
You have the honey still but these the gall;
So to be valiant is no praise at all.   145

PARIS Sir I propose not merely to myself
The pleasures such a beauty brings with it,
But I would have the soil of her fair rape
Wiped off in honourable keeping her.
What treason were it to the ransacked queen,   150
Disgrace to your great worths and shame to me,
Now to deliver her possession up
On terms of base compulsion! Can it be
That so degenerate a strain as this
Should once set footing in your generous bosoms?   155
There's not the meanest spirit on our party
Without a heart to dare or sword to draw
When Helen is defended, nor none so noble
Whose life were ill bestowed or death unfamed
Where Helen is the subject. Then I say,   160
Well may we fight for her whom we know well
The world's large spaces cannot parallel.

HECTOR Paris and Troilus, you have both said well,
And on the cause and question now in hand
Have glossed, but superficially – not much   165
Unlike young men whom Aristotle thought
Unfit to hear moral philosophy.
The reasons you allege do more conduce
To the hot passion of distempered blood
Than to make up a free determination   170
'Twixt right and wrong, for pleasure and revenge

---

145   In RSC 1976 Priam grew impatient and was about to leave. Paris detained him.
162   Priam left in 1965 NYSF. He buried his face in his hands in RSC 1985.

Have ears more deaf than adders to the voice
Of any true decision. Nature craves
All dues be rendered to their owners: now,
What nearer debt in all humanity   175
Than wife is to the husband? If this law
Of nature be corrupted through affection,
And that great minds, of partial indulgence
To their benumbèd wills, resist the same,
There is a law in each well-ordered nation   180
To curb those raging appetites that are
Most disobedient and refractory.
If Helen then be wife to Sparta's king,
As it is known she is, these moral laws
Of nature and of nations speak aloud   185
To have her back returned. Thus to persist
In doing wrong extenuates not wrong,
But makes it much more heavy. Hector's opinion
Is this in way of truth; yet ne'ertheless,
My sprightly brethren, I propend to you   190
In resolution to keep Helen still,
For 'tis a cause that hath no mean dependence
Upon our joint and several dignities.
TROILUS Why there you touched the life of our design!
Were it not glory that we more affected   195
Than the performance of our heaving spleens,
I would not wish a drop of Trojan blood
Spent more in her defence. But, worthy Hector,
She is a theme of honour and renown,
A spur to valiant and magnanimous deeds,   200
Whose present courage may beat down our foes
And fame in time to come canonise us.
For I presume brave Hector would not lose
So rich advantage of a promised glory

189 The Trojans rose as if the argument was over and were stopped in their tracks (RSC 1968). The
     Greek letter may be crumpled now or after Hector's closing speech. With Helen onstage for Miller
     (BBC 1981), Hector addressed his lines to her and Paris, who had been side-by-side since 145.
192 There has been applause by the princes at this point. In 1948 Troilus finally drank in relief. John
     Neville or Jeremy Brett, Guthrie's successive Troilus's, leaped on the table in joy, then resumed
     their dignity and came down to Priam during the ensuing speech (Old Vic 1956–7). Nunn had a
     spattering of applause as Hector announced his decision, and it became general at 208 when he
     spoke of the challenge, which Nunn showed being delivered in his next scene. After his speech,
     Shaw's Hector kissed Priam's hand at SMT 1954.

As smiles upon the forehead of this action   205
For the wide world's revenue.
HECTOR   I am yours,
You valiant offspring of great Priamus.
I have a roisting challenge sent amongst
The dull and factious nobles of the Greeks
Will strike amazement to their drowsy spirits.   210
I was advertised their great general slept
Whilst emulation in the army crept:
This I presume will wake him.

                                                    Exeunt

213   Barton's Trojans surrounded and toasted Hector, assisting Priam as they raised their glasses and
        shouted 'Hector' three times (RSC 1968). Quayle brought on Thersites to speak 2.3.63–6 after the
        Trojans left and before the first intermission (SMT 1948). Nunn followed this with 1.3.214ff.

ACT 2, SCENE 3

[2.3] *Enter* THERSITES *alone*

Occasionally 2.3 immediately followed 2.1 to avoid scene changes, as in Herbert or Macowan. Ajax talks more and more to himself, while the others comment (183–207), though much of the sequence is often cut. Like most of the humour in the play, this is diminishing, and Poel undercut Ajax further by having him drunk and clumsy. He could be heard falling offstage at 249 (promptbook, 1912).

The relationship of Patroclus and Achilles is often further developed between 35 and 61. Gaul didn't 'make much of the pansy implications of the text' at The Players (Percy Hammond, 8 June 1932), but by 1936 Norman Wooland (Achilles) and Basil Langton (Patroclus) were suggesting 'luxurious vice' (Crosse, Notebook xv, 146). Achilles seemed 'wildly neurotic' while 'Patroclus minced' for the Marlowe Society 1940 (*LT*, 7 March 1940). With daring for the 1950s, Shaw's promptbook directs Patroclus to lie on the stage steps and touch Achilles' leg as they question Thersites (40–60). Hall and Barton gave the two men little physical contact in 1960, but beginning with Barton in 1968, the emphasis has often been strong. Barton specified explicit gestures and touches, and even a phallic spear used to tease Thersites (promptbook). By 1981 Rutter was calling the gay relationship images Hands used clichéd (p. 138). In Nunn's production, despite the daybed, Achilles and Patroclus were circumspect during their thirty lines on stage with Thersites. And a year before, in Austria and Switzerland, Stefan Bachman had concentrated on Achilles' appearance: 'a swaggering, beer-bellied bruiser', very fat, in boots, black shorts, shades and a flowered bathing cap, sprawled in an overstuffed chair (*LT* photo, 26 August 1998, p. 28).

Beale felt Thersites is passive here, but able to distort others' motives and actions by his soliloquy (p. 168). Davies focused attention on Thersites by giving him elaborate opening business. The anachronistic phonograph was playing out-of-tune with an offstage piano as he entered. Armstrong turned it off, set down a carrier of food, pushed a broom about, spat on the table and polished it, threw a tin mug onto the balcony, and emptied an ashtray onto the floor before wiping and meticulously centering it on the table during his opening speech. Chairs that had been overturned as men jumped up during the Trojan debate in 2.2 were righted, and another one knocked over at 17 (RSC promptbook).

OSD In productions that played 2.1 merely as a bridge on the forestage while a new scene was being set behind the curtain, Achilles' tent must now be introduced or suggested. It was a tiny two-by-four canvas structure at The Players (Percy Hammond, *NYHT*, 6 June 1932). On

THERSITES How now, Thersites? What, lost in the labyrinth of thy
fury? Shall the elephant Ajax carry it thus? He beats me and
I rail at him: O worthy satisfaction! Would it were otherwise –
that I could beat him, whilst he railed at me. 'Sfoot, I'll learn
to conjure and raise devils but I'll see some issue of my spiteful   5
execrations. Then there's Achilles, a rare engineer. If Troy be not
taken till these two undermine it, the walls will stand till they fall
of themselves. O thou great thunder-darter of Olympus, forget that
thou art Jove the king of gods, and Mercury, lose all the serpentine
craft of thy caduceus, if ye take not that little little less than little   10
wit from them that they have, which short-armed ignorance itself
knows is so abundant scarce it will not in circumvention deliver a
fly from a spider without drawing their massy irons and cutting the
web. After this, the vengeance on the whole camp! Or rather the
Neapolitan bone-ache, for that methinks is the curse depending   15
on those that war for a placket. I have said my prayers and devil
Envy say 'Amen'. What ho, my Lord Achilles!
PATROCLUS [*Appearing at the entrance of the tent*] Who's there?
Thersites? – Good Thersites, come in and rail. [*Goes back inside
the tent*]   20

'Elizabethan' stages, the inner stage curtain was draped open (Poel; Payne) or an extra coarsely
woven cloth attached to a stage pillar (FTG 1983). A tent hanging served the Old Vic in 1956. At
Moshinsky's NT production, canvas backcloths on the platform behind the cockpit could have
represented the tent, but were ignored, and Achilles used the same entrances others had
employed (promptbook). A curtain partially drawn in front of the great stone head and metal
bars served Mendes in 1990 and the opening lines were accompanied by jangling harem music (F.
Shirley notes). The film of Nunn's NT production shows the flexible hangings spread to represent
the tent entrance, this time with a daybed, table and bowl of fruit in front of them. The tent was
imagined off stage in the three productions Barton was involved with at Stratford, and chairs and
emblems became the focus of action. Occasionally something substitutes for the tent – a camp
wagon at Stratford, Connecticut, or a Turkish bath at the NYTh (F. Shirley notes, 1961; Claire
Armstead, *FT*, 25 September 1987).

1ff   In keeping with the physicality of RSC 1968, Barton advanced Ajax's entrance, and he hit Thersites
and threw him down. Myrmidons with spears, 'cello-shaped shields and standards continued to
abuse him between 1 and 15, kicking and pushing him down (promptbook). In 1996 Judge
brought Thersites up the stage front steps, drinking from a bottle, and Achilles entered with food
at 35. At 8 Mendes introduced loud jazz from a radio to interrupt Thersites, and Beale turned to
slurring characters (Beale, p. 168).

17SD   There are no Q or F SDs for an entry, and Patroclus may call from within or pop his head out of
the tent. The face-to-face interchange seems to begin at 29–30. Patroclus was adjusting a tent
flap, Achilles called him, and he ran off laughing in SFC 2003 (Kidnie).

THERSITES If I could've remembered a gilt counterfeit, thou wouldst not have slipped out of my contemplation, but it is no matter: thyself upon thyself. The common curse of mankind, folly and ignorance, be thine in great revenue, heaven bless thee from a tutor, and discipline come not near thee. Let thy   25
blood be thy direction till thy death; then, if she that lays thee out says thou art a fair corpse, I'll be sworn and sworn upon't she never shrouded any but lazars. Amen.

[*Enter* PATROCLUS]

Where's Achilles?
PATROCLUS What, art thou devout, wast thou in prayer?   30
THERSITES Ay, the heavens hear me!
PATROCLUS Amen.
ACHILLES [*Within*] Who's there?
PATROCLUS Thersites, my lord.

[*Enter* ACHILLES]

ACHILLES Where, where, O where? Art thou come? Why, my cheese,   35
my digestion, why hast thou not served thyself in to my table so many meals? Come, what's Agamemnon?
THERSITES Thy commander, Achilles. Then tell me, Patroclus, what's Achilles?
PATROCLUS Thy lord, Thersites. Then tell me, I pray thee, what's   40
Thersites?
THERSITES Thy knower, Patroclus. Then tell me, Patroclus, what art thou?
PATROCLUS Thou must tell that knowest.

34SD In 1968 Patroclus had brought Thersites some food and Achilles entered with a spear, pushed the food away, and mounted Thersites. Barton's promptbook directs the teasing with the spear to continue until Ajax enters and chases Thersites off at 66. In 1985 the curtains on the balcony represented the tent and people were forced to look up to it. Achilles appeared on the balcony in a purple dressing gown, descended, and the three men sat around the table to talk until Achilles started up the stairs at 60. In highly suggestive SFC 2003, Patroclus had appeared adjusting a towel, followed by Achilles adjusting his robe (Kidnie).

36ff In Barton 1968, Thersites got Patroclus' tambourine. At the Folger, John Neville-Andrews had Achilles and Patroclus engage in a mouth-to-mouth kiss and long embrace before Thersites declared himself 'Thy knower, Patroclus' (42). Despite the body displays in Judge, 1996, there was apparently no physical contact beyond a few heavy slaps of greeting, though Patroclus chased Thersites after being declared 'a fool positive' at 57 (promptbook). Nunn's Achilles tossed the bowl of fruit to Thersites, who placed it in his bag before they went into the tent (NT 1999). In SFC 2003 Thersites stuck a rod between Patroclus' legs at 'knower' (Kidnie).

ACHILLES O tell, tell.   45

THERSITES I'll decline the whole question: Agamemnon commands
 Achilles, Achilles is my lord, I am Patroclus' knower, and Patroclus
 is a fool.

PATROCLUS You rascal!

THERSITES Peace, fool, I have not done.   50

ACHILLES He is a privileged man. Proceed, Thersites.

THERSITES Agamemnon is a fool, Achilles is a fool, Thersites is a fool,
 and as aforesaid Patroclus is a fool.

ACHILLES Derive this, come.

THERSITES Agamemnon is a fool to offer to command Achilles,   55
 Achilles is a fool to be commanded of Agamemnon, Thersites
 is a fool to serve such a fool, and Patroclus is a fool positive.

PATROCLUS Why am I a fool?

THERSITES Make that demand to the creator. It suffices me thou art.
 Look you, who comes here?   60

    Enter AGAMEMNON, ULYSSES, NESTOR,
      DIOMEDES, AND AJAX

ACHILLES Patroclus, I'll speak with nobody. Come in with me,
 Thersites.   *Exit*

THERSITES [*Aside*] Here is such patchery, such juggling, and such knav-
 ery: all the argument is a whore and a cuckold – a good quarrel
 to draw emulous factions and bleed to death upon. Now the dry   65
 serpigo on the subject, and war and lechery confound all!   [*Exit*]

AGAMEMNON Where is Achilles?

PATROCLUS Within his tent, but ill disposed my lord.

AGAMEMNON Let it be known to him that we are here.
  He shent our messengers and we lay by   70
  Our appertainings visiting of him;

51ff Achilles restrained Patroclus from hitting Thersites, and shifted to a fond embrace. The
  Myrmidons came forward to join in Barton 1968.

60SD The procession of Greek leaders has often been expanded. Poel added halberdiers, with Ajax
  bringing up the rear (1912) and four soldiers led the way downstage in SMT 1954. At the 1960
  sandpit Agamemnon had already begun the charade with Ajax and they entered arm-in-arm after
  Ulysses, who had been in time to see Achilles go. In Barton 1968, Ajax came first and chased
  Thersites off, then Agamemnon and the others entered less formally by 66. Nunn's Greek leaders
  immediately focused on the vacated daybed, with Nestor and Ulysses appropriating it, just as
  Barton's had focused on Patroclus' deck chair in 1968. Mendes had a very formal procession on
  the Swan's small stage (RSC 1990). In OX 1999 Dromgoole brought Nestor and others on
  informally in their worn khakis and combat boots.

> Let him be told so, lest perchance he think
> We dare not move the question of our place
> Or know not what we are.

PATROCLUS I shall say so to him.   [*Exit*]   75

ULYSSES We saw him at the opening of his tent:
> He is not sick.

AJAX Yes, lion-sick, sick of proud heart; you may call it melancholy
if you will favour the man but, by my head, 'tis pride. But why,
why? Let him show us the cause. A word, my lord.   80
> [*Takes Agamemnon aside*]

NESTOR What moves Ajax thus to bay at him?

ULYSSES Achilles hath inveigled his fool from him.

NESTOR Who, Thersites?

ULYSSES He.

NESTOR Then will Ajax lack matter, if he have lost his argument.   85

ULYSSES No, you see he is his argument that has his argument –
Achilles.

NESTOR All the better: their fraction is more our wish than their
faction. But it was a strong composure a fool could disunite.

ULYSSES The amity that wisdom knits not, folly may easily untie.   90
Here comes Patroclus.

> *Enter* PATROCLUS

NESTOR No Achilles with him.

ULYSSES The elephant hath joints but none for courtesy: his legs are
legs for necessity not for flexure.

PATROCLUS Achilles bids me say he is much sorry   95
> If anything more than your sport and pleasure
> Did move your greatness and this noble state
> To call upon him; he hopes it is no other
> But for your health and your digestion sake,
> An after-dinner's breath.

AGAMEMNON   Hear you Patroclus.   100
> We are too well acquainted with these answers,

78–80   Ajax angrily shouted his speech close to Achilles' tent in Judge 1996.

95   After ignoring Patroclus' entrance at 91, Quayle's Agamemnon used his stick to indicate where he should stand as he addressed him (SMT 1948). For Guthrie, Agamemnon rose and with a hand gesture stopped Patroclus dead (F. Shirley notes). Patroclus was about to leave after delivering Achilles' refusal, and was stopped by Agamemnon (SMT 1960). In 1985, Davies' Victorian Agamemnon had a swagger stick that he used to motion Patroclus into place. He banged it on the table at 100 to emphasize his reply, and at 109 poked him with it to underline his message and send him off.

But his evasion wing'd thus swift with scorn
Cannot outfly our apprehensions.
Much attribute he hath, and much the reason
Why we ascribe it to him, yet all his virtues   105
Not virtuously on his own part beheld
Do in our eyes begin to lose their gloss,
Yea, like fair fruit in an unwholesome dish,
Are like to rot untasted. Go and tell him
We come to speak with him, and you shall not sin   110
If you do say we think him over-proud
And under-honest, in self-assumption greater
Than in the note of judgement; and worthier than himself
Here tend the savage strangeness he puts on,
Disguise the holy strength of their command,   115
And underwrite in an observing kind
His humorous predominance, yea watch
His pettish lines, his ebbs, his flows, as if
The passage and whole carriage of this action
Rode on his tide. Go tell him this, and add   120
That if he overhold his price so much
We'll none of him, but let him, like an engine
Not portable, lie under this report:
'Bring action hither, this cannot go to war';
A stirring dwarf we do allowance give   125
Before a sleeping giant. Tell him so.
PATROCLUS I shall, and bring his answer presently.   [*Exit*]
AGAMEMNON In second voice we'll not be satisfied –
    We come to speak with him. Ulysses, enter you.

                                                  Exit Ulysses

AJAX What is he more than another?   130
AGAMEMNON No more than what he thinks he is.
AJAX Is he so much? Do you not think he thinks himself a better man than
    I am?
AGAMEMNON No question.
AJAX Will you subscribe his thought and say he is?   135
AGAMEMNON No, noble Ajax, you are as strong, as valiant, as wise, no
    less noble, much more gentle, and altogether more tractable.
AJAX Why should a man be proud? How doth pride grow? – I know
    not what pride is.
AGAMEMNON Your mind is the clearer, Ajax, and your virtues the   140
    fairer. He that is proud eats up himself; pride is his own glass, his
    own trumpet, his own chronicle, and whatever praises itself but in
    the deed devours the deed in the praise.

Enter ULYSSES

AJAX I do hate a proud man as I do hate the engendering of toads.
NESTOR [*Aside*] And yet he loves himself, is't not strange?   145
ULYSSES Achilles will not to the field tomorrow.
AGAMEMNON What's his excuse?
ULYSSES   He doth rely on none,
          But carries on the stream of his dispose
          Without observance or respect of any,
          In will peculiar and in self-admission.   150
AGAMEMNON Why will he not upon our fair request
          Untent his person and share the air with us?
ULYSSES Things small as nothing for request's sake only
          He makes important. Possessed he is with greatness
          And speaks not to himself but with a pride   155
          That quarrels at self-breath; imagined worth
          Holds in his blood such swoll'n and hot discourse
          That 'twixt his mental and his active parts
          Kingdomed Achilles in commotion rages
          And batters down himself. What should I say? –   160
          He is so plaguy proud that the death-tokens of it
          Cry 'No recovery'.
AGAMEMNON   Let Ajax go to him.
          Dear lord, go you and greet him in his tent:
          'Tis said he holds you well and will be led
          At your request a little from himself.   165
ULYSSES O Agamemnon, let it not be so.
          We'll consecrate the steps that Ajax makes
          When they go from Achilles; shall the proud lord
          That bastes his arrogance with his own seam
          And never suffers matter of the world   170
          Enter his thoughts, save such as doth revolve
          And ruminate himself, shall he be worshipped
          Of that we hold an idol more than he?
          No, this thrice worthy and right valiant lord
          Shall not so stale his palm nobly acquired,   175
          Nor, by my will, assubjugate his merit,
          As amply titled as Achilles' is,
          By going to Achilles.
          That were to enlard his fat-already pride,
          And add more coals to Cancer when he burns   180
          With entertaining great Hyperion.
          This lord go to him? Jupiter forbid,
          And say in thunder 'Achilles go to him!'

NESTOR [*Aside to Diomedes*] O this is well – he rubs the vein of him.

DIOMEDES [*Aside to Nestor*] And how his silence drinks up this
      applause!   185

AJAX If I go to him, with my armèd fist
      I'll pash him o'er the face.

AGAMEMNON O no, you shall not go.

AJAX An he be proud with me, I'll feeze his pride.
      Let me go to him.   190

ULYSSES Not for the worth that hangs upon our quarrel.

AJAX A paltry, insolent fellow.

NESTOR [*Aside*] How he describes himself.

AJAX Can he not be sociable?

ULYSSES [*Aside*] The raven chides blackness.   195

AJAX I'll let his humours blood.

AGAMEMNON [*Aside*] He will be the physician that should be the
      patient.

AJAX An all men were o'my mind –

ULYSSES [*Aside*] Wit would be out of fashion.   200

AJAX´ A should not bear it so, 'a should eat swords first; shall pride carry
      it?

NESTOR [*Aside*] An 'twould, you'd carry half.

ULYSSES [*Aside*] 'A would have ten shares.

AJAX I will knead him, I'll make him supple, he's not yet through warm. 205

NESTOR [*Aside*] Force him with praises, pour in, pour in: his ambition
      is dry.

ULYSSES [*To Agamemnon*] My lord, you feed too much on this dislike.

NESTOR Our noble general, do not do so.

DIOMEDES You must prepare to fight without Achilles.   210

ULYSSES Why, 'tis this naming of him does him harm.
      Here is a man – but 'tis before his face,
      I will be silent.

NESTOR   Wherefore should you so?
      He is not emulous as Achilles is.

ULYSSES Know the whole world he is as valiant –   215

AJAX A whoreson dog that shall palter with us thus. Would he were a
      Trojan.

NESTOR What a vice were it in Ajax now –

ULYSSES If he were proud.

DIOMEDES Or covetous of praise.   220

183ff   Having built up Ajax since 127, the Greeks began to draw away, leaving him alone by 192. He often
        strutted and flexed his muscles to make himself a more obvious target for Thersites' imitation in
        3.3. In RSC 1996 he again moved close to Achilles' tent to address it.

ULYSSES Ay, or surly borne.

DIOMEDES Or strange or self-affected.

ULYSSES [*To Ajax*] Thank the heavens, lord, thou art of sweet
composure:
Praise him that got thee, she that gave thee suck.
Famed be thy tutor and thy parts of nature   225
Thrice famed beyond, beyond all erudition.
But he that disciplined thine arms to fight,
Let Mars divide eternity in twain
And give him half; and for thy vigour
Bull-bearing Milo his addition yield   230
To sinewy Ajax. I will not praise thy wisdom
Which like a bourn, a pale, a shore, confines
Thy spacious and dilated parts. Here's Nestor:
Instructed by the antiquary times
He must, he is, he cannot but be wise;   235
But pardon, father Nestor, were your days
As green as Ajax' and your brain so tempered,
You should not have the eminence of him,
But be as Ajax.

AJAX [*To Nestor*]   Shall I call you father?

NESTOR Ay my good son.

DIOMEDES   Be ruled by him, Lord Ajax.   240

ULYSSES There is no tarrying here: the hart Achilles
Keeps thicket. Please it our great general
To call together all his state of war.
Fresh kings are come to Troy – tomorrow
We must with all our main of power stand fast.   245
And here's a lord, come knights from east to west
And cull their flower, Ajax shall cope the best.

AGAMEMNON Go we to council. Let Achilles sleep:
Light boats sail swift, though greater hulks draw deep.

Exeunt

239 Ajax has almost always made some move to show his respect for Nestor. He knelt (SMT 1936; RSC
1968; RSC 1990), embraced him (SMT 1954; NT 1999), did both in succession (RSC 1985) and
shook hands (Old Vic, 1956). The other Greeks have often shaken his hand or applauded,
sometimes with knowing looks.

249SD At the end of the scene, Ajax often made a final gesture. He flexed his muscles once more (RSC
1996), spat into the sand to show his disdain for Achilles' area (SMT 1960), and exited with
overdone dignity beside Agamemnon (Old Vic, 1956). At Hall's first sandpit there was a quick
change, with soldiers bringing on Helen's bed while others removed Achilles' chair and standard.
Macowan ended his first act here and the ironic juxtaposition of 3.2 and 3.3 was kept.

[3.1] *Music sounds within. Enter* PANDARUS *and a* SERVANT [*meeting*].

The scene is in Helen's quarters. The cause of it all, Helen, 'must simply be' (Rutter, p. 117), in her only scene. Dusinberre insisted she needs to be beautiful 'even if in the sex symbol rather than the classic mode', to make believable Troilus' measuring of Cressida's beauty by Helen's (Dusinberre, pp. 86–7). Hands (RSC 1981) turned Barbara Kingham into a Mae West prototype or 'fag-hag glamour puss' (Joe Tinker, *DM*, 8 July 1981) in her beaded flapper gown and feather boa, with a vanity mirror. Some directors have portrayed her as older, making her value more obviously an extrinsic Trojan construct. Yale solved its all-male cast problems by presenting her as older and less attractive in 1916. Papp chose a 'mature' actress in 1965, while at Trinity Rep she was 'a middle-aged slut . . . for whom neither Greek nor Trojan would have floated so much as a skiff' (Norton, *Record American*, 1 December 1971). In 1998 Nicola Duffert was a 'raddled . . . bottle blond vulgarian' (Charles Spencer, *Telegraph*, 15 June 1998). Blanche Yurka was criticized in 1932 because she 'lacked class' (Robert Garland, *World Telegram* 19 June). Angelika Waller wore 'a panniered Marie-Antoinette skirt', too much makeup and 'exaggeratedly round breasts' and played 'mechanically' in contrast to Cressida at the Berliner Ensemble (Martin Hoyle, *FT*, 19 August 1987). She and Paris represented 'ossified glamour' and were 'acting their roles' after seven years (Michael Billington, *Gdn*, 20 August 1987).

Often directors let Thersites be their guide, and Helen is either an aggressively sexy tart or a passive, painted whore. By 2001 Hall considered her 'clearly not someone worth fighting over . . . a bit of a bag and a bit of a boozer'. He chose dark-haired, voluptuous Cindy Katz, dressed her in a short skirt, and layered on mascara and rouge (Kastan). There may be a hint that Paris is tiring of her, as in his drunken, pro forma embraces for Guthrie. In 1985, he was a brutal Germanic type with a dueling scar, stiff collar and monocle (Michael Coveny, *FT*, 7 May 1986). Or the relationship with Paris may still include affection (Landau 1961), ardor (RSC 1968) or raging lust (NYSF 1995; RSC 1996; SFC 2003).

Troilus' alibi message that occasions Pandarus' visit is kept (64–6, 123–4), but often lost in the contrapuntal conversation with Helen. Hall (2001) added three revelers 'to tell us that Pandarus is not interrupting a private tryst . . . but a party' (Kastan). Many earlier directors also added other couples or numbers of attendants to liven the meeting. In productions that highlight the sexual relationship of Achilles and Patroclus, lust and self-indulgence in the Greek camp are now generally followed by a similar display in Troy. Where Pandarus is aggressively homosexual (RSC 1996; NYSF 1973; SFC 2003) he has often played the scene with more than friendly interest.

Designers and directors have often added domestic details appropriate to the period of choice. Payne (SMT 1936) and Neville-Andrews (FTG 1983) simply opened Elizabethan inner-stage curtains to reveal a daybed and stool, or a bed, respectively, with costumes providing ambience. Macowan and Guthrie went to the other extreme, with numerous properties. Glasses, bottles, cigarettes, magazines and other accoutrements of upper-class cocktail parties transformed the structurally sketchy sets. In 1938 Macowan used wrought-iron furniture, two upholstered pieces, and a floor lamp to indicate Helen's modern tastes. He introduced extra couples in the 'room in Helen's flat', and Pandarus (Max Adrian) accompanied himself on a white baby grand stage right while people embraced in ways that today seem quite decorous (production photos). Qualye's 1948 promptbook specifies six extras looking on as Paris holds grapes suggestively over Helen while they sit on a classical daybed. In 1954 Shaw included six additional couples. Servants pulled a figured gauze curtain across to indicate the delicate luxury of Paris and Helen's quarters and hide the distant panorama of the Greek camp and masts. Gold decorated cushions for Helen and Paris and trays of drinks for all completed the transformation of the set (Brown).

Ambience is important even when extras are not added to the principal trio. Guthrie quickly replaced Achilles' tent hanging with a pre-set truck carrying a piano and bench, chair and table. Helen in her high-fashion evening gown played or leaned provocatively on the piano when she and Paris weren't embracing. Audience imagination, aided by coloured cushions and a bolster, transformed the Hall/Barton sandpit in 1960, and Helen was given an attendant with a larger, more elaborate parasol than had shaded Cressida in 1.2 (production photos). Landau staged the scene in front of the Civil War mansion, and photographs show Helen with a beauty mark, hair in 1860 curls, and a low-cut light dress, mitts and a fan, leaning against Paris on the steps.

Papp (NYSF 1965) used draperies pulled between two columns stage left, and a chaise to relieve the severity of the set's permanent stone benches and blocks. The Berliner Ensemble projected rose petals on the stage floor in Edinburgh. They were revealed when the multi-functional white cloth fell partly forward (Andrew Rissick, *In*, 19 August 1987). The most unusual approach was the Sloane School's in 1955. The programme listed 3.1 as 'A Trojan Vision' and created a 'surprise effect'. Classically clad soldiers 'slept, relaxed or stood guard', radio music played, and 'Paris and Helen danced in modern evening dress, while Pandarus, in opera cape and top hat, watched from a small table' (W. A. Darlington, *DT*; Trewin, *ILN*, 2 April 1955). Nunn, having advanced 2.2, sandwiched this scene between 2.1 and 2.3.

OSD   Occasionally directors have cut Pandarus' preliminary exchange with the boy, which requires some music (SMT 1948; Old Vic 1956). Fry treated the episode as a conventional Shakespearean comic exchange between a clever servant and a visitor seeking information. At 'know me better' and two lines later, Pandarus tipped the servant (James O'Donnell Bennet, '"Troilus and Cressida" as staged in London', 23 June 1907), while Poel, Barton 1968, and Boyd cut lines 9–13. Poel used

PANDARUS Friend, you, pray you a word – do you not follow the young
    Lord Paris?
SERVANT Ay sir, when he goes before me.
PANDARUS You depend upon him I mean.
SERVANT Sir, I do depend upon the Lord.   5
PANDARUS You depend upon a notable gentleman: I must needs praise
    him.
SERVANT The Lord be praised!
PANDARUS You know me, do you not?
SERVANT Faith sir, superficially.   10
PANDARUS Friend, know me better, I am the Lord Pandarus.
SERVANT I hope I shall know your honour better.
PANDARUS I do desire it.
SERVANT You are in the state of grace.
PANDARUS Grace? Not so, friend, honour and lordship are my titles.   15
    What music is this?
SERVANT I do but partly know sir: it is music in parts.
PANDARUS Know you the musicians?
SERVANT Wholly, sir.
PANDARUS Who play they to?   20
SERVANT To the hearers, sir.

the crash of Ajax falling at the end of 2.3 to cue a string quartet while the tableau curtains closed.
His 3.1 opened in front of the curtains while the Paris/Helen tableau was arranged, with Paris
lolling on a couch and servants in attendance. In 2003, Monette made the episode a study in
attempted seduction, with Pandarus placing his fan between servant Kevin McKillip's legs and
later exchanging glances (Kidnie). It was 'the most carefully staged' part of the scene, 'filling the
stage with more erotic tension than the subsequent gymnastics of Lynda Prystawska's nympho
nightmare Helen and Tim Campbell's beach bum Paris' (Richard Ouzounian, *Toronto Star*, 17 May
2003).

  In 1972, at the Bristol Old Vic, Davies added a grotesque puppet show with drum
accompaniment to entertain Paris and Helen before Pandarus greeted them. At the RSC in 1985
he staged a rowdy party at the officers' club, with Paris and Helen almost incidental participants.
Cowbells rang, glasses were clinked, Pandarus was welcomed and his hat and stick were taken.
Just before Paris and Helen entered, he was carried to the landing, handed upside down to three
men, and his trousers stripped off. Helen helped him pull his trousers back on, and joined Paris in
pushing him to the piano stool by 45. 'There was a Brecht/Weill decadence as Paris and Helen
humililated Pandarus.' (Stephen Wall, 'Bridging the Homeric Gap', *TLS* 12 July 1985.) In Judge's
1996 staging, a red cloth pulled along the platform and a settee with cushions on and around it on
the main level signalled Helen's apartment. The servant leaned on the couch while talking to
Pandarus (production photos).

PANDARUS At whose pleasure, friend?
SERVANT At mine sir, and theirs that love music.
PANDARUS Command I mean, friend.
SERVANT Who shall I command, sir?   25
PANDARUS Friend, we understand not one another. I am too courtly
    and thou too cunning. At whose request do these men play?
SERVANT That's to't indeed sir. Marry sir, at the request of Paris my
    lord, who is there in person, with him the mortal Venus, the heart-
    blood of beauty, love's invisible soul.   30
PANDARUS Who, my cousin Cressida?
SERVANT No sir, Helen. Could you not find out that by her attributes?
PANDARUS It should seem, fellow, thou hast not seen the Lady Cressid.
    I come to speak with Paris from the Prince Troilus. I will make a
    complimental assault upon him, for my business seethes.   35
SERVANT Sodden business? There's a stewed phrase indeed!

36SD   Helen, a 'wonderfully trivial' Edwardian chorus girl 'who had married into the peerage' was
playing a sentimental Edwardian song as Guthrie's scene opened (Berry, *On Directing
Shakespeare*, p. 17; Wood and Clarke). In 1968 Barton pulled aside masking drapes on a large
circular bed. Extras held fans and ten male guards formed a V behind the bed while Pandarus
leaned over the lovers (promptbook details). In 1981 Hands added half a dozen scantly clad
young men with curly wings who threw feathers like darts. They joined Paris in lolling with Helen,
who enjoyed the revelry. In 1976 Barton and Kyle made Helen into a captive sex slave, led in by
Paris with a golden chain around her neck. Actions were formalized, and Helen spoke 135–8
slowly and grimly under constraint. In 1986 Dorn had her carried in on a litter by six slaves, her
head covered by a golden veil (Olivia Fuchs, *PP* July 1987, p. 35). Mendes seemed to echo Dorn,
and treated Helen as prize in 1990. She was carried in on a large dish or circle, wrapped in
shining gold. Paris unwrapped her to the accompaniment of exotic flute music, while red light
shone on the great stone head. The circle in the floor was the ritual centre, where Pandarus
reclined with Helen, in her off-shoulder tight red gown. Paris joined them as they spoke of Troilus
and she embraced Pandarus but scarcely touched Paris. Gary O'Connor found her 'straight out of
Watergate . . . which makes Paris and his backers, although more clean and courtly [than the
Greeks] . . . even shorter on wit' (*PP*, August 1990). In Judge's 1996 production, 'having . . .
lovebirds Paris and Helen emerge naked from a sunken steam bath for some determined
foreplay . . . make[s] the audience uneasily compliant in the rampant voyeuristic oglings onstage
of Clive Francis' raddled, flesh-creeping queen of a Pandarus' (Paul Taylor, *In*, 26 July 1996, p. 5).
Helen draped herself, sari-fashion, in a towel, then Pandarus and the servant held a bath sheet
and she dressed behind it, while Paris lounged on the settee. Incense smoke added to the
hedonism, as did Helen's dance gestures (F. Shirley notes). At the Folger in 1983 John
Neville-Andrews brought back the two children who had spoken the Prologue. During the

Enter PARIS *and* HELEN

PANDARUS Fair be to you, my lord, and to all this fair company, fair
    desires in all fair measure fairly guide them – especially to you,
    fair queen, fair thoughts be your fair pillow!

HELEN Dear lord, you are full of fair words.   40

PANDARUS You speak your fair pleasure, sweet queen. Fair prince, here
    is good broken music.

PARIS You have broke it, cousin, and by my life you shall make it whole
    again – you shall piece it out with a piece of your performance.
    Nell, he is full of harmony.   45

PANDARUS Truly lady, no.

HELEN O sir!

PANDARUS Rude in sooth, in good sooth very rude.

PARIS Well said, my lord, well, you say so in fits.

PANDARUS I have business to my lord, dear queen. My lord, will you   50
    vouchsafe me a word?

HELEN Nay this shall not hedge us out, we'll hear you sing certainly.

PANDARUS Well, sweet queen, you are pleasant with me. But, marry
    thus my lord: my dear lord and most esteemed friend, your brother
    Troilus –   55

HELEN My Lord Pandarus, honey-sweet lord –

PANDARUS Go to, sweet queen, go to – commends himself most affec-
    tionately to you.

HELEN You shall not bob us out of our melody: if you do, our melan-
    choly upon your head.   60

ensuing fifty lines they built a little house from a small wagon full of wood, engaged in a pillow
fight on the rumpled sheets, and finally mimed the three monkeys, seeing, hearing and speaking
no evil. In Nunn's exotic NT 1999 staging, slow music played while purple, green and blue carpets
were spread with four big cushions. Firebowls marked the corners of the carpet area and four
attendants placed torches into holes on the Olivier stage (promptbook).

49ff Georgine Anderson (Helen) and Robert Robinson (Paris) had Ralph Nossek (Pandarus) on his
      back on the cushions at the Birmingham Rep, and tickled him (*Birmingham Post and Mail* photo,
      1963). At the 1985 officers' club party, Helen was pushed onto Pandarus' knee, and later held him
      when he tried to rise from the stool at 51. In Colorado John Churchill and Noel True, though in
      Civil War costumes, 'are like teenagers – they roughhouse, show affection, unaware or uncaring
      about the havoc around them' (Sandra Brooks-Dillard, 'Smartly Staged *Troilus and Cressida*
      Disparages War', *Denver Post*, 1 August 1977, F 9). There was a bed centre stage in the mansion
      set in Strachan's 1998 OA where 'dapper' Pandarus joined 'bleached blonde Helen' and 'smug
      little Paris' (Charles Spencer, *Telegraph*, 15 June 1998). Langham used a double-width chaise at
      SFC 1963, and William Hutt joined the lovers and flicked a flywhisk suggestively (F. Shirley notes).

PANDARUS Sweet queen, sweet queen, that's a sweet queen, i'faith –

HELEN And to make a sweet lady sad is a sour offence.

PANDARUS Nay that shall not serve your turn, that shall it not, in truth, la! Nay I care not for such words, no, no. And, my lord, he desires you that if the King call for him at supper you will make 65
his excuse.

HELEN My Lord Pandarus –

PANDARUS What says my sweet queen, my very, very sweet queen?

PARIS What exploit's in hand? Where sups he tonight?

HELEN Nay but my lord – 70

PANDARUS What says my sweet queen? My cousin will fall out with you.

HELEN You must not know where he sups.

PARIS I'll lay my life with my disposer Cressida.

PANDARUS No, no, no such matter, you are wide: come, your disposer 75
is sick.

PARIS Well I'll make's excuse.

PANDARUS Ay, good my lord. Why should you say Cressida? – no, your poor disposer's sick.

PARIS I spy – 80

PANDARUS You spy? What do you spy? [*To a musician*] Come, give me an instrument: now sweet queen –

HELEN Why this is kindly done.

PANDARUS My niece is horribly in love with a thing you have, sweet queen. 85

HELEN She shall have it my lord, if it be not my Lord Paris.

PANDARUS He? No, she'll none of him: they two are twain.

HELEN Falling in after falling out may make them three.

PANDARUS Come, come, I'll hear no more of this. I'll sing you a song now. 90

HELEN Ay, ay, prithee now. By my troth, sweet lord, thou hast a fine forehead.

81ff Pandarus occasionally called for one of the instruments the musicians played during the earlier 'broken music'. On 'Elizabethan' stages, he may play a lute, the casual instrument of the time (Payne 1936; OSF 1958), or guitar, which Helen 'twanged' while offstage musicians actually played (Poel). Landau had an appropriate banjo in 1961. Shaw called for a lyre in 1954, when two servant girls also played pipes, though one photograph shows a small harp. When there is a piano on stage, Pandarus has played that (Macowan; Guthrie; Trinity Rep; and Davies 1985).

91 In 1968 Helen pulled Pandarus down and stroked his forehead, and after the song Paris leaned across him to kiss Helen. Although Helen flirted a bit in Davies 1985, stroking Pandarus' head and sitting on Paris' lap through the song, some of her moves seemed pro forma self-preservation rather than sensuous enjoyment in the rowdy surroundings. At The Players, Paris and Helen were

PANDARUS Ay you may, you may –

HELEN Let thy song be love: this love will undo us all, O Cupid,
Cupid, Cupid –   95

PANDARUS Love, ay, that it shall i'faith.

PARIS Ay good now: [*Sings*] Love, love, nothing but love –

PANDARUS In good troth, it begins so.

    [*Sings*] Love, love, nothing but love, still love, still more!

        For O love's bow   100

        Shoots buck and doe.

        The shaft confounds

        Not that it wounds

    But tickles still the sore.

    These lovers cry, O, O, they die,   105

        Yet that which seems the wound to kill

    Doth turn 'O, O' to 'ha ha he',

        So dying love lives still.

    'O, O' a while, but 'ha ha ha'

    'O, O' groans out for 'ha ha ha' – Heigh-ho!   110

HELEN In love, i'faith, to the very tip of the nose.

PARIS He eats nothing but doves, love, and that breeds hot blood, and
hot blood begets hot thoughts, and hot thoughts beget hot deeds,
and hot deeds is love.

PANDARUS Is this the generation of love: hot blood, hot thoughts,   115
and hot deeds? Why, they are vipers; is love a generation of
vipers? Sweet lord, who's afield today?

'only incidental' and 'don't engage in the cooing we expect' (Brooks Atkinson, *NYT*, 5 June 1932,
10.1). Quayle made them more daring in 1948. Paris pushed Pandarus onto one end of the
daybed while he and Helen reclined on the other end. Just before the song, Helen tapped
Pandarus on the nose with her toe (SMT promptbook).

99   Pandarus has generally had a reasonably decent singing voice. At The Players, however, Eugene
Powers was 'wonderfully cast and unctuous' and 'stole his scenes', but 'should have had a
substitute singer' (Stephen Rathburn, 'Players Club Presents "Troilus and Cressida", a Pictorially
Effective Production', *NYS*, 7 June 1932). While Pandarus sang and Helen stroked Paris' head in
1948, one of Quayle's extras put a cloak over them, amidst much giggling (promptbook).

105 The groping 'rises to an orgasm at the top note of Pandarus' song' (Wardle, *LT*, 8 July 1981), with
Hands' pseudo cupids engaging in a 'group grope' as opposed to the 'gang grope' of 4.5
(Nightingale, *New Statesman*), making sex 'a spectator sport' (Michael Billington, *Gdn*,
8 July 1981). In 1936 Payne had five ladies-in-waiting dance with Pandarus as he repeated the
refrain, then Paris and a servant finally lifted him in the air in a sort of lavolta.

PARIS Hector, Deiphobus, Helenus, Antenor, and all the gallantry of
    Troy. I would fain have armed today, but my Nell would not have
    it so. How chance my brother Troilus went not?   120

HELEN He hangs the lip at something – you know all, Lord Pandarus.

PANDARUS Not I, honey-sweet queen. I long to hear how they sped
    today. You'll remember your brother's excuse?

PARIS To a hair.

PANDARUS Farewell, sweet queen.   125

HELEN Commend me to your niece.

PANDARUS I will, sweet queen.   [*Exit*]

                 Sound a retreat

PARIS They're come from field: let us to Priam's hall
    To greet the warriors. Sweet Helen, I must woo you
    To help unarm our Hector: his stubborn buckles,   130
    With these your white enchanting fingers touched,
    Shall more obey than to the edge of steel
    Or force of Greekish sinews; you shall do more
    Than all the island kings t'disarm great Hector.

HELEN 'Twill make us proud to be his servant, Paris;   135
    Yea, what he shall receive of us in duty
    Gives us more palm in beauty than we have,
    Yea, overshines ourself.

PARIS Sweet, above thought I love thee.

                                  Exeunt

127SD   In 1956 Helen played a march on the piano then moved lightly into the exchange with Paris.
      Virtually every production retains 128–39 uncut. At the end of the Berliner Ensemble scene, the
      canvas was lifted and flowers covered the entire stage to become Cressida's garden, while
      stagehands twisted part of the cloth to represent a tree trunk (Taylor, p. 300).

ACT 3, SCENE 2

[**3.2**] *Enter* PANDARUS *and Troilus'* MAN [*meeting*]

Monette was not successful in moving from the heightened tone of 3.1 to the quieter meeting of Troilus and Cressida (Kidnie). The scene is the orchard of Calchas' house, where she lives with Pandarus (see 4.1.38). Many directors have cut the first four lines so eager Troilus appears immediately. In the restrained Yale Rep production, Walter Kerr found 'the sense . . . is that of a positively chaste shyness. Troilus, played by a strapping Dan Hamilton, confesses to the whirl his head is in by standing utterly rigid, frozen to that stoniness that overtakes teen-aged boys at their first proms.' (*NYT*, 18 April 1976, II 5.) Guthrie interpreted the giddiness as a mix of drink and expectation. Rosemary Harris, in an evening dress with a hobble skirt, was a 'calculating' Cressida, and David called Troilus a 'thoughtless undergraduate seduced by a bitch', though, with the production's emphasis on satire of the military, 'their first meeting was trifled away' (*SS 10* 1957, p. 131). Moshinsky also diminished the scene. Robert Eddison was kindly, 'without vicarious lechery', but the production was fragmented 'by driving the love story off from the main action' (Sally Emerson, *PP*, September 1976). Troilus became more active and excited in 1981, pawing Cressida, making her 'seem like a tart' and himself 'a nincompoop' (Milton Schulman, *NS*, 8 July 1981). Kenneth Albers described their first meeting as 'tainted and poisoned' (OSF 2001 Programme note).

Over a dozen lines are usually cut before 36 to increase focus on the actual meeting. The entire scene was often mercilessly slashed in earlier productions, with Poel omitting a third and Payne almost a quarter of the lines. By comparison, promptbooks show that Barton in his shortest version, in 1976, cut only a tenth, including 60–2, 67b–69a, and 78b–84, which are seldom played. Boyd, like many others directors, tightened the oaths, removing 154b–61 and 171b–74. Nunn, after all the earlier rearrangement, now let scenes run in their original order and removed only two dozen lines from 3.2.

The actor and director must decide how shy or truly calculating Cressida should be. Papp felt she came 'too easy' (p. 36). At the Old Vic in 1923, when she was expected to be the villain, 'Florence Saunders does well by showing Cressida's wanton spirit – even as she protests fidelity.' (*LT*, 6 November 1923, p. 12.) Pamela Brown's 'Elizabethan doll' was 'attractive enough to attract Troilus, yet light-minded and unworthy' and W. A. Darlington found her protestations 'false'

(*DT*, 25 April, 1936). Robert Harris made Troilus 'a bit of a bore', while Ruth Lodge was 'sensual and shallow, yet has an air of distinction' in Macowan's 1938 modern-dress production (anonymous review). *The Times*, responding to a letter to the Editor, said 'Don't be too hard on Cressida.' She is 'not evil or vicious, merely light' (25 September 1938). Juliet Stevenson gave the appearance of genuine thoughtfulness as she tried to assess the course she was embarking on in 1985, while Victoria Hamilton 'moved away from him, came back to his arms, in a way that, through instinct or design, imparted the maximum urgent energy to their exit to the bedroom' (Smallwood, *SS 50*, p. 214). Hall 2001 had replaced Cressida's 1.2 orange skirt and heavy blouse with revealing pants and filmy poncho (Kastan).

Pandarus has helped determine the atmosphere by playing up his voyeuristic delight at their gradually growing closeness or by 'being the uncle who merely wants to see them happy'. Occasionally a sexual interest in Troilus has conflicted with his pandering. In earlier productions, he tended to be more restrained. Randle Ayrton looked like a 'stock schoolmaster' in 1936. At the Marlowe Society in 1964, Pandarus resembled 'an Irish priest at Aintree, or an Anglican vicar entertaining a honeymoon couple (Christopher Driver, *Gdn*, 10 March 1964). Clive Merrison, younger than many in the role, was the kindly uncle 'helping them to overcome their shyness of each other' (Russell, p. 37). By contrast, Tony Church (SC 1981) was 'in a lather' at the prospect of Troilus and Cressida together (Frances Kay, *ST*, 17 July 1981). In 1996 Clive Francis 'swayed and writhed and minced his way through his pandering, making it perfectly clear that he would be delighted to supply Cressida's place in Troilus' bed if she continued to delay' (Smallwood, *SS 50*, p. 212). Bernard Hopkins, 'reminiscent of Dame Edna', longed for either lover (Richard Ouzounian, *Toronto Star*, 17 August 2003). In BBC 1981, Charles Gray was 'too loud' and 'over the top', and 'venery becomes dull when overstated' (Michael Ratcliff, 'Wit is First Casualty', 9 November 1981).

OSD   Although line 14 sets the scene in an orchard, designers and directors have often moved it indoors. Poel staged it neutrally in front of his tableau curtains, allowing the Greeks to get posed for 3.3. Payne opened the penthouse curtains slightly to give a glimpse of a room offstage. Quayle added many indoor details: a chair, rug, stove and classical couch different from the one in 3.1. Although action centred on the couch, Cressida's room (their goal) was offstage. In 1956, as the Helen truck rolled off right, Guthrie brought a truck in from the left with chairs, table and lamp in a more sombre tone (F. Shirley notes). At Stratford, Connecticut, the lattice screen 'looks like a lofty wall leading into a gracious mansion' (Howard Taubman, *NYT*, 24 July 1961). A single small orange tree behind an L-shaped bench in the sand pit served Hall and Barton in 1960, while Barton used a small tree and straight bench for the increased activity of 1968. Nunn projected mottled light on the dark red earth of the Olivier stage and the white costumes stood out.

PANDARUS How now, where's thy master? At my cousin Cressida's?
MAN No sir, he stays for you to conduct him thither.

Enter TROILUS

PANDARUS O here he comes: how now, how now!
TROILUS Sirrah, walk off.

                                                          [Exit Man]

PANDARUS Have you seen my cousin?   5
TROILUS No Pandarus, I stalk about her door
        Like a strange soul upon the Stygian banks
        Staying for waftage. O, be thou my Charon
        And give me swift transportation to those fields
        Where I may wallow in the lily beds   10
        Proposed for the deserver. O gentle Pandar,
        From Cupid's shoulder pluck his painted wings
        And fly with me to Cressid.
PANDARUS Walk here i'th'orchard, I'll bring her straight.   *Exit*
TROILUS I am giddy: expectation whirls me round.   15
        Th'imaginary relish is so sweet
        That it enchants my sense – what will it be
        When that the wat'ry palate tastes indeed
        Love's thrice repurèd nectar? Death, I fear me,
        Sounding destruction, or some joy too fine,   20
        Too subtle-potent, tuned too sharp in sweetness
        For the capacity of my ruder powers.
        I fear it much and I do fear besides
        That I shall lose distinction in my joys,
        As doth a battle when they charge on heaps   25
        The enemy flying.

2SD   Photographs of classically garbed productions generally show Troilus in a short tunic or peplum, occasionally with a longer cloak. Dromgoole had him in a suit and tie when he called on Cressida, in contrast to the informality of most of the costuming, and Pandarus also donned a coat to add to the importance of impressions on this first date (F. Shirley notes). In Guthrie 1956, Edwardian evening wear meant Pandarus in white tie and tails, and Troilus in a mess jacket and bow tie.

14ff   Merrison went up and down the mansion stairs in Davies 1985. The balcony curtain now represented Cressida's rooms. Rodway put on his blazer in 1990, adding a note of formality as he got ready to oversee the meeting.

Enter PANDARUS

PANDARUS She's making her ready, she'll come straight; you must be
witty now. She does so blush and fetches her wind so short as if she
were frayed with a sprite. I'll fetch her; it is the prettiest villain –
she fetches her breath as short as a new-ta'en sparrow.   *Exit*   30

TROILUS Even such a passion doth embrace my bosom:
    My heart beats thicker than a feverous pulse
    And all my powers do their bestowing lose,
    Like vassalage at unawares encount'ring
    The eye of majesty.   35

Enter PANDARUS *and* CRESSIDA

PANDARUS Come, come, what need you blush? – shame's a baby. Here
she is now: swear the oaths now to her that you have sworn to me.
[*Cressida draws away*] What are you gone again? – you must be
watched ere you be made tame, must you? Come your ways, come
your ways: an you draw backward, we'll put you i'th'thills. Why do   40
you not speak to her? Come, draw this curtain and let's see your picture [*Removing her veil*]. Alas the day, how loath you are to offend
daylight: an 'twere dark you'd close sooner. So, so, rub on and kiss
the mistress. How now, a kiss in fee-farm! Build there carpenter, the
air is sweet. Nay you shall fight your hearts out ere I part you, the   45
falcon as the tercel, for all the ducks i'th'river. Go to, go to.

TROILUS You have bereft me of all words, lady.

PANDARUS Words pay no debts, give her deeds; but she'll bereave you
o'th'deeds too, if she call your activity in question. What, billing
again? Here's 'In witness whereof the parties interchangeably . . .'   50
Come in, come in, I'll go get a fire.   [*Exit*]

CRESSIDA Will you walk in my lord?

TROILUS O Cressida, how often have I wished me thus!

CRESSIDA Wished my lord? The gods grant – O my lord –

TROILUS What should they grant? What makes this pretty abruption?   55
What too curious dreg espies my sweet lady in the fountain of our
love?

42   There is no SD, but Cressida must have entered wearing a veil to emphasize her shyness.
Pandarus draws it off, revealing the prize and trying to end her modesty so they may kiss at 44. In
1956, Paul Rogers wrapped Rosemary Harris' light veil around his own head and 'quivered with
expectation' (Wood and Clarke). The first kiss is generally a tentative peck, but Judge made it a
long kiss and clench in 1996.

CRESSIDA More dregs than water if my fears have eyes.

TROILUS Fears make devils of cherubims, they never see truly.

CRESSIDA Blind fear that seeing reason leads, finds safer footing than   60
blind reason stumbling without fear: to fear the worst oft cures
the worse.

TROILUS O let my lady apprehend no fear: in all Cupid's pageant there
is presented no monster.

CRESSIDA Nor nothing monstrous neither?   65

TROILUS Nothing but our undertakings, when we vow to weep seas,
live in fire, eat rocks, tame tigers, thinking it harder for our mistress
to devise imposition enough than for us to undergo any difficulty
imposed. This is the monstrosity in love, lady, that the will is
infinite and the execution confined, that the desire is boundless   70
and the act a slave to limit.

CRESSIDA They say all lovers swear more performance than they are
able, and yet reserve an ability that they never perform, vowing
more than the perfection of ten and discharging less than the tenth
part of one. They that have the voice of lions and the act of hares,   75
are they not monsters?

TROILUS Are there such? Such are not we. Praise us as we are tasted,
allow us as we prove. Our head shall go bare till merit crown it: no
perfection in reversion shall have a praise in present; we will not
name desert before his birth and, being born, his addition shall be   80
humble. Few words to fair faith: Troilus shall be such to Cressid
as what envy can say worst shall be a mock for his truth, and what
truth can speak truest not truer than Troilus.

CRESSIDA Will you walk in my lord?

Enter PANDARUS

PANDARUS What, blushing still? Have you not done talking yet?   85

CRESSIDA Well uncle, what folly I commit I dedicate to you.

PANDARUS I thank you for that: if my lord get a boy of you, you'll give
him me. Be true to my lord; if he flinch chide me for it.

78   In RSC 1985, as Anton Lesser's Troilus became more poetic, Stevenson responded. Brockbank
found her 'balanced between drawing closer and going away'. She knows how women are
treated in a man's world, and her responses to the courtship are 'balanced between spontaneity
and calculation' (p. 47).

85SD   The amount of talk before supposedly eager Troilus can act suggests the risk Cressida is taking
(Papp, p. 33). When Pandarus returns, despite a few interjections, he is more and more the
watcher until 176. In 1985 Merrison looked down from the mansion stairs and blocked her
attempted escape at 120.

TROILUS You know now your hostages: your uncle's word and my firm
    faith.   90

PANDARUS Nay I'll give my word for her too: our kindred, though they
    be long ere they be wooed, they are constant being won; they are
    burrs I can tell you: they'll stick where they are thrown.

CRESSIDA Boldness comes to me now and brings me heart:
    Prince Troilus, I have loved you night and day   95
    For many weary months.

TROILUS Why was my Cressid then so hard to win?

CRESSIDA Hard to seem won, but I was won my lord
    With the first glance that ever – pardon me,
    If I confess much, you will play the tyrant;   100
    I love you now, but till now not so much
    But I might master it – in faith I lie,
    My thoughts were like unbridled children grown
    Too headstrong for their mother – see, we fools!
    Why have I blabbed? Who shall be true to us   105
    When we are so unsecret to ourselves?
    But though I loved you well, I wooed you not,
    And yet, good faith, I wished myself a man
    Or that we women had men's privilege
    Of speaking first. Sweet, bid me hold my tongue,   110
    For in this rapture I shall surely speak
    The thing I shall repent. See, see your silence,
    Coming in dumbness, from my weakness draws
    My very soul of counsel. Stop my mouth.

TROILUS And shall, albeit sweet music issues thence.   115

                    [*Kisses her*]

PANDARUS Pretty i'faith.

---

94   At Stratford, Connecticut, when Cressida yields, 'the play shifts into the nostalgic, romantic' with
     her 'the southern belle' (Howard Taubman, 'Stratford Puts Troilus and Cressida to 1860's', *NYT*, 24
     July 1961). She was more eager at SFC 1963, and a photograph shows Cressida leaning over
     Troilus, mouth open, while Pandarus hovers close behind them. Sophie Okonedo 'was smiling
     and excited in the confession of love and the vows' (Smallwood, *SS 53*, p. 257), but clapped her
     hand to her mouth after revealing her love. Hall 2001 emphasized their youthful innocence here
     'only to contrast with the other scenes in which . . . [it] is soiled and crushed' (Kastan).

98ff The pauses and shifts in 98–114 have been either the 'mocking innocence' Roger Warren found in
     Carol Royle (*SS 35*, p. 149) or signs that she is genuinely upset and 'ashamed' (117–20), with the
     conflicting sides of her personality shown.

CRESSIDA My lord I do beseech you, pardon me –
    'Twas not my purpose thus to beg a kiss;
    I am ashamed – O heavens, what have I done?
    For this time will I take my leave, my lord.   120
TROILUS Your leave, sweet Cressid?
PANDARUS Leave? An you take leave till tomorrow morning –
CRESSIDA Pray you, content you –
TROILUS What offends you lady?
CRESSIDA Sir, mine own company.   125
TROILUS You cannot shun yourself.
CRESSIDA Let me go and try.
    I have a kind of self resides with you,
    But an unkind self that itself will leave
    To be another's fool. I would be gone.   130
    Where is my wit? I know not what I speak.
TROILUS Well know they what they speak that speak so wisely.
CRESSIDA Perchance my lord I show more craft than love
    And fell so roundly to a large confession
    To angle for your thoughts; but you are wise,   135
    Or else you love not – for to be wise and love
    Exceeds man's might; that dwells with gods above.
TROILUS O that I thought it could be in a woman –
    As, if it can, I will presume in you –
    To feed for aye her lamp and flames of love,   140
    To keep her constancy in plight and youth,
    Outliving beauty's outward with a mind
    That doth renew swifter than blood decays,
    Or that persuasion could but thus convince me
    That my integrity and truth to you   145
    Might be affronted with the match and weight
    Of such a winnowed purity in love –
    How were I then uplifted! But, alas,
    I am as true as truth's simplicity
    And simpler than the infancy of truth.   150
CRESSIDA In that I'll war with you.
TROILUS   O virtuous fight,
    When right with right wars who shall be most right!
    True swains in love shall in the world to come
    Approve their truth by Troilus: when their rhymes,
    Full of protest, of oath and big compare,   155

---

120   Pamela Brown curtsied, taking her leave in Elizabethan fashion in SMT 1936. Pandarus has always made some move to block her exit by 122, then often again moved aside to watch.

Want similes, truth tired with iteration –
As true as steel, as plantage to the moon,
As sun to day, as turtle to her mate,
As iron to adamant, as earth to th'centre –
Yet after all comparisons of truth,   160
As truth's authentic author to be cited,
'As true as Troilus' shall crown up the verse
And sanctify the numbers.
CRESSIDA   Prophet may you be!
If I be false or swerve a hair from truth,
When time is old and hath forgot itself,   165
When waterdrops have worn the stones of Troy
And blind oblivion swallowed cities up
And mighty states characterless are grated
To dusty nothing, yet let memory
From false to false among false maids in love   170
Upbraid my falsehood: when they've said 'as false
As air, as water, wind or sandy earth,
As fox to lamb, or wolf to heifer's calf,
Pard to the hind or stepdame to her son',
Yea, let them say to stick the heart of falsehood,   175
'As false as Cressid'.
PANDARUS Go to, a bargain made: seal it, seal it, I'll be the witness.
Here I hold your hand, here my cousin's. If ever you prove false
one to another, since I have taken such pains to bring you together,
let all pitiful goers-between be called to the world's end after my   180
name: call them all panders; let all constant men be Troiluses, all
false women Cressids, and all brokers-between panders. Say Amen.
TROILUS Amen.
CRESSIDA Amen.

165 Cressida, allowed by Hands to add some mocking gestures, pertly drew her hair around to form a beard (Warren, *SS 35*, p. 149).

177 Despite Pandarus' language of commerce, directors retain the allusion to a marriage ceremony after the overblown vows of fidelity. Pandarus generally stands behind or between them and takes their hands, joining them by the last 'Amen'. Occasionally they have knelt for a while, with him standing over them at the end (SMT 1948; RSC 1960 and 1990; NAO 1978). At first Scofield was seated, while Cressida and Pandarus stood and Pandarus pulled their hands together in SMT 1948 (production photographs). Pandarus, with glasses and a large wallet hanging from his belt, stood before slightly open penthouse curtains to join Elizabethan dandy Troilus and Cressida with her large fan in a stiff gesture (SMT 1936 production photo). In 2001 they knelt in the sand and immediately began to kiss (Kastan).

PANDARUS Amen. Whereupon I will show you a chamber with a bed,   185
     which bed, because it shall not speak of your pretty encounters,
     press it to death, away!

                              Exeunt [*Troilus and Cressida*]
          And Cupid grant all tongue-tied maidens here
          Bed, chamber, pander, to provide this gear.   *Exit*

188   Pandarus' couplet makes a good curtain line, and in modern productions the interval generally
      comes here. Poel had a distant drum and Cassandra crossed the stage, then his first act ended to
      string quartet music.

ACT 3, SCENE 3

[3.3] *Flourish. Enter* AGAMEMNON, ULYSSES, DIOMEDES, NESTOR, [AJAX,] MENELAUS, and CALCHAS

The second-longest scene of the play, 3.3 has proven easier to stage for modern audiences because of its variety, with the shock value of the exchange arrangements, the tension between Achilles and the Greek commanders and the humour at the end. The irony of Shakespeare's juxtaposition of 3.2 and 3.3.1–37 is reduced by an interval, and earlier productions that had two breaks preserved Shakespeare's effect. It is Calchas' only appearance unless directors bring him on silently at 4.5 to watch the kissing from the side or have him appear to present Cressida to Diomedes in 5.2. For Davies 1985 his manner here was a dignified statement of facts with notes of the points he needed to make. It was 'unctuous pleading' in BBC 1981, with Peter Whitbread 'smiling and sweating' and Michael Ratcliff found his appearance 'a surprise stroke' on the heels of 3.2 ('Wit is the First Casualty', 9 November 1981).

The opening exchanges have occasionally been cut by four or five lines, and Payne inexplicably substituted 'Margarelon' for 'Antenor', but the opening section is generally left intact. Directors often prune segments of Achilles' and Ulysses' speeches before and after 'Time hath . . . a wallet' (145–53a) so that the message and the later reference to Ajax' activity compared to Achilles' withdrawal (181–9a) are not lost in multiple examples. Quayle and Shaw cut the references to Polyxena that add complexity to Achilles' reason for not fighting and to his relationship with Patroclus. Guthrie as well as Hall and Barton cut 196–203a, typically keeping essentials and sharpening the focus. Comparison of cuts in particular scenes shows the emphasis of a production. In 3.3 Guthrie excised only about thirty lines to Hall and Barton's sixty (RSC 1962). In 1999 Nunn kept most of the scene through 240, then slashed over two-thirds of the final segment with Thersites, as did Landau in 1961, to retain focus on the more serious parts. Conversely, Poel considered Achilles a different person in this scene, 'more intelligent' and not 'simply a prize-fighter' (*Shakespeare in the Theatre*, p. 111), but felt the scene interfered with the play's progress (Programme note). He preserved most of the Calchas and Thersites episodes, but reduced Ulysses' segment by over half (promptbook 1912).

OSD The setting normally repeats 2.3, and has occasionally been run together with it. Quayle's SMT 1948 promptbook placed the rest of 3.3 earlier, then ran lines 1–37 just before 4.1, with a bodyguard announcing 'the Trojan Calchas' and Diomedes introducing him to Agamemnon as if

CALCHAS   Now, princes, for the service I have done,
     Th'advantage of the time prompts me aloud
     To call for recompense. Appear it to your mind
     That through the sight I bear in things to come
     I have abandoned Troy, left my possession,   5
     Incurred a traitor's name, exposed myself
     From certain and possessed conveniences
     To doubtful fortunes, sequest'ring from me all
     That time, acquaintance, custom, and condition
     Made tame and most familiar to my nature,   10
     And here to do you service am become
     As new into the world – strange, unacquainted.
     I do beseech you, as in way of taste,
     To give me now a little benefit
     Out of those many registered in promise   15
     Which you say live to come in my behalf.
AGAMEMNON   What wouldst thou of us, Trojan? Make demand.
CALCHAS   You have a Trojan prisoner called Antenor
     Yesterday took: Troy holds him very dear.
     Oft have you (often have you thanks therefor)   20
     Desired my Cressid in right great exchange
     Whom Troy hath still denied; but this Antenor
     I know is such a wrest in their affairs
     That their negotiations all must slack
     Wanting his manage, and they will almost   25
     Give us a prince of blood, a son of Priam,
     In change of him. Let him be sent, great princes,

they had never met. Guthrie's Calchas, an intellectual priest in frock coat and fur hat, met the Greek commanders and Antenor in front of the curtain to begin the second act (Wood and Clarke, p. 51). Payne's actors were before the penthouse curtains, which opened to a trumpet call as Calchas left (promptbook 1936). Barton and Hall again placed soldiers with crossed spears across the rear of the sandpit, facing away, as guards. Barton elaborated on this in 1968. Calchas and Achilles had deck chairs, and Achilles exercised with a discus while Calchas sat. Four Myrmidons paced stage left and three stood guard by Achilles' chair, one holding a bull emblem. They had a camp upstage with an armour stand with a sword, a helmet and 'cello-shaped shields (F. Shirley notes). Davies (1985) repeated the 1.3 council setting with the telegraph ticker to the right and papers and pens on the large table. A small table and chair were added to the balcony area in front of the curtains, which again represented Achilles' tent. In 1999 Nunn opened all the massive panels surrounding the Olivier stage and had jangling metallic 'banners' at the rear. In NYSF 1965 curtains between the stage left columns now represented the tent.

>   And he shall buy my daughter, and her presence
>   Shall quite strike off all service I have done
>   In most accepted pain.

AGAMEMNON   Let Diomedes bear him   30
>   And bring us Cressid hither; Calchas shall have
>   What he requests of us. Good Diomed,
>   Furnish you fairly for this interchange;
>   Withal bring word if Hector will tomorrow
>   Be answered in his challenge: Ajax is ready.   35

DIOMEDES This shall I undertake and 'tis a burden
>   Which I am proud to bear.

>   [*Exeunt Diomedes and Calchas*]

ACHILLES *and* PATROCLUS [*appear in the doorway of*] *their tent*

ULYSSES Achilles stands i'th'entrance of his tent:
>   Please it our general pass strangely by him
>   As if he were forgot, and, princes all,   40
>   Lay negligent and loose regard upon him;
>   I will come last. 'Tis like he'll question me
>   Why such unplausive eyes are bent, why turned, on him;
>   If so, I have derision medicinable
>   To use between your strangeness and his pride,   45
>   Which his own will shall have desire to drink.
>   It may do good: pride hath no other glass
>   To show itself but pride, for supple knees
>   Feed arrogance and are the proud man's fees.

AGAMEMNON We'll execute your purpose and put on   50
>   A form of strangeness as we pass along;

---

30 Calchas had stood taking notes in 1985 while bugles offstage and occasional bursts from the ticker tape suggested events beyond the meeting. As the conversation ended, Agamemnon signed an exchange order and placed it in a file folder. Smallwood noted that in 1996 Philip Voss' 'foxy' and 'patient' Ulysses looked 'disbelieving' when the exchange was announced (*SS 50*, p. 212).

37SD Guthrie's curtain rose to reveal Achilles in an open-necked silk shirt, trousers and dressing gown, smoking a cigarette (Wood and Clarke, p. 31). In the 1960 sandpit, Patroclus wore a leopard skin and Achilles a long robe, mixing pride and indolence. They sat outside the sandpit, and the Greek commanders were gathered within it, looking downstage at the pair (SMT 1960 photo).

50ff This sequence has generally been played for comedy as the Greek commanders studiously ignore Achilles. They may hum to themselves when not talking (1985), circle elaborately (1960) or pass unnecessarily close to the tent as they cold-shoulder the watching Achilles (NYSF 1965).

So do each lord and either greet him not
Or else disdainfully, which shall shake him more
Than if not looked on – I will lead the way.
              [*They file past Achilles' tent*]
ACHILLES What, comes the general to speak with me?   55
       You know my mind, I'll fight no more 'gainst Troy.
AGAMEMNON What says Achilles? Would he aught with us?
NESTOR Would you, my lord, aught with the general?
ACHILLES No.
NESTOR Nothing, my lord.   60
AGAMEMNON The better.
ACHILLES Good day, good day.
MENELAUS How do you, how do you?
ACHILLES What, does the cuckold scorn me?
AJAX How now, Patroclus?   65
ACHILLES Good morrow, Ajax.
AJAX Ha!
ACHILLES Good morrow.
AJAX Ay, and good next day too.
              Exeunt [*Agamemnon, Nestor, Menelaus, and Ajax*]
ACHILLES What mean these fellows? Know they not Achilles?   70
PATROCLUS They pass by strangely: they were used to bend,
       To send their smiles before them to Achilles,
       To come as humbly as they use to creep
                        To holy altars.
ACHILLES   What, am I poor of late?
       'Tis certain greatness, once fall'n out with fortune,   75

70ff   Ulysses does not join the general exit. He often stays to one side, reading. In Miller, BBC 1981, he wandered casually towards Achilles' cot. Achilles, focused on himself, may not notice him until 92b. 1938 photographs show Robert Speaight, in civilian blazer and slacks, talking with uniformed, pipe-smoking Achilles, both sitting on camp stools within a pedimented doorframe. Patroclus, on the steps below in a plain uniform, looked like an orderly, as he would in 1956. In 1954 Patroclus, scantily clad, lounged on the downstage steps at the SMT, propped on his elbow and listening, while 'Leo McKern plays well on Achilles' vanity' (*LT*, 14 July 1954, p. 11). Mairowitz found Robin Ellis' Achilles (RSC 1976) 'more like a ballet dancer gone to seed than a warrior . . . a whining queen, frivolous instead of arrogant, displaying girlishness rather than dispirited manhood' (*PP*, October 1976, pp. 20–1). In RSC 1981 the bond between Achilles and Patroclus was 'not effeminate'. Patroclus 'oiled and massaged Suchet fondly and listened intently to Ulysses' (Warren, *SS 35*, p. 149). In 1985 Ulysses remained at the large table, and Achilles and Patroclus noticed him as they came down from the balcony.

Must fall out with men too. What the declined is,
He shall as soon read in the eyes of others
As feel in his own fall; for men, like butterflies,
Show not their mealy wings but to the summer,
And not a man for being simply man   80
Hath any honour, but honour for those honours
That are without him, as place, riches, and favour –
Prizes of accident as oft as merit,
Which, when they fall, as being slippery standers,
The love that leaned on them, as slippery too,   85
Doth one pluck down another and together
Die in the fall. But 'tis not so with me;
Fortune and I are friends: I do enjoy
At ample point all that I did possess,
Save these men's looks, who do methinks find out   90
Something not worth in me such rich beholding
As they have often given. Here is Ulysses,
I'll interrupt his reading. How now, Ulysses!

ULYSSES Now, great Thetis' son!

ACHILLES What are you reading?

ULYSSES   A strange fellow here   95
Writes me that man, how dearly ever parted,
How much in having, or without or in,
Cannot make boast to have that which he hath,
Nor feels not what he owes, but by reflection –
As when his virtues shining upon others   100
Heat them, and they retort that heat again
To the first givers.

ACHILLES   This is not strange, Ulysses:
The beauty that is borne here in the face
The bearer knows not, but commends itself
To others' eyes; nor doth the eye itself,   105
That most pure spirit of sense, behold itself,
Not going from itself, but eye to eye opposed,
Salutes each other with each other's form,
For speculation turns not to itself
Till it hath travelled and is mirrored there   110
Where it may see itself. This is not strange at all.

ULYSSES I do not strain at the position –
It is familiar – but at the author's drift,
Who in his circumstance expressly proves
That no man is the lord of anything,   115
Though in and of him there be much consisting,
Till he communicate his parts to others;

Nor doth he of himself know them for aught
Till he behold them formed in the applause
Where they're extended, who like an arch reverb'rate   120
The voice again, or like a gate of steel
Fronting the sun, receives and renders back
His figure and his heat. I was much rapt in this,
And apprehended here immediately
The unknown Ajax.   125
Heavens what a man is there! – a very horse
That has he knows not what. Nature, what things there are
Most abject in regard and dear in use!
What things again most dear in the esteem
And poor in worth! Now shall we see tomorrow –   130
An act that very chance doth throw upon him –
Ajax renowned. O heavens, what some men do
While some men leave to do;
How some men creep in skittish Fortune's hall,
Whiles others play the idiots in her eyes;   135
How one man eats into another's pride,
While pride is fasting in his wantonness!
To see these Grecian lords – why even already
They clap the lubber Ajax on the shoulder
As if his foot were on brave Hector's breast   140
And great Troy shrieking.
ACHILLES   I do believe it, for they passed by me
As misers do by beggars: neither gave to me
Good word nor look. What, are my deeds forgot?
ULYSSES   Time hath, my lord, a wallet at his back   145
Wherein he puts alms for oblivion,
A great-sized monster of ingratitudes;
Those scraps are good deeds past, which are devoured
As fast as they are made, forgot as soon
As done. Perseverance, dear my lord,   150
Keeps honour bright: to have done is to hang
Quite out of fashion like a rusty mail
In monumental mock'ry. Take the instant way,
For honour travels in a strait so narrow
Where one but goes abreast; keep then the path,   155

145ff   'From the mass of swaggering Greeks [at SFC 2003], the only one who makes a positive
impression is Peter Donaldson as Ulysses. He delivers the great speech about time with such
clarity and resonance you suddenly say: My God, this is Shakespeare and it's good!' (Richard
Ouzounian, 'Queer Eye for Shakespare's Greeks', *Toronto Star*, 17 August 2003.)

For emulation hath a thousand sons
That one by one pursue. If you give way
Or hedge aside from the direct forthright,
Like to an entered tide they all rush by
And leave you hindmost;   160
Or like a gallant horse fall'n in first rank,
Lie there for pavement to the abject rear,
O'er-run and trampled on: then what they do in present,
Though less than yours in past, must o'er-top yours;
For Time is like a fashionable host   165
That slightly shakes his parting guest by th'hand,
And with his arms outstretched as he would fly
Grasps in the comer; Welcome ever smiles
And Farewell goes out sighing. O let not virtue seek
Remuneration for the thing it was,   170
For beauty, wit,
High birth, vigour of bone, desert in service,
Love, friendship, charity, are subjects all
To envious and calumniating Time.
One touch of nature makes the whole world kin: 175
That all with one consent praise new-born gauds,
Though they are made and moulded of things past,
And give to dust that is a little gilt
More laud than gilt o'er-dusted.
The present eye praises the present object;   180
Then marvel not, thou great and complete man,
That all the Greeks begin to worship Ajax,
Since things in motion sooner catch the eye
Than what stirs not. The cry went once on thee,
And still it might, and yet it may again,   185
If thou wouldst not entomb thyself alive
And case thy reputation in thy tent,
Whose glorious deeds but in these fields of late
Made emulous missions 'mongst the gods themselves
And drove great Mars to faction.
ACHILLES   Of this my privacy   190
        I have strong reasons.
ULYSSES   But 'gainst your privacy

190–209 Patroclus paced as Ulysses talked of Polyxena. Guthrie cut about half the lines but Patroclus'
         agitation showed (F. Shirley notes, 11 January 1957). In 1981 he stopped oiling Achilles and stared
         at the mention of Polyxena (Warren, *SS 35*, p. 149). Colin Hurly, as Ulysses, had incriminating
         photographs of Polyxena and Achilles in RSC 1998.

The reasons are more potent and heroical.
'Tis known, Achilles, that you are in love
With one of Priam's daughters.
ACHILLES Ha, known?   195
ULYSSES Is that a wonder?
The providence that's in a watchful state
Knows almost every grain of Pluto's gold,
Finds bottom in th'uncomprehensive deeps,
Keeps place with thought and, almost like the gods,   200
Does thoughts unveil in their dumb cradles.
There is a mystery, with whom relation
Durst never meddle, in the soul of state,
Which hath an operation more divine
Than breath or pen can give expressure to.   205
All the commerce that you have had with Troy
As perfectly is ours as yours, my lord,
And better would it fit Achilles much
To throw down Hector than Polyxena.
But it must grieve young Pyrrhus now at home,   210
When fame shall in our islands sound her trump,
And all the Greekish girls shall tripping sing:
'Great Hector's sister did Achilles win
But our great Ajax bravely beat down him.'
Farewell my lord; I as your lover speak –   215
The fool slides o'er the ice that you should break.   [*Exit*]
PATROCLUS To this effect, Achilles, have I moved you.
A woman impudent and mannish grown
Is not more loathed than an effeminate man
In time of action. I stand condemned for this: 220
They think my little stomach to the war,
And your great love to me, restrains you thus.
Sweet, rouse yourself, and the weak, wanton Cupid
Shall from your neck unloose his amorous fold
And, like a dew-drop from the lion's mane,   225
Be shook to air.
ACHILLES   Shall Ajax fight with Hector?
PATROCLUS Ay, and perhaps receive much honour by him.

---

216 Achilles fell to his knees with a loud cry and Ulysses pushed his face into the sand as he left
     (SMT 1960).
217 Patroclus knelt for his speech as if pleading (Shaw 1954 promptbook).

ACHILLES I see my reputation is at stake,
     My fame is shrewdly gored.
PATROCLUS   O then beware!
     Those wounds heal ill that men do give themselves;   230
     Omission to do what is necessary
     Seals a commission to a blank of danger,
     And danger like an ague subtly taints
     Even then when we sit idly in the sun.
ACHILLES Go call Thersites hither, sweet Patroclus,   235
     I'll send the fool to Ajax and desire him
     T'invite the Trojan lords after the combat
     To see us here unarmed. I have a woman's longing,
     An appetite that I am sick withal,
     To see great Hector in his weeds of peace,   240

Enter THERSITES

     To talk with him and to behold his visage
     Even to my full of view. A labour saved!
THERSITES A wonder!
ACHILLES What?
THERSITES Ajax goes up and down the field asking for himself.   245
ACHILLES How so?
THERSITES He must fight singly tomorrow with Hector and is so
    prophetically proud of an heroical cudgelling that he raves in say-
    ing nothing.
ACHILLES How can that be?   250

240SD   Beale found this 'very difficult'. The 'comic turn' after a beautiful scene 'has to be funny' (p. 170).
    In 1936 Thersites entered laughing and 'stalked about as he describes Ajax' for Payne. In the older
    productions he was less active or the promptbooks don't record the action as precisely as more
    recent ones. Barton's notation in 1968 that the actors could move as they desired during the long
    Achilles/Ulysses interchange may suggest what older directors did. Barton, however, included
    specific directions for the Thersites segment, including having two Myrmidon guards stop him as
    he entered with the tambourine. In 1985 Armstrong had a carryall full of groceries and equipment
    for the officers' club.

250ff   The most devastating take-off of Ajax was Armstrong's in 1985. As the others watched, he did a
    peacock walk, then climbed onto the large table with a rolled-up paper (the challenge?) and
    pulled a saucepan from the carryall. Thersites put the saucepan on his head, handle to the front,
    and as he and Patroclus played a conversation with Ajax, he strutted and puffed out his chest, and
    finally climbed down at 292. Patroclus hit the saucepan with a stick, ramming it down on his head
    (production film). Barton's 1968 Myrmidons came downstage to provide a larger audience,

THERSITES Why 'a stalks up and down like a peacock – a stride and
a stand; ruminates like an hostess that hath no arithmetic but her
brain to set down her reckoning; bites his lip with a politic regard
as who should say 'There were wit in this head an 'twould out';
and so there is, but it lies as coldly in him as fire in a flint, which   255
will not show without knocking. The man's undone for ever: for
if Hector break not his neck i'th'combat, he'll break't himself in
vainglory. He knows not me – I said 'Good morrow, Ajax' and he
replies 'Thanks, Agamemnon.' What think you of this man that
takes me for the general? He's grown a very land-fish, language-   260
less, a monster. A plague of opinion! – A man may wear it on both
sides like a leather jerkin.

ACHILLES Thou must be my ambassador to him, Thersites.

THERSITES Who, I? Why, he'll answer nobody, he professes not answering – speaking is for beggars; he wears his tongue in's arms.   265
I will put on his presence: let Patroclus make demands to me, you
shall see the pageant of Ajax.

ACHILLES To him Patroclus. Tell him I humbly desire the valiant Ajax
to invite the most valorous Hector to come unarmed to my tent,
and to procure safe-conduct for his person of the magnanimous   270
and most illustrious six-or-seven-times-honoured captain-general
of the Grecian army, Agamemnon, *et cetera*. Do this.

PATROCLUS Jove bless great Ajax!

THERSITES H'm –

PATROCLUS I come from the worthy Achilles –   275

THERSITES Ha?

PATROCLUS Who most humbly desires you to invite Hector to his
tent –

THERSITES H'm –

PATROCLUS And to procure safe-conduct from Agamemnon –   280

THERSITES Agamemnon?

PATROCLUS Ay, my lord.

THERSITES Ha!

PATROCLUS What say you to't?

THERSITES God be wi'you, with all my heart.   285

PATROCLUS Your answer, sir?

and Thersites grabbed Achilles' sword as he began his performance. Barton's promptbook
directions included Thersites' putting a leg over Patroclus and hitting Achilles, who bit him on the
wrist and took back his sword between 280 and 292. In BBC 1981,'Orlando' went through some
body-building motions as he started the imitation. Dromgoole (OX 2000) let Lucas imitate
Mussolini's arm gestures and add business to steal the scene (F. Shirley notes).

THERSITES If tomorrow be a fair day, by eleven o'clock it will go one
    way or other; howsoever, he shall pay for me ere he has me.
PATROCLUS Your answer, sir?
THERSITES Fare ye well, with all my heart.   290
ACHILLES Why, but he is not in this tune is he?
THERSITES No, but he's out o'tune thus. What music will be in him
    when Hector has knocked out his brains I know not, but I am sure
    none, unless the fiddler Apollo get his sinews to make catlings on.
ACHILLES Come, thou shalt bear a letter to him straight.   295
THERSITES Let me bear another to his horse, for that's the more capable
    creature.
ACHILLES My mind is troubled like a fountain stirred,
       And I myself see not the bottom of it.
                              [Exeunt Achilles and Patroclus]
THERSITES Would the fountain of your mind were clear again, that I   300
    might water an ass at it. I had rather be a tick in a sheep than
    such a valiant ignorance.   *[Exit]*

302   As Armstrong followed Achilles and Patroclus up the steps, he was tugging at the saucepan stuck
       on his head (1985 production film). In 1936 Payne had Thersites close the penthouse curtains as
       he left, preparing for 4.1, which took place in front of the curtains. Poel changed the limelight to
       dawn (promptbook), but the 4.1 SD requires torches, indicating to Elizabethan audiences that it
       was dark. Barton closed the scene with a bull roar in 1968.

ACT 4, SCENE 1

[**4.1**] *Enter at one door* AENEAS *with a torch, at another* PARIS,
DEIPHOBUS, ANTENOR, DIOMEDES *the Grecian, with torches*

PARIS See ho, who is that there?
DEIPHOBUS It is the Lord Aeneas.
AENEAS Is the prince there in person?
      Had I so good occasion to lie long
      As you, Prince Paris, nothing but heavenly business   5
      Should rob my bed-mate of my company.
DIOMEDES That's my mind too. Good morrow, Lord Aeneas.
PARIS A valiant Greek, Aeneas, take his hand,
      Witness the process of your speech, wherein
      You told how Diomed a whole week by days   10
      Did haunt you in the field.

Fry omitted this scene. It has usually been done in a static fashion that suits the careful courtesy of men subduing their animosity, until Diomedes' discussion with Paris strikes sparks. To move the action along, a tradition has developed of cutting much of the courteous/threatening interchange characterized by Paris' oxymoron (33–4), leaving only a few words of greeting, the details of the trade and Diomedes' exchange with Paris at the end (Poel; Payne; Quayle; Shaw; Guthrie; Barton and Hall 1960; and Barton 1968, for example). Nunn kept the entire scene.

OSD Where there is a curtain, the scene occured on the forestage, while properties are changed to Cressida's quarters. Even Payne's Elizabethan revival used the penthouse curtain to indicate a change of locale in 1936. The torches called for in Q and F conventionally signal that it is still dark, and are almost always included. Barton's enhanced staging in 1968 included ten extras with Greek and Trojan emblems and banners. Servants brought in drinks and Paris entered with seven ladies (F. Shirley notes). In 1960 Barton and Hall had merely given torches to all the named characters. Lines 37–41 indicate that it takes place outside, on the way to Calchas' house, but Davies placed it inside in 1985. The red Trojan and grey Greek uniforms contrasted slightly. Paris entered in a robe, with tea and a newspaper. During Diomedes' comments he changed into a green civilian jacket. Stage rear, some debris from the earlier party (3.1), which had not been lighted in 3.2 and 3.3, was now being cleaned up by servants (RSC promptbook).

AENEAS   Health to you, valiant sir,
    During all question of the gentle truce;
    But when I meet you armed, as black defiance
    As heart can think or courage execute.
DIOMEDES The one and other Diomed embraces.   15
    Our bloods are now in calm and, so long, health!
    But when contention and occasion meet,
    By Jove I'll play the hunter for thy life
    With all my force, pursuit, and policy.
AENEAS And thou shalt hunt a lion that will fly   20
    With his face backward. In humane gentleness,
    Welcome to Troy; now, by Anchises' life,
    Welcome indeed! By Venus' hand I swear
    No man alive can love in such a sort
    The thing he means to kill more excellently.   25
DIOMEDES We sympathise. Jove, let Aeneas live,
    If to my sword his fate be not the glory,
    A thousand complete courses of the sun;
    But in mine emulous honour let him die
    With every joint a wound, and that tomorrow.   30
AENEAS We know each other well.
DIOMEDES We do and long to know each other worse.
PARIS This is the most despiteful gentle greeting,
    The noblest hateful love, that e'er I heard of.
    What business, lord, so early?   35
AENEAS I was sent for to the king, but why I know not.
PARIS His purpose meets you: 'twas to bring this Greek
    To Calchas' house and there to render him
    For the enfreed Antenor the fair Cressid.
    Let's have your company or, if you please,   40
    Haste there before us. [*Aside to Aeneas*] I constantly believe –
    Or rather call my thought a certain knowledge –
    My brother Troilus lodges there tonight.
    Rouse him and give him note of our approach,
    With the whole quality wherefore; I fear   45
    We shall be much unwelcome.
AENEAS [*To Paris*]   That I assure you.
    Troilus had rather Troy were borne to Greece
    Than Cressid borne from Troy.
PARIS [*To Aeneas*]   There is no help:
    The bitter disposition of the time
    Will have it so. – On, lord, we'll follow you.   50
AENEAS Good morrow all.   *Exit*

PARIS And tell me, noble Diomed, faith, tell me true,
   Even in the soul of sound good fellowship,
   Who in your thoughts deserves fair Helen best,
   Myself or Menelaus?
DIOMEDES   Both alike: 55
   He merits well to have her that doth seek her,
   Not making any scruple of her soil,
   With such a hell of pain and world of charge;
   And you as well to keep her that defend her,
   Not palating the taste of her dishonour,   60
   With such a costly loss of wealth and friends.
   He like a puling cuckold would drink up
   The lees and dregs of a flat tamèd piece;
   You like a lecher out of whorish loins
   Are pleased to breed out your inheritors.   65
   Both merits poised, each weighs nor less nor more,
   But he as he, the heavier for a whore.
PARIS You are too bitter to your countrywoman.
DIOMEDES She's bitter to her country. Hear me Paris,
   For every false drop in her bawdy veins,   70
   A Grecian's life hath sunk; for every scruple
   Of her contaminated carrion weight,
   A Trojan hath been slain; since she could speak
   She hath not given so many good words breath
   As for her Greeks and Trojans suffered death.   75
PARIS Fair Diomed, you do as chapmen do,
   Dispraise the thing that you desire to buy;
   But we in silence hold this virtue well:
   We'll not commend what we intend to sell.
   Here lies our way.   80
             Exeunt

52ff Paris and Diomedes conversed lit by Jeep headlights in the NYTh 1987 Middle East war zone. The
   jeep had brought the exchange party (Robert Hanks, *In*, 30 September 1987). In 1985 the servants
   stopped cleaning and listened as Diomedes spoke.
80SD Mendes sent them up the Swan Theatre aisles.

ACT 4, SCENE 2

[4.2] *Enter* TROILUS *and* CRESSIDA

TROILUS Dear, trouble not yourself, the morn is cold.
CRESSIDA Then, sweet my lord, I'll call mine uncle down,
      He shall unbolt the gates.
TROILUS   Trouble him not.
      To bed, to bed; sleep kill those pretty eyes,
      And give as soft attachment to thy senses   5
      As infants empty of all thought.
CRESSIDA Good morrow then.

The setting is inside Cressida's home, and with a few exceptions 4.3 is cut, so 4.2 flows into 4.4 without interruption.

OSD   Birch used music by Byrd and others to accompany the classically garbed lovers in 1922. Generally Cressida has come in wearing a nightdress, which can serve as an undergarment if a servant later brings outer garments. Helen Mirren was the first Cressida to emerge nude (for Barton, 1968). She robed as they spoke. Macowan (1938) had Pandarus still in a dressing gown and slippers, but Troilus and Cressida were already dressed. Paul Scofield was putting on his coat and blowing up the fire in a stove as the lights came up on Quayle's 1948 production. O'Connor pointed out the great contrast between 'Greeks in leather greatcoats' and 'the under-clad lovers', part of a mix of effects, costumes and acting in Mendes' production (*PP*, August 1990, p. 29). Dromgoole's modern Cressida was in shorts, while Troilus had his shirt-tail out. In Hall 2001, Troilus entered 'pulling on his shirt' and Cressida's 'body and underclothes are now covered by nothing but the diaphanous shawl she had on in the earlier scene' (Kastan).

    Payne (1936) used the steps in front of the tiring house balcony suggested by Monck, and Troilus and Cressida came down to the main stage, as they did in Quayle's 1948 multi-level Trojan setting. Guthrie had Pandarus' house truck pushed on as Paris left at the end of 4.1. Photographs of it show Cressida's room above with dressing table and bench, and the lower half of a flight of steps coming through an arch onto a platform with a table and some bottles at stage level. Occasionally Troilus and Cressida come outdoors, tying into the reference to cold and gates at 1–3. Barton (1968) had them return to the bench and tree, and Landau brought them out of the ante-bellum mansion. Moshinsky's NT 1976 promptbook has Troilus and Cressida using different entrances, and their kiss suggests a meeting rather than a parting.

TROILUS   I prithee now to bed.

CRESSIDA Are you a-weary of me?

TROILUS O Cressida, but that the busy day,

   Waked by the lark, hath roused the ribald crows   10

   And dreaming night will hide our joys no longer,

   I would not from thee.

CRESSIDA   Night hath been too brief.

TROILUS Beshrew the witch! With venomous wights she stays

   As tediously as hell, but flies the grasps of love

   With wings more momentary-swift than thought.   15

   You will catch cold and curse me.

CRESSIDA   Prithee tarry;

   You men will never tarry.

   O foolish Cressid, I might have still held off

   And then you would have tarried. Hark, there's one up.

PANDARUS (*Within*) What's all the doors open here?   20

TROILUS It is your uncle.

CRESSIDA A pestilence on him! Now will he be mocking – I shall have
such a life.

Enter PANDARUS

PANDARUS How now, how now, how go maidenheads? Hear you, maid,
  where's my cousin Cressid?   25

CRESSIDA Go hang yourself, you naughty mocking uncle!
   You bring me to do, and then you flout me too.

PANDARUS To do what? To do what? Let her say what. What have I
  brought you to do?

CRESSIDA Come, come, beshrew your heart! You'll ne'er be good nor 30
  suffer others –

PANDARUS Ha, ha! Alas, poor wretch, ah, poor *chipochia*! Has't not slept
  tonight? Would he not, a naughty man, let it sleep? A bugbear take
  him!

CRESSIDA Did not I tell you? Would he were knocked i'th'head. 35

One knocks

Who's that at door? Good uncle, go and see.

23SD Pandarus brought morning tea to Cressida's modern bedroom suite in Macowan's production
   (Crosse, Notebook XVII, p. 31), and in 1968 Barton provided a jug of wine and cups, and Pandarus
   toasted them. In BBC 1981 he brushed past them in the hall and entered the bedroom to check
   the bed.

31 Using a text with 'capochia' (see textual note in Dawson, p. 173), Francis addressed '"Has't not
   slept tonight?" directly to Troilus' private parts' in 1996 (Smallwood, *SS 50*, p. 213).

My lord, come you again into my chamber.
You smile and mock me as if I meant naughtily.
TROILUS Ha, ha!
CRESSIDA Come, you are deceived: I think of no such thing.   40
                    Knock
How earnestly they knock. Pray you, come in –
I would not for half Troy have you seen here.
                    Exeunt [*Troilus and Cressida*]
PANDARUS Who's there? What's the matter, will you beat down the
door? [*He opens the door*]

        [*Enter* AENEAS]

How now, what's the matter?   45
AENEAS Good morrow, lord, good morrow.
PANDARUS Who's there? My Lord Aeneas! By my troth, I knew you
not; what news with you so early?
AENEAS Is not Prince Troilus here?
PANDARUS Here? What should he do here?   50
AENEAS Come, he is here, my lord, do not deny him.
It doth import him much to speak with me.
PANDARUS Is he here say you? It's more than I know, I'll be sworn –
for my own part, I came in late. What should he do here?
AENEAS Whoa – nay then! Come, come, you'll do him wrong ere   55
you are ware; you'll be so true to him to be false to him. Do not
you know of him, but yet go fetch him hither, go.

        Enter TROILUS

TROILUS How now, what's the matter?
AENEAS My lord, I scarce have leisure to salute you,
        My matter is so rash: there is at hand   60
        Paris your brother, and Deiphobus,
        The Grecian Diomed, and our Antenor
        Delivered to us, and for him forthwith,
        Ere the first sacrifice, within this hour,
        We must give up to Diomedes' hand   65

44SD   Pandarus put on his suit jacket to answer the door and let in Aeneas in Dromgoole's often
       informal production. In 1936 Payne sent Troilus and Cressida back up to the balcony at the knock,
       and Troilus came halfway down at 57. He reappeared in the arch on Guthrie's multi-level set
       (F. Shirley notes). Troilus had left his cloak on a bench before 44 in 1948. Aeneas spotted it and
       picked it up at 51, ending Pandarus' show of innocence. He returned it to Troilus as they left
       (SMT promptbook).

> The Lady Cressida.

TROILUS   Is it so concluded?

AENEAS By Priam and the general state of Troy;
        They are at hand and ready to effect it.

TROILUS How my achievements mock me!
        I will go meet them, and, my Lord Aeneas,   70
        We met by chance – you did not find me here.

AENEAS Good, good, my lord, the secrets of nature
        Have not more gift in taciturnity.

                              Exeunt [Troilus and Aeneas]

PANDARUS Is't possible? No sooner got but lost? The devil take
        Antenor! The young prince will go mad – a plague upon Antenor! I   75
        would they had broke 's neck.

                         Enter CRESSIDA

CRESSIDA How now, what's the matter? Who was here?

PANDARUS Ah, ah!

CRESSIDA Why sigh you so profoundly? Where's my lord?
        Gone? Tell me, sweet uncle, what's the matter?   80

PANDARUS Would I were as deep under the earth as I am above.

CRESSIDA O the gods! what's the matter?

PANDARUS Pray thee, get thee in; would thou hadst ne'er been born!
        I knew thou wouldst be his death. O poor gentleman! A plague
        upon Antenor!   85

CRESSIDA Good uncle I beseech you, on my knees I beseech you, what's
        the matter?

PANDARUS Thou must be gone, wench, thou must be gone: thou art
        changed for Antenor. Thou must to thy father and be gone from
        Troilus; 'twill be his death, 'twill be his bane, he cannot bear it.   90

66b Smallwood noted that in contrast to his highly emotional delivery elsewhere, Joseph Fiennes'
     'uncomplaining compliance seemed even calmer than it usually does' (*SS 50*, p. 214).

74   Pandarus conventionally sits after Troilus leaves and Cressida finds him with his head bowed, on
     the steps (1956), on the edge of the sandpit (1960) or on a stool (1990). 'Roy Hamilton's
     Pandarus . . . was very much the romantic at heart, delighted at bringing the lovers together and
     absolutely shattered by the defeat of his plans.' (Smallwood, *SS 53*, p. 260.)

77ff Pandarus and Cressida have often started by holding each other, and she gradually works up her
     emotions while Pandarus offers no comfort. Sophie Okonedo ran off hysterical at the Olivier in
     1999. The BBC cameras could follow Cressida into her room, where she lay sobbing on her bed.
     In Hall 2001 Pandarus let Cressida rage helplessly. 'Her relative nakedness has nothing prurient
     about it; rather, it highlights her terrible vulnerability.' (Kastan.)

CRESSIDA O you immortal gods, I will not go.

PANDARUS Thou must.

CRESSIDA I will not uncle: I have forgot my father,
       I know no touch of consanguinity,
       No kin, no love, no blood, no soul so near me   95
       As the sweet Troilus. O you gods divine,
       Make Cressid's name the very crown of falsehood
       If ever she leave Troilus. Time, force, and death
       Do to this body what extremes you can,
       But the strong base and building of my love   100
       Is as the very centre of the earth
       Drawing all things to it. I'll go in and weep –

PANDARUS Do, do.

CRESSIDA Tear my bright hair and scratch my praisèd cheeks,
       Crack my clear voice with sobs and break my heart   105
       With sounding Troilus. I will not go from Troy.

Exeunt

ACT 4, SCENE 3

[4.3] *Enter* PARIS, TROILUS, AENEAS, DEIPHOBUS, ANTENOR, *and* DIOMEDES

PARIS It is great morning, and the hour prefixed
      For her delivery to this valiant Greek
      Comes fast upon. Good my brother Troilus,
      Tell you the lady what she is to do,
      And haste her to the purpose.
TROILUS   Walk into her house;   5
      I'll bring her to the Grecian presently,
      And to his hand, when I deliver her,
      Think it an altar and thy brother Troilus
      A priest there off'ring to it his own heart.

                                        [*Exit*]

PARIS [*Aside*] I know what 'tis to love   10
      And would, as I shall pity, I could help! –
      Please you walk in, my lords.

                                  Exeunt

Despite the flexibility of his 'Elizabethan' stage, Poel cut 4.3, and like most directors, including Miller, ran 4.2 into 4.4. Payne (SMT 1936) did it as a night scene, with torches, watchmen and singing people moving about in front of the penthouse curtains, which reopened at the end to continue the Cressida scene. Barton and Hall retained it in 1960. Barton at first planned to include it then changed his mind in 1968 (promptbook). In 1996 Judge brought in torches at the rear and Pandarus and Cressida remained at the side while a few lines of 4.3 were spoken. At the NT 1999 Troilus rushed out into a bright light on the Olivier stage, then returned to Cressida. Occasionally a few lines (3b–5a and 10–11) are slipped in at 4.4.107.

    When kept, the scene gives Cressida a chance to change into traveling attire from her nightclothes. Rutter notes the importance of Cressida's departure costume, in which she will appear at the Greek camp. 'Designers have overtly simplified things in far from impartial designs that load Cressida's costume change with significance and so over-determine her later scenes.' (p. 126.)

OSD Although 5b indicates a street location, on Guthrie's bi-level set the men approached the downstairs hall area, Aeneas stepping onto the platform. They remained there between the end of 4.3 and 4.4.107, with Aeneas calling up. Photographs show that Macowan had a similar arrangement with a doorframe separating Cressida's rooms from an outer platform down a few steps, where the soldiers waited.

ACT 4, SCENE 4

[4.4] *Enter* PANDARUS *and* CRESSIDA

PANDARUS Be moderate, be moderate.
CRESSIDA Why tell you me of moderation?
        The grief is fine, full, perfect that I taste
        And violenteth in a sense as strong
        As that which causeth it. How can I moderate it?   5
        If I could temporise with my affection,
        Or brew it to a weak and colder palate,
        The like allayment could I give my grief.
        My love admits no qualifying dross,
        No more my grief in such a precious loss.   10

Enter TROILUS

PANDARUS Here, here, here he comes! Ah, sweet ducks!
CRESSIDA [*Embracing him*] O Troilus, Troilus!

In 1922 Enid Clinton-Baddeley played Cressida for laughs, 'so much of a spoiled child that it seems impossible for her to achieve the reaction towards dignity which is necessary to such a scene as the farewell to Troilus' (*LT*, 21 June 1922). More recently, Cressida has emphasized dismay at Troilus' behaviour. Juliet Stevenson's approach to the role made the 'weakest moment . . . the normally intensely touching scene of the morning' because of her doubts about men (Shrimpton, *SS 39*, p. 205), but did suit her gradual dismay at Troilus' ineffectuality. Many productions cut a number of Troilus' self-indulgent lines, making Cressida's half lines and growing impatience less striking. Papp felt all Troilus' talk prepared Cressida for Diomedes. He is 'caught up in his own speech' and 'fills her ears'. She is almost silent and 'knows it is over' (pp. 53–5).

OSD When the escort remained visible below in Guthrie's production it fit the production's downplaying of the love story. 'Even then the lovers were not allowed to claim undivided attention . . . with the impatient escort as prominent as the protagonists. Pandarus, fooling with his shawl and bustling about also distracted the audience' (David, *SS 10*, p. 131).

11SD When Troilus reentered in Guthrie's production, he helped Cressida fasten her travelling attire. 'The parting became comic, with Troilus trying to pin Cressida into her clothes between sobs' (Tylee, p. 67). Photographs show a grey walking suit with hat and ermine muff. In 1998 Ashbourne in her anguish had 'grabbed her suitcase from Pandarus, opened it, and hurled

PANDARUS   What a pair of spectacles is here – let me embrace too! 'O
heart', as the goodly saying is,
>   O heart, heavy heart!   15
>   Why sigh'st thou without breaking?
where he answers again:
>   Because thou canst not ease thy smart
>   By friendship nor by speaking.
There was never a truer rhyme. Let us cast away nothing, for we   20
may live to have need of such a verse – we see it, we see it. How
now, lambs!
TROILUS   Cressid, I love thee in so strained a purity
>   That the blest gods, as angry with my fancy,
>   More bright in zeal than the devotion which   25
>   Cold lips blow to their deities, take thee from me.
CRESSIDA   Have the gods envy?
PANDARUS   Ay, ay, ay, ay, 'tis too plain a case.
CRESSIDA   And is it true that I must go from Troy?
TROILUS   A hateful truth.
CRESSIDA   What, and from Troilus too?   30
TROILUS   From Troy and Troilus.
CRESSIDA   Is't possible?
TROILUS   And suddenly – where injury of chance
>   Puts back leave-taking, jostles roughly by
>   All time of pause, rudely beguiles our lips
>   Of all rejoindure, forcibly prevents   35
>   Our locked embrasures, strangles our dear vows
>   Even in the birth of our own labouring breath.
>   We two that with so many thousand sighs
>   Did buy each other must poorly sell ourselves
>   With the rude brevity and discharge of one.   40
>   Injurious time now with a robber's haste

clothes about' (Rutter, p. 114). At the Berliner Ensemble, 1987, Cressida became 'physically
aggressive', flailed her fists and clutched Troilus.

13ff   Pandarus may put his arms around them. In 1936 he pushed their heads together by 22 and
backed away. William Hutt's lower jaw quivered under stress at SFC 1963; he was 'easily roused'
but 'dashed by setbacks' (Alan Pryce Jones, *TA*, August 1963). At NYSF 1965 Pandarus reached
over the back of a stone bench while Troilus and Cressida sat close. In 1981 he was on his knees,
hugging Troilus' legs and showing concern for him rather than his niece. Quayle as director in
1948 had him merely put his hands on their shoulders, while in 1954 Quayle as Pandarus got
between them for a hug. In Barton 1968 he knelt over them as they lay on the floor. Joseph
Fiennes pushed him off in 1996 and he went to the stage right platform steps and hunched in an
almost foetal position.

Crams his rich thiev'ry up he knows not how:
As many farewells as be stars in heaven,
With distinct breath and consigned kisses to them,
He fumbles up into a loose adieu, 45
And scants us with a single famished kiss
Distasted with the salt of broken tears.
AENEAS (*Within*) My lord, is the lady ready?
TROILUS Hark, you are called. Some say the Genius so
Cries 'come' to him that instantly must die. 50
[*To Pandarus*] Bid them have patience, she shall come anon.
PANDARUS Where are my tears, rain to lay this wind, or my heart will
be blown up by the root! [*Exit*]
CRESSIDA I must then to the Grecians?
TROILUS   No remedy.
CRESSIDA A woeful Cressid 'mongst the merry Greeks. 55
When shall we see again?
TROILUS Hear me my love, be thou but true of heart –
CRESSIDA I true? How now, what wicked deem is this?
TROILUS Nay, we must use expostulation kindly,
For it is parting from us. 60
I speak not 'be thou true' as fearing thee,
For I will throw my glove to Death himself
That there's no maculation in thy heart,
But 'be thou true' say I to fashion in
My sequent protestation: be thou true 65
And I will see thee.
CRESSIDA O you shall be exposed, my lord, to dangers
As infinite as imminent – but I'll be true.
TROILUS And I'll grow friend with danger. Wear this sleeve.
CRESSIDA And you this glove. When shall I see you? 70

43–5   Speaight complained that by omitting 43–5 Poel missed the 'very essence of Shakespeare as well as the melodic line and symmetry of the whole speech' (*William Poel*, p. 198), but most directors cut those lines along with a number of others in Troilus' long protestations.

58ff   In Poel 1912, Edith Evans was interested in her reflection in a mirror as she adjusted a fashionable Elizabethan hat. More recently Cressida has shown dismay, becoming cold as Carol Royle did (RSC 1981), or throwing up her hands and moving away (Sophie Okonedo in NT 1999).

69–70 Rutter said Barton cut the token exchange in 1968 but restored it in 1976 (pp. 126, 29). (The promptbook shows it at 106, just before the Greeks enter, in 1968.) The exchange has often been updated with the costumes, since Elizabethan detachable sleeves don't fit modern or period clothing. Guthrie had both present gloves. Sometimes Troilus hands her a ribbon or band and she may give a scarf.

TROILUS I will corrupt the Grecian sentinels
         To give thee nightly visitation.
         But yet be true!
CRESSIDA   O heavens, 'be true' again?
TROILUS Hear why I speak it, love:
         The Grecian youths are full of quality,   75
         Their loving well composed, with gifts of nature flowing,
         And swelling o'er with arts and exercise;
         How novelty may move, and parts with person –
         Alas a kind of godly jealousy,
         Which I beseech you call a virtuous sin,   80
         Makes me afeard.
CRESSIDA   O heavens, you love me not!
TROILUS Die I a villain then!
         In this I do not call your faith in question
         So mainly as my merit: I cannot sing,
         Nor heel the high lavolt, nor sweeten talk,   85
         Nor play at subtle games – fair virtues all
         To which the Grecians are most prompt and pregnant.
         But I can tell that in each grace of these
         There lurks a still and dumb-discoursive devil
         That tempts most cunningly. But be not tempted.   90
CRESSIDA Do you think I will?
TROILUS No,
         But something may be done that we will not,
         And sometimes we are devils to ourselves
         When we will tempt the frailty of our powers,   95
         Presuming on their changeful potency.
AENEAS (*Within*) Nay, good my lord –
TROILUS   Come, kiss and let us part.
PARIS (*Within*) Brother Troilus!
TROILUS   Good brother, come you hither,
         And bring Aeneas and the Grecian with you.
CRESSIDA My lord, will you be true?   100

73ff During the ensuing talk of being true, Boyd had Troilus fold the clothing Cressida had scattered
      earlier, then close the suitcase and hand it to her (Rutter 114). Edith Evans was the first to show
      impatience with the reiteration. 'The exquisite by-play of this "woman of quick sense", and later
      her sprightly response to the kisses of the Greek lords, was beautifully natural . . . Cressida as a
      fashionable Elizabethan lady, with the languid airs and affected graces of a Court beauty, had the
      positive merit of creating, with cunning artistic detail, a real woman.' Troilus was, by comparison,
      'a study in absorbed, brooding passion' (Edward Garland, *The Contemporary Review*, February
      1913). Recent Cressidas have moved away during his speeches, or kissed perfunctorily at 96.

TROILUS Who I? Alas it is my vice, my fault:
        Whiles others fish with craft for great opinion,
        I with great truth catch mere simplicity;
        Whilst some with cunning gild their copper crowns,
        With truth and plainness I do wear mine bare; 105
        Fear not my truth. The moral of my wit
        Is 'plain and true': there's all the reach of it.

    Enter [AENEAS, PARIS, ANTENOR, DEIPHOBUS, *and* DIOMEDES]

        Welcome Sir Diomed! Here is the lady
        Which for Antenor we deliver you;
        At the port, lord, I'll give her to thy hand 110
        And by the way possess thee what she is.
        Entreat her fair and by my soul, fair Greek,
        If e'er thou stand at mercy of my sword,
        Name Cressid and thy life shall be as safe
        As Priam is in Ilium.
DIOMEDES   Fair Lady Cressid, 115
        So please you save the thanks this prince expects:
        The lustre in your eye, heaven in your cheek,
        Pleads your fair usage, and to Diomed
        You shall be mistress and command him wholly.
TROILUS Grecian, thou dost not use me courteously 120
        To shame the seal of my petition to thee
        In praising her. I tell thee, lord of Greece,

107SD A photograph of Hands' 1981 production shows her in a peignoir. She donned a loose dark overcoat and picked up bundles as she left. Pip Miller's Diomedes seemed far more mature than Troilus. In 1985, as the Greeks entered, Lesser placed his coat over Stevenson's shoulders, for she was still in her nightgown. A servant brought suitcases downstairs and sat on them while Troilus and Diomedes challenged each other. Although covered, Stevenson became more vulnerable and the man's coat seemed to mark her as a possession. 'It was an impropriety as great, given this production's vocabulary of costume, as setting Florence Nightingale naked in the officers' mess at Sebastapol.' (Rutter, p. 115.) In Payne's Elizabethan production Cressida curtsied to Diomedes. In BBC 1981, she was helped out of bed, as if in a trance.

114ff In 1938 Cressida was in a fashionable business dress and pumps from her entrance at 4.2.8, and added a jacket and hat. As she left she picked up a large purse. At ASF 1961 she had been in a white, eyelet-trimmed petticoat with dark ribbons. By the time she arrived in the Greek camp she had on an appropriate light, flower-sprigged dress (F. Shirley notes). In 1968 Barton rearranged some lines and made the action more physical than any hint in the text. Diomedes brushed past Troilus and raised Cressida from her seat on the bench and kissed her hand. Troilus hit him in the stomach, Diomedes fell, Cressida backed away, and Diomedes rose by 127 (promptbook).

She is as far high-soaring o'er thy praises
As thou unworthy to be called her servant.
I charge thee use her well, even for my charge,   125
For by the dreadful Pluto, if thou dost not,
Though the great bulk Achilles be thy guard,
I'll cut thy throat.
DIOMEDES   O be not moved, Prince Troilus.
Let me be privileged by my place and message
To be a speaker free; when I am hence   130
I'll answer to my lust. And know you, lord,
I'll nothing do on charge: to her own worth
She shall be prized, but that you say be't so,
I speak it in my spirit and honour, no.
TROILUS Come, to the port. I tell thee Diomed,   135
This brave shall oft make thee to hide thy head.
Lady, give me your hand and as we walk
To our own selves bend we our needful talk.
                    [*Exeunt Troilus, Cressida, and Diomedes*]
                    Sound trumpet
PARIS Hark, Hector's trumpet!
AENEAS How have we spent this morning!   140
The prince must think me tardy and remiss
That swore to ride before him to the field.
PARIS 'Tis Troilus' fault. Come, come to field with him.
DEIPHOBUS Let us make ready straight.
AENEAS Yea, with a bridegroom's fresh alacrity   145
Let us address to tend on Hector's heels:
The glory of our Troy doth this day lie
On his fair worth and single chivalry.

                    Exeunt

138   In 1956 Rosemary Harris had to dash back to pick up the token glove (Wood and Clarke). Barton
1968 had them exit through an arch of spears held by extras. In BBC 1981 she was still in her
nightgown, but a waiting woman followed with the tan dress she wore when she appeared in 4.5.
Guthrie put a second interval after Cressida's departure, as did Quayle and Macowan.

ACT 4, SCENE 5

[4.5] *Enter* AJAX, *armed*, ACHILLES, PATROCLUS, AGAMEMNON, MENELAUS, ULYSSES, NESTOR [*and others, with a trumpeter*]

Nunn considered the exchange of Cressida the play's 'watershed event' (*In*, 10 March 1999). The Greeks have assembled with a trumpeter at the start of 4.5, ready to sound their own challenge. In some productions they have seemed surprised to see, instead of Hector's party, 'Diomed with Calchas' daughter'. The Berliner Ensemble joined the two segments of the scene – Cressida's reception and the duel – by having Ajax jog past, 'warming up for the fight' during the kissing (Taylor, p. 229). Other productions have had Ajax present throughout, armed and ready, and not part of the kissing. He joined Diomedes in watching or, for Dromgoole, he groped Cressida as she was passed to Nestor.

Agamemnon almost always greets her with a courteous kiss. Her treatment after Ulysses' suggestion that she be 'kissed in general' has changed greatly during the twentieth century. In earlier productions, Cressida was dressed properly for her arrival and the men were polite to her, despite the banter, young Patroclus' grabbing two kisses, and Ulysses' comments (55–63) that often came after she had left. More recently she has appeared sending various signals: a conservative dress (ASF 1961), her nightgown (Davies in 1985), a revealing dress (Hands 1981; Judge, 1996) and the men have acted like any soldiers in an overseas camp, starved for female company. They have handed her around with varying degrees of roughness, sometimes threatening gang rape, and the kisses have become more possessive than polite. In 1990 she 'became soiled and perverted when treated like a parcel' (Neil Taylor, *PI*, August 1990, p. 21). Gary O'Connor found her 'more roughly handled than false (*PP*, August 1990, p. 29).

Cressida's reaction has also varied widely, though as Greene says, the men in this play are 'predatory' and her habit is to 'oblige expectation' (135–6). The most victimized was 'Jayne Ashbourne's plump, round-faced Cressida, cheerful, naive, and spontaneous, yearning for physical affection, . . . destroyed by the transfer to the Greek camp, the "kissing in general" . . . [and] a sinister orgiastic tango dance whose steps she had to quickly master or be destroyed, a drum beating all the time at the back of the auditorium to implicate us' (Smallwood, *SS 53*, p. 260). The following year Sophie Okonedo was also goaded into a dance and touched by the men as she swirled by them. In 1985 'Cressida [Juliet Stevenson] is emotionally raw and experiences the kissing game as a brutal sexual assault from which she defends herself by her only weapon: sarcasm' (Tylee, p. 73). In 1996 Hamilton found Achilles' kisses more interesting.

AGAMEMNON Here art thou in appointment fresh and fair,
　　　　　Anticipating time with starting courage.
　　　　　Give with thy trumpet a loud note to Troy,
　　　　　Thou dreadful Ajax, that the appallèd air
　　　　　May pierce the head of the great combatant　　　　　5
　　　　　And hale him hither.
AJAX　　　　　　　　　　　Thou, trumpet, there's my purse:
　　　　　Now crack thy lungs and split thy brazen pipe,
　　　　　Blow, villain, till thy spherèd bias cheek
　　　　　Outswell the colic of puffed Aquilon;

'Patroclus clearly aroused her, her leg wrapping itself around him in a way that Ulysses registered.' (Smallwood, *SS 50*, p. 214.) Earlier Cressida's have flirted and enjoyed the experience, though more decorously than Hamilton. Writing of Mendes' production, Holland considered Amanda Root best in 3.2. In the Greek camp there was 'no disjunction, no creative confusion out of which the ambivalence of character could emerge' (*SS 44*, p. 172).

OSD　The Greek camp is now generally devoid of tents, and the whole stage is used. Poel had the Greeks in front of the tableau curtain in straw-coloured limelight for the kissing segment. Payne (SMT 1936) opened his penthouse curtains to reveal a painted backdrop of Troy's walls, looking like Carcassonne. (In 2000 Dromgoole had a smaller scene of a distant city behind his scaffold.) 4.5 began Quayle's last act, and the house curtains rose on the Greeks and extra soldiers, two uncoiling a rope and bowing to Agamemnon as they set up a rectangle for the duel, with benches and shields on poles at either end (SMT 1948 promptbook). Guthrie cut lines 1–13 and opened with Cressida and Diomedes already on. In 1960 Hall and Barton had preparations in progress: stools were placed in and out of the sandpit, and there were banners. In 1968 Barton had one large and two small bull emblems for the Greeks. Davies (1985) established the ambience of the officers' club with drinks, a camera set up to record the match, and a billiard table under the balcony. Ajax practised with his foil while Agamemnon played billiards. Patroclus came down for a drink and returned to the balcony before 17. For the first time, Achilles was in uniform (promptbook). Thrust stages, like SFC's Festival Theatre or The RSC Swan, are left uncluttered and people generally stand. Small bleachers were set up in Ottawa (1978).

　　　Both Q and F include Calchas among the Greeks, and Monette brought him on to produce a sense of added degradation, for he is powerless to help his daughter (Kidnie). He also appeared in OSF 2001, with a 'look of fear . . . as he left her to the Greeks' kisses . . . but . . . if he . . . cared as much as this actor made him care, why send for her at all?' (Mike Jensen unpublished comment, 16 September 2003.) He may exit at some time before Diomedes offers to take her to him, or remain upstage, with Diomedes leading her to him and the three exiting at 63.

6b–10　There were extra trumpet calls here for fun in NYSF 1965, and Miller had jeers in the distance as Cressida came through the camp in BBC 1981.

Come stretch thy chest and let thy eyes spout blood,   10
Thou blowest for Hector.
                              [*Trumpet sounds*]
ULYSSES No trumpet answers.
ACHILLES   'Tis but early days.
AGAMEMNON Is not yond Diomed with Calchas' daughter?

Enter DIOMEDES *and* CRESSIDA]

ULYSSES 'Tis he – I ken the manner of his gait:
          He rises on the toe; that spirit of his,   15
          In aspiration lifts him from the earth.
AGAMEMNON Is this the Lady Cressid?
DIOMEDES   Even she.
AGAMEMNON Most dearly welcome to the Greeks, sweet lady.
                              [*Kisses her*]
NESTOR Our general doth salute you with a kiss.
ULYSSES Yet is the kindness but particular –   20
                  'Twere better she were kissed in general.
NESTOR And very courtly counsel. I'll begin.
                              [*Kisses her*]
          So much for Nestor.
ACHILLES I'll take that winter from your lips, fair lady.
          Achilles bids you welcome.   25
                              [*Kisses her*]
MENELAUS I had good argument for kissing once.
PATROCLUS But that's no argument for kissing now,

13SD Poel accompanied Diomedes and Cressida's entrance by Halberds. Francesca Annis had left Troy
      in a jeballah and had somehow changed en-route (Rutter, p. 129), becoming a replica of the stiff
      pottery Minoan snake goddess or priestess, with tiered heavy skirt and scale-like bodice, but
      revealing gauze over her breasts (RSC 1976). Diomedes removed a scarf to reveal Annis' upper
      bodice. Cressida entered in a black cloak in the Barton (1968) and Hands (1981) productions. In
      1981 Diomedes unwrapped her 'like a gift in figure-hugging red silk'. 'She is a new person, and
      her later switch is a peccadillo' (Michael Billington, *Gdn*, 12 July 1981). In 1996 'Victoria Hamilton's
      arrival in the Greek camp was a remarkable scene . . . Pushing her through the gate in the great
      wall of Troy, Diomedes stripped off the stole that covered her bare shoulders and upper breast.
      There she stood in a pale lemon, highly revealing dress, riveting the gaze of every man.'
      (Smallwood, *SS 50*, p. 214.)

18ff The blocking of the kissing has varied from a formal line-up, with Greeks stepping forward for
      their kiss and then stepping back into place (SMT 1954), to a fluid circle or grouping. At
      NYSF 1965, they started in a line in their armour, then became unruly as the kissing progressed.

> For thus popped Paris in his hardiment,
> And parted thus you and your argument.
>   [*Kisses her*]
> ULYSSES O deadly gall and theme of all our scorns   30
>   For which we lose our heads to gild his horns.
> PATROCLUS The first was Menelaus' kiss, this mine:
>   [*Kisses her again*]
>   Patroclus kisses you.
> MENELAUS   O this is trim.
> PATROCLUS Paris and I kiss evermore for him.
> MENELAUS I'll have my kiss, sir. Lady, by your leave –   35

Papp said 'The kiss substitutes for sexual assault' but is 'just as devastating' to Cressida (pp. 60–1), and his actors egged each other on with laughter and ribaldry. At Glasgow Citizens' in 1972 Achilles (Mike Gwilym) and scantily clad Patroclus (Rayner Bourton) were at the side at first, ignoring Cressida in her décolleté among the roughly clad Greeks. Sexuality was emphasized in the body poses (production photographs). In the earlier productions, where the men were restrained, Cressida seemed to enjoy the kisses and flirtation, and her behaviour was in keeping with the sensuous and light-hearted character revealed in 1.2. A Sloane School programme note shows the traditional interpretation: she is 'a heartless, inconstant person flattered by Troilus' love', and 'quick to distribute favours to the Greeks and accept Diomedes as a hard substitute for Troilus'. In RSC 1976, Francesca Annis was not troubled by the kisses (Styan, p. 264).

Since the 1980s the action has threatened to become a sanctioned gang rape, with Diomedes finally rescuing her. In 1985 Achilles and Patroclus came down from the mansion balcony when she entered. Stevenson slapped Agamemnon and was slapped in return, and the others reacted aggressively. Nestor pushed her toward Achilles, he picked her up, Patroclus grabbed her several times, pushed Troilus' coat aside and pulled her gown off her shoulder, then pushed her toward Menelaus (production film). By contrast, Barton's handling of the scene in 1968 had been restrained, though intensity built. Agamemnon held her hand and kissed her wrist, Nestor and Achilles gave straightforward kisses, and Achilles offered her somewhat forcefully to Patroclus (F. Shirley notes). More complex responses have been attempted in later productions. Sophie Okonedo, her head swathed in a veil, tried to wipe off Agamemnon's kiss. In 1996 Smallwood noted that Ulysses registered Hamilton's action, 'which fed directly into his savage denunciation of her' (*SS 50*, pp. 214–15). At OSF 2001, Tyler Lawton became 'hauntingly vacant, [the] ill-used love-token blond' (Winn, *San Francisco Chronicle*, 19 June 2001, p. E1).

27ff   By having Elaine Pyke play Patroclus, was Boyd having 'a Lesbian fantasy' as 'he' kissed Cressida, thus making Achilles' reaction more complex? (Rutter, p. 141.)

35ff   Cressida's exchange of wit has been either a genuinely flirtatious response to the men, or her handling of a situation that Yoder noted she is powerless to refuse, so she 'plays the game with wit and spirit, for that is her best defense' (p. 22).

CRESSIDA In kissing do you render or receive?
MENELAUS Both take and give.
CRESSIDA   I'll make my match to live,
    The kiss you take is better than you give.
    Therefore, no kiss.
MENELAUS I'll give you boot: I'll give you three for one.   40
CRESSIDA You're an odd man: give even or give none.
MENELAUS An odd man, lady? Every man is odd.
CRESSIDA No, Paris is not, for you know 'tis true
    That you are odd and he is even with you.
MENELAUS You fillip me o'th'head.
CRESSIDA   No, I'll be sworn.   45
ULYSSES It were no match, your nail against his horn.
    May I, sweet lady, beg a kiss of you?
CRESSIDA You may.
ULYSSES   I do desire it.
CRESSIDA   Why, beg then.
ULYSSES Why then, for Venus' sake, give me a kiss
    When Helen is a maid again and his.   50
CRESSIDA I am your debtor: claim it when 'tis due.
ULYSSES Never's my day, and then a kiss of you.
DIOMEDES Lady, a word. I'll bring you to your father.
        [Diomedes and Cressida talk aside]
NESTOR A woman of quick sense.
ULYSSES   Fie, fie upon her!
    There's language in her eye, her cheek, her lip,   55
    Nay her foot speaks, her wanton spirits look out

46ff   Stevenson (1985) had difficulty with the lines and hit upon pointing to the floor at 'Why, beg then.'
      Peter Jeffrey refused and became angry. In 1996 'Philip Voss' Ulysses is annoyed by Cressida's
      wit' (Paul Taylor, *In*, 26 July 1996). Styan felt Ulysses prided himself on being in control, and was
      angry at being outwitted (p. 265).

53SD   There is no indication of movement here in Q or F, but directors have occasionally had Cressida
      and Diomedes leave before Ulysses' comment at the end of the kissing. At SMT 1954 she bowed
      formally to Menelaus before leaving. The F 'exeunt' at 63 can't refer to the Greeks in general, who
      must remain, waiting for Hector, and may indicate Diomedes and Cressida as well as Calchas.

54b   On the Delacorte's huge stage, (NYSF 1965), Diomedes and Cressida gradually moved off, so they
      could be seen during Ulysses' description. In 1996, 'Cressida [Victoria Hamilton] remained on
      stage for that denunciation, taking it straight in the face and glaring defiantly back at him . . . not
      quite succeeding in hiding the damage it was doing to her – a painful, powerful piece of theatre.'
      (Smallwood, *SS* 50, p. 215.) Paul Taylor felt she was 'visibly shaken' (*In*, 26 July 1996, p. 6). In Utah
      Ulysses' description was cut, as it was by Guthrie, where Rosemary Harris was obviously a vamp.

At every joint and motive of her body.
O these encounterers, so glib of tongue,
That give a coasting welcome ere it comes,
And wide unclasp the tables of their thoughts   60
To every ticklish reader. Set them down
For sluttish spoils of opportunity
And daughters of the game.

> *Exeunt [Diomedes and Cressida]*
> *Flourish*

ALL   The Trojans' trumpet!
AGAMEMNON   Yonder comes the troop.

> *Enter all of Troy:* HECTOR [*armed*], PARIS, AENEAS,
> [TROILUS], HELENUS, *and Attendants*

AENEAS   Hail all the state of Greece! What shall be done   65
To him that victory commands, or do you purpose
A victor shall be known? Will you the knights
Shall to the edge of all extremity
Pursue each other, or shall they be divided
By any voice or order of the field?   70
Hector bade ask.
AGAMEMNON   Which way would Hector have it?
AENEAS   He cares not, he'll obey conditions.
AGAMEMNON   'Tis done like Hector.
ACHILLES   But securely done:

63SD   In Hands 1981, a 'steel grille clanged into place behind her, a maze that literalized her alienation from home, and her new vulnerability . . . or her new vocation' (Rutter, p. 129). The Greek shout 'The Trojans' trumpet' is often elided into 'The Trojan strumpet!' becoming a final comment and an announcement of the next episode. By having Cassandra say it carefully in Utah, the original words were preserved, as they were in Davies 1985.

   The kissing episode is generally played in its entirety, and the cutting in the scene occurs in the speeches leading up to the duel. Aeneas' mention of the relationship between Hector and Ajax, as well as the description of Troilus, are most frequently omitted. Hector's gracious words after the fight (119b–138a) are also often cut, and attention is focused on the duel and the later war of words with Achilles.

65ff   There often has been some preliminary humour as Ajax practises with his sword or spear. In 1985 the tables were moved into a square in Davies' officers' club and referees got into place and chalked back footmarks on the tables. The Greeks and Trojans poured drinks, placed bets and arranged themselves in chairs or up the mansion stairs. Achilles and Patroclus watched from the balcony. The combatants, in shirtsleeves, donned white protective aprons and goggles (RSC Promptbook). In Adrian Hall's 1971 TR production, they removed most of their modern outer garments, Ajax strapped on a phallus and Hector wore an athletic support and bandoleer.

A little proudly and great deal misprizing
The knight opposed.

AENEAS   If not Achilles, sir,   75
What is your name?

ACHILLES   If not Achilles, nothing.

AENEAS Therefore Achilles. But, whate'er, know this:
In the extremity of great and little,
Valour and pride excel themselves in Hector,
The one almost as infinite as all,   80
The other blank as nothing. Weigh him well,
And that which looks like pride is courtesy:
This Ajax is half made of Hector's blood,
In love whereof half Hector stays at home,
Half heart, half hand, half Hector comes to seek   85
This blended knight, half Trojan and half Greek.

ACHILLES A maiden battle, then. O, I perceive you.

[*Enter* DIOMEDES]

AGAMEMNON Here is Sir Diomed. Go, gentle knight,
Stand by our Ajax; as you and Lord Aeneas
Consent upon the order of their fight,   90
So be it, either to the uttermost
Or else a breath. The combatants being kin
Half stints their strife before their strokes begin.

[*Ajax and Hector enter the lists*]

93SD   Q and F rely on Ulysses' words to indicate when the fight has started. The combat has been
staged as anything from a brawl to a formal duel. Hector's challenge in chivalric terms mentioned
lances, which would suggest a Medieval tilt on horseback. In earlier productions, swords and
shields were used. On Payne's cramped Elizabethan stage, supers formed a barrier with their
spears, with spectators in a shallow inverted V behind them. Shaw had more of the SMT stage to
work with and used soldiers with staves, torches and tape to mark off the ground for a formal
fight. Poel had his duel offstage and used drums, the sound of blows, a crash, an alarum, and a
final long drum roll before Ajax returned, followed by Hector and Troilus (promptbook).
Dromgoole and Langham had both sides watch an offstage combat. Macowan probably did the
same, despite Crosse's note that it was completely cut (Notebook XVII). Parker complained about
'the taps of Ajax and Hector, arrayed in "mortal combat"' at Yale (*BET*, 19 June 1916). Wardle
noted that Hands' Hector (Bruce Purchase) was 'undercut by being presented as a comic opera
hero, and by the poorest swordfights' (*LT*, 8 July 1981) and Thersites 'groveled in the muddy stage
cloth' as they fought (Frances King, *ST*, 17 July 1981). Other weapons have been used. In Ottawa,
'some of [Mr. Wood's] staging is remarkable. The half serious duel between Hector and the
doltish Ajax is cleverly done. The battleaxes cross and cut at each other as if in an argument
rather than a fight. When Ajax finds the axe point aimed at his throat after each pass, it is a steel

ULYSSES They are opposed already.

AGAMEMNON What Trojan is that same that looks so heavy?   95

ULYSSES The youngest son of Priam, a true knight,
        Not yet mature, yet matchless firm of word,
        Speaking in deeds and deedless in his tongue,
        Not soon provoked nor, being provoked, soon calmed;
        His heart and hand both open and both free,   100
        For what he has he gives, what thinks he shows,
        Yet gives he not till judgement guide his bounty
        Nor dignifies an impare thought with breath;
        Manly as Hector, but more dangerous:
        For Hector in his blaze of wrath subscribes   105
        To tender objects, but he in heat of action
        Is more vindicative than jealous love.
        They call him Troilus and on him erect
        A second hope as fairly built as Hector.
        Thus says Aeneas, one that knows the youth   110
        Even to his inches and with private soul
Did in great Ilium thus translate him to me.

                    Alarum [*Hector and Ajax fight*]

AGAMEMNON They are in action.

NESTOR Now, Ajax, hold thine own!

TROILUS Hector thou sleep'st; awake thee!   115

AGAMEMNON His blows are well disposed; there, Ajax!

DIOMEDES You must no more.

                    Trumpets cease

AENEAS   Princes, enough, so please you.

AJAX I am not warm yet: let us fight again.

DIOMEDES As Hector pleases.

---

syllogism that pins him.' (Richard Eder, *NYT*, 26 January 1978.) Occasionally, as at the Old Vic 1956, stage traps are lowered slightly to make a fighting pit. The sandpit provided a space for a 'convincing' and 'well-developed' fight in 1960. Barton 1968 and Hall 2001 used follow spots to rivet audience attention. In 1996 Judge started the fight as a TV-style wrestling match, but the men moved on to sticks, conveniently placed in a large can nearby, and finally Hector heaved the can at Ajax (F. Shirley notes). In Nunn's 1999 production, white Ajax fought in tight black, while black Hector was in flowing white. They lost swords, banged shields, Ajax retrieved his sword, Hector grabbed it and threw Ajax. The spectators tend to give the combatants as much space as possible, even when a specific fighting area has not been designated. Achilles paid particular attention to Hector in NYSF 1965, and Hector tried to ignore him.

117   Diomedes may come between them. Papp felt his attention was on his future meeting with Cressida.

HECTOR   Why then will I no more.
        Thou art, great lord, my father's sister's son,   120
        A cousin-german to great Priam's seed.
        The obligation of our blood forbids
        A gory emulation 'twixt us twain.
        Were thy commixtion Greek and Trojan so
        That thou couldst say 'This hand is Grecian all,   125
        And this is Trojan, the sinews of this leg
        All Greek and this all Troy, my mother's blood
        Runs on the dexter cheek and this sinister
        Bounds in my father's', by Jove multipotent,
        Thou shouldst not bear from me a Greekish member   130
        Wherein my sword had not impressure made
        Of our rank feud. But the just gods gainsay
        That any drop thou borrow'dst from thy mother,
        My sacred aunt, should by my mortal sword
        Be drained. Let me embrace thee, Ajax;   135
        By him that thunders, thou hast lusty arms!
        Hector would have them fall upon him thus.
        Cousin, all honour to thee.
AJAX   I thank thee, Hector,
        Thou art too gentle and too free a man.
        I came to kill thee, cousin, and bear hence   140
        A great addition earnèd in thy death.
HECTOR Not Neoptolemus so mirable,
        On whose bright crest Fame with her loud'st Oyez
        Cries 'This is he', could promise to himself
        A thought of added honour torn from Hector.   145
AENEAS There is expectance here from both the sides
        What further you will do.
HECTOR   We'll answer it:
        The issue is embracement. Ajax, farewell.
AJAX If I might in entreaties find success,
        As seld I have the chance, I would desire   150
        My famous cousin to our Grecian tents.
DIOMEDES 'Tis Agamemnon's wish, and great Achilles
        Doth long to see unarmed the valiant Hector.
HECTOR Aeneas, call my brother Troilus to me,
        And signify this loving interview   155
        To the expecters of our Trojan part;

120ff   Directors have staged a variety of embraces, conciliatory gestures, hospitable invitations and a
        gradual relaxation until 179 when Hector mentions Helen. Armourers may help them disarm, as
        they did in 1960 Hall and Barton. The most frequent cuts come in Nestor's long speech (183–200).

Desire them home. [*To Ajax*] Give me thy hand, my cousin,
I will go eat with thee and see your knights.
                    Agamemnon and the rest [come forward]
AJAX Great Agamemnon comes to meet us here.
HECTOR The worthiest of them tell me name by name –   160
        But for Achilles my own searching eyes
        Shall find him by his large and portly size.
AGAMEMNON Worthy all arms! As welcome as to one
        That would be rid of such an enemy –
        But that's no welcome; understand more clear,   165
        What's past and what's to come is strewed with husks
        And formless ruin of oblivion.
        But in this extant moment, faith and truth,
        Strained purely from all hollow bias-drawing,
        Bids thee with most divine integrity,   170
        From heart of very heart, great Hector, welcome!
HECTOR I thank thee, most imperious Agamemnon.
AGAMEMNON [*To Troilus*] My well-famed lord of Troy, no less to you.
MENELAUS Let me confirm my princely brother's greeting:
        You brace of warlike brothers, welcome hither!   175
HECTOR Who must we answer?
AENEAS   The noble Menelaus.
HECTOR O you, my lord, by Mars his gauntlet thanks!
        Mock not that I affect th'untraded oath:
        Your quondam wife swears still by Venus' glove.
        She's well, but bade me not commend her to you.   180
MENELAUS Name her not now, sir, she's a deadly theme.
HECTOR O pardon, I offend.
NESTOR I have, thou gallant Trojan, seen thee oft,
        Labouring for destiny, make cruel way
        Through ranks of Greekish youth; and I have seen thee   185
        As hot as Perseus spur thy Phrygian steed,
        Despising many forfeits and subduements,
        When thou hast hung thy advancèd sword i'th'air
        Not letting it decline on the declined,
        That I have said to some my standers-by   190
        'Lo, Jupiter is yonder dealing life';
        And I have seen thee pause and take thy breath
        When that a ring of Greeks have hemmed thee in,
        Like an Olympian wrestling. This have I seen
        But this thy countenance, still locked in steel,   195
        I never saw till now. I knew thy grandsire
        And once fought with him; he was a soldier good,
        But by great Mars, the captain of us all,

Never like thee. O, let an old man embrace thee,
And, worthy warrior, welcome to our tents!   200
AENEAS 'Tis the old Nestor.
HECTOR Let me embrace thee, good old chronicle,
        That hast so long walked hand in hand with time;
        Most reverend Nestor, I am glad to clasp thee.
NESTOR I would my arms could match thee in contention   205
        As they contend with thee in courtesy.
HECTOR I would they could.
NESTOR Ha!
        By this white beard, I'd fight with thee tomorrow.
        Well, welcome, welcome – I have seen the time,   210
ULYSSES I wonder now how yonder city stands,
        When we have here her base and pillar by us.
HECTOR I know your favour, Lord Ulysses, well.
        Ah sir, there's many a Greek and Trojan dead
        Since first I saw yourself and Diomed   215
        In Ilium on your Greekish embassy.
ULYSSES Sir, I foretold you then what would ensue;
        My prophecy is but half his journey yet.
        For yonder walls that pertly front your town,
        Yon towers whose wanton tops do buss the clouds,   220
        Must kiss their own feet.
HECTOR   I must not believe you.
        There they stand yet, and modestly I think
        The fall of every Phrygian stone will cost
        A drop of Grecian blood; the end crowns all,
        And that old common arbitrator Time   225
        Will one day end it.
ULYSSES   So to him we leave it.
        Most gentle and most valiant Hector, welcome!
        After the general I beseech you next
        To feast with me and see me at my tent.
ACHILLES I shall forestall thee, Lord Ulysses, thou!   230
        Now Hector I have fed mine eyes on thee,
        I have with exact view perused thee, Hector,
        And quoted joint by joint.

230ff   Finally Hector and Achilles meet, and all the looking in the scene becomes a contest. In 1948
        Achilles touched Hector with his flywhisk as he mentioned where he would kill him
        (promptbook). Overt sexual fascination had been an element since the 1960s. Achilles posed
        scantily clad in 1968, and in 1996 he paraded in front of the Trojans, back to the audience, and
        opened his robe to show off his body or possibly to flash them.

HECTOR   Is this Achilles?

ACHILLES I am Achilles.

HECTOR Stand fair, I pray thee, let me look on thee.   235

ACHILLES Behold thy fill.

HECTOR   Nay I have done already.

ACHILLES Thou art too brief. I will the second time,
      As I would buy thee, view thee limb by limb.

HECTOR O, like a book of sport thou'lt read me o'er,
      But there's more in me than thou understand'st.   240
      Why dost thou so oppress me with thine eye?

ACHILLES Tell me, you heavens, in which part of his body
      Shall I destroy him – whether there or there or there? –
      That I may give the local wound a name,
      And make distinct the very breach whereout   245
      Hector's great spirit flew. Answer me, heavens.

HECTOR It would discredit the blest gods, proud man,
      To answer such a question. Stand again!
      Think'st thou to catch my life so pleasantly
      As to prenominate in nice conjecture   250
      Where thou wilt hit me dead?

ACHILLES   I tell thee yea.

HECTOR Wert thou an oracle to tell me so
      I'd not believe thee. Henceforth guard thee well,
      For I'll not kill thee there, nor there, nor there,
      But, by the forge that stithied Mars his helm,   255
      I'll kill thee everywhere, yea o'er and o'er.
      You wisest Grecians, pardon me this brag:
      His insolence draws folly from my lips,
      But I'll endeavour deeds to match these words
      Or may I never –

AJAX   Do not chafe thee, cousin.   260
      And you, Achilles, let these threats alone
      Till accident or purpose bring you to't.
      You may have every day enough of Hector
      If you have stomach; the general state, I fear,
      Can scarce entreat you to be odd with him.   265

HECTOR I pray you, let us see you in the field.
      We have had pelting wars since you refused
      The Grecians' cause.

254–6   Hector went berserk for an instant in 1968. In 1996 he pointed to Patroclus as the third place he
      would kill Achilles (F. Shirley notes).

ACHILLES   Dost thou entreat me Hector?
        Tomorrow do I meet thee fell as death,
        Tonight all friends.
HECTOR   Thy hand upon that match.   270
AGAMEMNON First, all you peers of Greece, go to my tent;
        There in the full convive we. Afterwards,
        As Hector's leisure and your bounties shall
        Concur together, severally entreat him.
        Beat loud the tabourins, let the trumpets blow,   275
        That this great soldier may his welcome know.
                [Trumpets and drums]
                        Exeunt [all but Troilus and Ulysses]
TROILUS My Lord Ulysses, tell me I beseech you
        In what place of the field doth Calchas keep?
ULYSSES At Menelaus' tent, most princely Troilus.
        There Diomed doth feast with him tonight,   280
        Who neither looks on heaven nor on earth
        But gives all gaze and bent of amorous view
        On the fair Cressid.
TROILUS Shall I, sweet lord, be bound to you so much
        After we part from Agamemnon's tent   285
        To bring me thither?
ULYSSES   You shall command me, sir.
        But gentle tell me, of what honour was
        This Cressida in Troy? Had she no lover there
        That wails her absence?
TROILUS O sir, to such as boasting show their scars   290
        A mock is due. Will you walk on, my lord?
        She was belov'd, she loved, she is and doth,
        But still sweet love is food for Fortune's tooth.
                                Exeunt

---

270   In 1981, Suchet did a finger-snapping dance, entrancing Hector. In NT 1999 'Dhobi Oparei,
      somewhat naively found himself swept up in an erotic dance with Achilles' (Smallwood, *SS* 53,
      p. 259). They had also danced in 1968, while in earlier performances as well as many later ones,
      there was the handshake the text indicates.

ACT 5, SCENE I

[**5.1**] *Enter* ACHILLES *and* PATROCLUS

ACHILLES I'll heat his blood with Greekish wine tonight,
        Which with my scimitar I'll cool tomorrow.
        Patroclus, let us feast him to the height.
PATROCLUS Here comes Thersites.

Enter THERSITES

ACHILLES How now, thou cur of envy,   5
        Thou crusty botch of nature, what's the news?
THERSITES Why thou picture of what thou seem'st, and idol of idiot
    worshippers, here's a letter for thee.
ACHILLES From whence, fragment?
THERSITES Why thou full dish of fool, from Troy.   10
        [*Achilles takes letter and reads apart*]
PATROCLUS Who keeps the tent now?
THERSITES The surgeon's box or the patient's wound.

This scene is often heavily cut to speed the action to Cressida's dramatic turn to Diomedes. Shaw (1954) eliminated all but Thersites' final speech. Nunn excised everything after line 44 except Troilus' exchange with Ulysses at the end. Generally the cutting is more selective – part of Thersites' invective and some of the lines of the returning Greeks. In 1968 Barton focused on the letter, as Guthrie had done. In 1990, Mendes let Beale dominate with his curses and reductive comments.

OSD   The setting has often been treated as a revisiting of 2.3 or 3.3, with Achilles' tent. Despite his textual cuts, Barton added many details in 1968. Patroclus entered with the bull's head, put it in front of the deck chair, and ten Myrmidons came with banners and crouched or sat until 44, then stood guard (F. Shirley notes). Moshinsky's treatment was static, with Thersites holding the centre of the cockpit for his long speeches. Davies (1985) considered it a continuum of the post-duel camaraderie, with Achilles putting bottles in a crate and Thersites entering with a tray and cloth as well as the letter (promptbook). Mendes staged it in very low light, very quietly, as a bridge between the activity of 4.5 and the emotion of 5.2. Nunn emphasized the tenderness of the Achilles/Patroclus relationship, and its good nature, with them wrestling on the ground as the scene opened, in preparation for the anguish at Patroclus' death.

PATROCLUS Well said, adversity, and what need these tricks?

THERSITES Prithee be silent, boy, I profit not by thy talk. Thou art
said to be Achilles' male varlet.   15

PATROCLUS Male varlet, you rogue, what's that?

THERSITES Why, his masculine whore. Now the rotten diseases of the
south, the guts-griping, ruptures, catarrhs, loads o'gravel in the
back, lethargies, cold palsies, raw eyes, dirt-rotten livers, wheezing
lungs, bladders full of imposthume, sciaticas, lime-kilns i'th'palm,   20
incurable bone-ache, and the rivelled fee-simple of the tetter, take
and take again such preposterous discoveries.

PATROCLUS Why thou damnable box of envy, thou, what mean'st thou
to curse thus?

THERSITES Do I curse thee?   25

PATROCLUS Why no, you ruinous butt, you whoreson indistinguishable
cur, no.

THERSITES No? Why art thou then exasperate, thou idle immaterial
skein of sleave-silk, thou green sarcenet flap for a sore eye, thou
tassel of a prodigal's purse thou? Ah, how the poor world is   30
pestered with such waterflies, diminutives of nature!

PATROCLUS Out, gall!

THERSITES Finch egg!

ACHILLES My sweet Patroclus, I am thwarted quite
       From my great purpose in tomorrow's battle: 35
       Here is a letter from Queen Hecuba,
       A token from her daughter, my fair love,
       Both taxing me and gaging me to keep
       An oath that I have sworn. I will not break it.
       Fall Greeks, fail fame, honour or go or stay,   40
       My major vow lies here: this I'll obey.
       Come, come Thersites, help to trim my tent,
       This night in banqueting must all be spent.
       Away, Patroclus.

                 [*Exeunt Achilles and Patroclus*]

17ff   In 1996, Patroclus and Thersites had grappled then embraced. Thersites kissed him and was
thrown off violently, and this caused the string of invective. In 1990 Beale used the entire list of
diseases, chanting and drawing them out. Menelaus has 'little or no personality', and Thersites
'pins his frustrations' on him (Beale, pp. 171–2).

33   In BBC 1981 'The Incredible Orlando', 'sibilant, bone bald, relished his lines' and 'made "finch
egg" a real insult' (Michael Ratcliff).

34ff   Miller heavily emphasized the letter, which the camera could focus on. In 1985 Achilles gave it to
Patroclus at 41, and he tore it up. Nunn (1999) showed Achilles kissing Patroclus tenderly just
after talking of 'my fair love' (Polyxena) at 40–1.

THERSITES With too much blood and too little brain, these two may   45
run mad; but if with too much brain and too little blood they do,
I'll be a curer of madmen. Here's Agamemnon, an honest fellow
enough and one that loves quails, but he has not so much brain as
earwax, and the goodly transformation of Jupiter there, his brother
the bull, the primitive statue and oblique memorial of cuckolds, a   50
thrifty shoeing-horn in a chain hanging at his brother's leg – to
what form but that he is should wit larded with malice and malice
farced with wit turn him to? To an ass were nothing, he is both
ass and ox; to an ox were nothing, he is both ox and ass. To be a
dog, a mule, a cat, a fitchew, a toad, a lizard, an owl, a puttock,   55
or a herring without a roe, I would not care, but to be Menelaus
I would conspire against destiny. Ask me not what I would be if
I were not Thersites, for I care not to be the louse of a lazar, so I
were not Menelaus. Hey-day, sprites and fires!

Enter HECTOR, [TROILUS,] AJAX, AGAMEMNON, ULYSSES,
NESTOR, [MENELAUS,] *and* DIOMEDES, *with lights*

AGAMEMNON We go wrong, we go wrong.
AJAX   No, yonder 'tis,   60
There, where we see the lights.
HECTOR   I trouble you.
AJAX No, not a whit.

Enter ACHILLES

ULYSSES   Here comes himself to guide you.
ACHILLES Welcome brave Hector, welcome princes all!
AGAMEMNON So now, fair prince of Troy, I bid good night.
Ajax commands the guard to tend on you.   65

45ff   Payne's 1936 promptbook directed Thersites to move 'ad libitum' during his soliloquy, ending up
in a 'watching position' right of the right stage column as the Trojans and Greeks entered laughing
from the left at 59SD. Barton (1968 promptbook) had him move and examine the bull's head,
finally pushing it back to the deck chair and spitting; singing and giggling could be heard offstage,
and the drunks returned. Occasionally the Greeks have begun to drift back in as Thersites talks
about them. In 1985, they were served drinks by extras and sang and drank.

59SD   The 'lights' are not only the conventional Elizabethan signal for darkness, but also provide the
'torch' that Diomedes will take when he leaves at 79.

62SD   In 1968 Achilles was born in on a litter with two large fans, his blond wig and languorous position
making the somewhat drunken Greeks at first mistake him for Helen. If Menelaus was made fun
of earlier in a production, he was often reeling drunk in this scene and had to be helped off by
Agamemnon and others at 70.

HECTOR Thanks and good night to the Greeks' general.

MENELAUS Good night, my lord.

HECTOR Good night, sweet lord Menelaus.

THERSITES Sweet draught! 'Sweet' quoth'a, sweet sink, sweet sewer.

ACHILLES Good night and welcome, both at once to those   70
        That go or tarry.

AGAMEMNON Good night.

                          Exeunt Agamemnon [and] Menelaus

ACHILLES Old Nestor tarries, and you too, Diomed,
        Keep Hector company an hour or two.

DIOMEDES I cannot, lord, I have important business,   75
        The tide whereof is now. Good night, great Hector.

HECTOR Give me your hand.

ULYSSES [*Aside to Troilus*] Follow his torch, he goes to Calchas' tent;
        I'll keep you company.

TROILUS   Sweet sir, you honour me.

HECTOR And so good night.

        [*Exit Diomedes, Ulysses and Troilus following*]

ACHILLES   Come, come, enter my tent.   80

        Exeunt [Achilles, Hector, Ajax, and Nestor]

THERSITES That same Diomed's a false-hearted rogue, a most unjust
knave. I will no more trust him when he leers than I will a serpent
when he hisses; he will spend his mouth and promise like Brabbler
the hound, but when he performs, astronomers foretell it, it is
prodigious: there will come some change; the sun borrows of the   85
moon when Diomed keeps his word. I will rather leave to see
Hector than not to dog him. They say he keeps a Trojan drab and
uses the traitor Calchas' tent. I'll after. Nothing but lechery – all
incontinent varlets!   [*Exit*]

80SD   In 1968 Barton's Myrmidons surrounded and escorted Hector and Achilles off hospitably.

ACT 5, SCENE 2

[5.2] *Enter* DIOMEDES

Over the years the scene has gained in complexity of interpretation as Cressida has been made less culpable. At first she was the shallow flirt and jilt, perhaps even 'whore' (113) in mind and action, interested in any man and quick to forget hero Troilus. The most flattering assessment was that, in Marlowe Society 1922, she 'was unable to resist compliments, well-meaning but unstable' (*BET*, March 1922). At The Players Edith Barrett became 'the glamourous symbol of the weakness that does corrupt, or else turns life to bitterness' (Richard David Skinner, 'The Play "Troilus and Cressida"', *The Commonweal*, 29 June 1932, p. 246). At Yale 1916, with its all-male cast, 'The great dramatic scene of the play . . . was particularly beautiful, and it brought out quite naturally the best piece of acting' from Troilus when he was betrayed (Tucker Brooke, *Yale News*, 20 June 1916). At the Old Vic 1956, Rosemary Harris was 'a slow, sensual, treacherous strumpet' and Jeremy Brett was 'straightforward' in his disbelief' (Brooks Atkinson, 'Mars is Mauled', *NYT*, 27 December 1956, p. 21). Guthrie had the scene played in full light, however, with the characters moving in a 'kind of blind man's buff', and the scene became funny, so Troilus' passion was not allowed to come through (David, *SS 10*, p. 131.)

More recently Cressida has been conflicted, or a victim who must seek the only means of self-preservation, or even a person frightened into yielding by Diomedes' roughness. W. H. W. found Cressida's 'switch from sincerity to wantonness' hard to accept, though Jennifer Hilary was 'baffled' rather than 'glib and predictable' (*Birmingham Mail*, 2 February 1963). Anna Calder-Marshall at BOV was also 'bewildered by the discovery of her own sensuality' (Michael Anderson, *PP*, July 1972, p. 72). At SFC 2003 Claire Jullien's performance 'grew enormously over the course of the run', and this scene became more complex (Kidnie). In William's earlier Ontario staging Lorne Kennedy's Diomedes used 'symbolic violence' and 'physical menace' toward Peggy Coffee and left her 'near hysteria' (Helms, p. 202). As usual, there are few stage directions except entrances and exits, but the lines suggest what is happening, and the director and actors have chosen different slants to put on the actions that are mentioned. Cressida has teased with the sleeve or been genuinely sentimental. Diomedes has been slightly playful or threateningly rough. Generally very few lines are cut until Cressida leaves. Poel, Barton (1969) and Nunn cut 36–43 and a dozen scattered lines before 111. Troilus' long lament is often shortened. Landau, Davies (1985) and Boyd, for example, retained the general shape of his thoughts by selective cutting. Most consistently excised are 141–51. Quayle and Shaw cut two dozen of the 68 lines before Aeneas' entrance, and even Hall and Barton (1962) shortened Troilus' laments almost as much.

DIOMEDES What, are you up here, ho? Speak.
CALCHAS [*Within*] Who calls?
DIOMEDES Diomed. Calchas, I think. Where's your daughter?
CALCHAS [*Within*] She comes to you.

Enter TROILUS *and* ULYSSES [*at a distance; after them* THERSITES]

ULYSSES Stand where the torch may not discover us.   5

Enter CRESSIDA

0SD Calchas occasionally appears, hands her to Diomedes and retreats into his tent (NYSF 1963; RSC 1985, 1996; NT 1999). Guthrie's Thersites, the reporter sniffing out a story, beat Diomedes to Calchas' tent. Characteristic of the additions in RSC 1976, Barton and Kyle provided a large Helen doll. Moshinsky had Thersites actually bow to Diomedes as he walked to the cockpit wall, climbed up, and commented from near the audience.

4SD The blocking can help the audience believe that Troilus, Ulysses and Thersites aren't seen or heard. Poel placed them to the rear, dimly lit by blue light, though they had to comment across Diomedes and Cressida. In 1936 a heavy bench stood in front of the penthouse curtains that represented Calchas' tent. Ulysses hid his lantern under it, and he and Troilus retreated behind the left pillar while Thersites went behind the right (SMT promptbook). The pillars of Payne's Elizabethan stage framed Diomedes and Cressida and concentrated audience gazes. Hodgdon wrote that Cressida and Diomedes were 'framed by male gazes', which 'are split as is Cressida's vision' (p. 277). In NT 1999 the onlookers carefully avoided the light of Diomedes' torch. Barton and Kyle placed Ulysses and Troilus in the same balcony Cressida had used in 1.2 to watch Troilus, and put Thersites in the opposite balcony. In 2001 Hall stationed them where Pandarus had watched the foreplay of Troilus and Cressida in 3.2 (Kastan).

5SD Cressida's appearance is important here, as is her conduct, which contrasts sharply with her actions as she entered in 3.2 (see Rutter). Brown, Payne's painted, lisping doll, initiated repeated kissing (forward behaviour in 1936). Ruth Lodge's Cressida (Macowan 1938) was 'not sluttish enough to make an ironic tragedy of Troilus' breaking his heart over her' (Ivor Brown, *Obs*, 25 September 1938). Rosemary Harris wore a 'flame-colored tea gown, slit to the knee, black stockings, high heels' (Wood and Clarke). The Berliner Ensemble Cressida had gone to the camp barefooted, but with Diomedes she wore 'trashy red high heels' (Taylor, p. 299). Victoria Hamilton appeared in a very revealing red dress that made 'her arousal of his desires by alternating passionate embraces, her legs twining around him, with sudden self-distancing, even more blatant' (Smallwood, *SS 50*, p. 215). Diomedes was bare to the waist, and Hamilton's sequins sparkled in the torchlight. Papp (1965) called Cressida 'assured' in contrast to 3.2. In RSC 1976 she wore a cloak to suggest the chill of the night. She also had on a cap and as she left, turned to reveal a second, courtesan's face on the back of her head. In 1985 Stevenson could do less to shift the balance in 5.2 than she could in 4.5, and was not helped by her costume. Suddenly provocative, she came down the stairs in a dirndle skirt and off-the-shoulder gypsy

TROILUS Cressid comes forth to him.
DIOMEDES   How now, my charge?
CRESSIDA Now, my sweet guardian, hark, a word with you.
                    [*She whispers to Diomedes*]
TROILUS Yea, so familiar?
ULYSSES She will sing any man at first sight.
THERSITES And any man may sing her, if he can take her clef: she's   10
    noted.
DIOMEDES Will you remember?
CRESSIDA Remember, yes.
DIOMEDES Nay, but do then!
                    And let your mind be coupled with your words.   15
TROILUS What shall she remember?
ULYSSES List!
CRESSIDA Sweet honey Greek, tempt me no more to folly.
THERSITES Roguery!
DIOMEDES Nay then –   20
CRESSIDA I'll tell you what –
DIOMEDES Fo, fo, come tell a pin! You are forsworn.
CRESSIDA In faith, I cannot – what would you have me do?
THERSITES A juggling trick – to be secretly open.
DIOMEDES What did you swear you would bestow on me?   25
CRESSIDA I prithee do not hold me to mine oath.
                    Bid me do anything but that, sweet Greek!
DIOMEDES Good night.
TROILUS Hold, patience!
ULYSSES How now, Trojan?   30
CRESSIDA Diomed –
DIOMEDES No no, good night. I'll be your fool no more.
TROILUS Thy better must.
CRESSIDA Hark, a word in your ear.
TROILUS O plague and madness!   35

blouse, her hair in a braid on one side, to meet Diomedes who stood under the steps smoking. For Stevenson and Hamilton, 'costumes . . . hijacked the scene . . . leaving no doubt how the assignation . . . would end' (Rutter, p. 130). Hall 2001 had a final costume change into 'a Grecian black leather jacket, with Diomedes' dark cloak . . . as a skirt. Her hair, which tumbled freely in Troy, has been tied back severely . . . Her body is now closely walled and defended. She will decide when to open the gates' (Kastan).

35–44a   Poel had a dumb show of Diomedes and Cressida courting while Ulysses and Troilus talked. Depending on the production, there may be tender touching or rougher pushing and pulling. In both NT 1976 and RSC 1996 they engaged in a long kiss and tight embrace.

ULYSSES You are moved, prince, let us depart, I pray,
    Lest your displeasure should enlarge itself
    To wrathful terms; this place is dangerous,
    The time right deadly. I beseech you, go.
TROILUS Behold, I pray you.
ULYSSES   Nay, good my lord, go off;   40
    You flow to great distraction, come, my lord.
TROILUS I prithee, stay.
ULYSSES   You have not patience, come.
TROILUS I pray you stay. By hell and all hell's torments,
    I will not speak a word.
DIOMEDES   And so good night.
CRESSIDA Nay, but you part in anger.
TROILUS   Doth that grieve thee?   45
    O withered truth!
ULYSSES   How now, my lord?
TROILUS   By Jove,
    I will be patient.
CRESSIDA   Guardian, why Greek –
DIOMEDES Fo, fo, adieu, you palter.
CRESSIDA In faith I do not; come hither once again.
ULYSSES You shake, my lord, at something, will you go?   50
    You will break out.
TROILUS   She strokes his cheek.
ULYSSES   Come, come.
TROILUS Nay stay, by Jove I will not speak a word.
    There is between my will and all offences
    A guard of patience. Stay a little while.
THERSITES How the devil Luxury with his fat rump and potato finger   55
    tickles these together. Fry, lechery, fry!
DIOMEDES Will you then?
CRESSIDA In faith, I will, la, never trust me else.
DIOMEDES Give me some token for the surety of it.
CRESSIDA I'll fetch you one.   *Exit*   60
ULYSSES You have sworn patience.
TROILUS   Fear me not, my lord.
    I will not be myself, nor have cognition
    Of what I feel. I am all patience.

    Enter CRESSIDA [*with Troilus' sleeve*]

63SD At the Berliner Ensemble the token was a red ribbon. 'Diomedes takes it, makes it a choker, holds
     her head back for a brutal kiss' (Taylor, p. 299). Peter Hall (Shapiro interview, *NYT*, 1 April 2001,
     p. 5:1) noted the importance of the sleeve 'as the last physical token of Cressida's past'.

THERSITES Now the pledge, now, now, now!
CRESSIDA Here Diomed, keep this sleeve.   65
TROILUS O beauty, where is thy faith?
ULYSSES   My lord –
TROILUS I will be patient outwardly, I will.
CRESSIDA You look upon that sleeve, behold it well:
          He loved me – O false wench! – Give't me again.
DIOMEDES Whose was't?   70
CRESSIDA It is no matter now I have't again.
          I will not meet with you tomorrow night.
          I prithee Diomed, visit me no more.
THERSITES Now she sharpens, well said, whetstone!
DIOMEDES I shall have it.
CRESSIDA   What, this?
DIOMEDES   Ay, that.   75
CRESSIDA O all you gods – O pretty, pretty, pledge,
          Thy master now lies thinking on his bed
          Of thee and me, and sighs and takes my glove
          And gives memorial dainty kisses to it,
          As I kiss thee.
          [*As she is kissing the sleeve, Diomedes snatches it*]
                    Nay do not snatch it from me;   80
          He that takes that doth take my heart withal.
DIOMEDES I had your heart before – this follows it.
TROILUS I did swear patience.
CRESSIDA You shall not have it, Diomed, faith, you shall not.
          I'll give you something else.   85
DIOMEDES I will have this – whose was it?
CRESSIDA It is no matter.

65ff   The ensuing teasing with the sleeve aroused Diomedes at NYSF 1965. Papp had her cry a bit at
       76, and he 'savagely pulls the sleeve from her hand' at 80. Payne's Cressida (1936) tied the favour
       around her arm, then pulled it off and dodged as he tried to get it back. In 1985 Stevenson
       dropped the sleeve over the balcony, then ran down to try to reclaim it. In the BBC 1981 tent,
       Diomedes leaned above her on a cot with the sleeve. Jeremy Brett's reactions (Guthrie 1957)
       were so overdone that they made his feelings seem less genuine, and made it harder to accept
       the convention that he was not heard by Cressida and Diomedes. In 1960, by having Troilus and
       Ulysses upstage and Cressida and Diomedes sitting on the front edge of the sandpit, Hall and
       Barton shifted the focus to Cressida. In most productions they are standing, and there is much
       more movement as they grab for the sleeve.

87ff   In Shaw 1954, Diomedes seemed more interested in the sleeve's former owner, though he might
       have guessed Troilus from 4.4, unless he was implying Cressida had a collection of tokens. After

DIOMEDES Come, tell me whose it was.
CRESSIDA 'Twas one's that loved me better than you will.
      But now you have it, take it.
DIOMEDES   Whose was it?   90
CRESSIDA By all Diana's waiting-women yond,
      And by herself, I will not tell you whose.
DIOMEDES Tomorrow will I wear it on my helm
      And grieve his spirit that dares not challenge it.
TROILUS [*Aside*] Wert thou the devil and wor'st it on thy horn,   95
      It should be challenged.
CRESSIDA Well well, 'tis done, 'tis past, and yet it is not:
      I will not keep my word.
DIOMEDES   Why then, farewell,
      Thou never shalt mock Diomed again.
CRESSIDA You shall not go; one cannot speak a word   100
      But it straight starts you.
DIOMEDES   I do not like this fooling.
THERSITES Nor I, by Pluto, but that that likes not you pleases me best.
DIOMEDES What, shall I come? The hour?
CRESSIDA Ay, come. O Jove! – do come – I shall be plagued.
DIOMEDES Farewell till then.
CRESSIDA   Good night! I prithee, come.   105
                           Exit [*Diomedes*]
      Troilus farewell, one eye yet looks on thee,
      But with my heart the other eye doth see.
      Ah, poor our sex, this fault in us I find:

he had the sleeve his thoughts turned from Cressida to the next day's battle and a challenge (Hodgdon, 277). Diomedes tended to be gentler in earlier productions, but by the 1960s the pair became more demonstrative and overtly sensual.

106ff   Poel closed the curtains on Cressida after her soliloquy, with the remainder of the scene on the forestage, while the Trojan 5.3 tableau was set. Shaw cut the soliloquy. At SFC 1987 Peggy Coffee was so hysterical that her soliloquy was 'virtually unintelligible'. The 'text of her collusion' gave way before the stage image of the terror of rape. William's production 'deconstructed the patriarchal representation of the vain and shallow coquette' and also 'deconstructed Troilus' vilifying of her' (Helms, p. 202). In 1996 Hamilton 'encapsulated [her] vacillation . . . "Troilus" was wailed out in a grief-stricken dying fall; "farewell" followed in a crisp, matter-of-fact dismissive tone' (Smallwood, *SS 50*, p. 215). Peter Hall (2001) said Cressida 'will hide her emotion' in her last soliloquy. 'All the spoken grief is centered in Troilus.' In 1965 Papp found the women in his audience sympathetic, but the actors were less happy with the idea of Cressida as the 'victim of men, their wars, their desires and their double standards' (p. 70).

                The error of our eye directs our mind.
                What error leads must err: O then conclude,   110
                Minds swayed by eyes are full of turpitude.   *Exit*
THERSITES A proof of strength she could not publish more,
                Unless she said 'My mind is now turned whore.'
ULYSSES All's done my lord.
TROILUS   It is.
ULYSSES   Why stay we then?
TROILUS To make a recordation to my soul   115
                Of every syllable that here was spoke.
                But if I tell how these two did co-act,
                Shall I not lie in publishing a truth?
                Sith yet there is a credence in my heart,
                An esperance so obstinately strong,   120
                That doth invert th'attest of eyes and ears,
                As if those organs had deceptious functions,
                Created only to calumniate.
                Was Cressid here?
ULYSSES   I cannot conjure, Trojan.
TROILUS She was not, sure.
ULYSSES   Most sure she was.   125
TROILUS Why, my negation hath no taste of madness.
ULYSSES Nor mine, my lord. Cressid was here but now.
TROILUS Let it not be believed for womanhood.
                Think we had mothers, do not give advantage
                To stubborn critics, apt without a theme   130

---

109   John Harrison (BR 1963) had the line spoken to suggest Cressida was 'not so much a daughter of the game as a Juliet who had faltered' (Sprague, p. 67).

111SD   In RSC 1976 Cressida stayed on through Thersites' couplet and laughed. Hodgdon wondered if she heard and agreed (p. 278).

115ff   In 1960 Denholm Elliott 'had no reserve of power to transform himself into a cold, resolved, "savage" for the last scenes, so he could only become tense and shout his anger' (John Russell Brown, SS 14, p. 130). Troilus' vocal tour de force is frequently shortened to make him seem less self-centred. In RSC 1976 'Mike Gwilym's fiery Troilus weaves a clamorous passion, setting the love affair inside its own verbal whirlpool . . . [and] moves marvelously into fury and despair.' (Mairowitz, PP, October 1976, p. 21.) In 1990 Ralph Fiennes was on his knees, holding her scarf, at several times during his speeches, then rising as Aeneas entered. In 1996 Joseph Fiennes' reaction built to a 'voice-cracking crescendo . . . though more technically dexterous than emotionally involving, a quality that seemed true of the presentation of the lovers throughout' (Smallwood, SS 50, p. 215). David Murray found Fiennes' tremolo 'tiring' ('All Sweat and Tangas', FT, 6 December 1996, p. 17).

For depravation, to square the general sex
By Cressid's rule. Rather, think this not Cressid.
ULYSSES What hath she done, prince, that can soil our mothers?
TROILUS Nothing at all, unless that this were she.
THERSITES Will 'a swagger himself out on's own eyes? 135
TROILUS This she? No, this is Diomed's Cressida.
    If beauty have a soul this is not she,
    If souls guide vows, if vows be sanctimonies,
    If sanctimony be the gods' delight,
    If there be rule in unity itself, 140
    This is not she. O madness of discourse
    That cause sets up with and against itself –
    Bifold authority, where reason can revolt
    Without perdition, and loss assume all reason
    Without revolt! This is and is not Cressid. 145
    Within my soul there doth conduce a fight
    Of this strange nature: that a thing inseparate
    Divides more wider than the sky and earth,
    And yet the spacious breadth of this division
    Admits no orifex for a point as subtle 150
    As Ariachne's broken woof to enter.
    Instance, O instance, strong as Pluto's gates,
    Cressid is mine, tied with the bonds of heaven.
    Instance, O instance, strong as heaven itself,
    The bonds of heaven are slipped, dissolved, and loosed, 155
    And with another knot, five-finger-tied,
    The fractions of her faith, orts of her love,
    The fragments, scraps, the bits and greasy relics
    Of her o'er-eaten faith, are given to Diomed.
ULYSSES May worthy Troilus be half attached 160
    With that which here his passion doth express?
TROILUS Ay Greek, and that shall be divulgèd well
    In characters as red as Mars his heart
    Inflamed with Venus; never did young man fancy
    With so eternal and so fixed a soul. 165
    Hark Greek, as much as I do Cressid love,
    So much by weight hate I her Diomed.
    That sleeve is mine that he'll bear in his helm:
    Were it a casque composed by Vulcan's skill,
    My sword should bite it; not the dreadful spout, 170
    Which shipmen do the hurricano call,
    Constringed in mass by the almighty sun,
    Shall dizzy with more clamour Neptune's ear
    In his descent than shall my prompted sword
    Falling on Diomed. 175

THERSITES He'll tickle it for his concupy.

TROILUS O Cressid, O false Cressid, false, false, false!
　　　　Let all untruths stand by thy stainèd name
　　　　And they'll seem glorious.

ULYSSES　　　　　　　　　　　O contain yourself:
　　　　Your passion draws ears hither.　　　　　　　　　　180

Enter AENEAS

AENEAS I have been seeking you this hour, my lord.
　　　　Hector by this is arming him in Troy;
　　　　Ajax your guard stays to conduct you home.

TROILUS Have with you, prince. [*To Ulysses*] My courteous lord, adieu.
　　　　Farewell, revolted fair; and Diomed,　　　　　　　185
　　　　Stand fast and wear a castle on thy head.

ULYSSES I'll bring you to the gates.

TROILUS　　　　　　　　　Accept distracted thanks.
　　　　　　Exeunt Troilus, Aeneas, and Ulysses

THERSITES Would I could meet that rogue Diomed. I would croak like a
　　　　raven, I would bode, I would bode. Patroclus will give me anything
　　　　for the intelligence of this whore: the parrot will not do more for　　190
　　　　an almond than he for a commodious drab. Lechery, lechery, still
　　　　wars and lechery, nothing else holds fashion – a burning devil take
　　　　them!　　　　　　　　　　　　　　　　　　　　　　　*Exit*

180SD In 1985, Troilus took a drink left over from the earlier party and finished it before he left.

188 Here and elsewhere in RSC 1976 John Nettles (Thersites) loses 'the moral rancour which *drives*
　　him to observe, to comment. He shows neither [the] cause nor the true anger . . . which makes
　　sense of his *concerned* witnessing of Cressida's seduction' (Mairowitz, *PP*, October 1976, p. 21). In
　　1990 Troilus dropped Cressida's scarf token as he left. Thersites picked it up, sniffed it, but
　　couldn't understand its import (Holland, p. 73). In 1996 Troilus dropped the scarf into the pit
　　where Thersites had viewed the scene and he brought it up for his final lines. Nunn's Thersites
　　spoke his lines very slowly and pointed to the audience at 191. In 1954 Shaw placed another
　　interval at the end of Thersites' speech, before the final movement to battle.

ACT 5, SCENE 3

[5.3] *Enter* HECTOR *and* ANDROMACHE

ANDROMACHE When was my lord so much ungently tempered
　　　　To stop his ears against admonishment?
　　　　Unarm, unarm and do not fight today.
HECTOR You train me to offend you – get you in.
　　　　By all the everlasting gods, I'll go.　　　　　　　　　　　　5
ANDROMACHE My dreams will sure prove ominous to the day.
HECTOR No more I say.

Enter CASSANDRA

Unless she had been brought in for 2.2 at a dinner, or earlier, as in Boyd, Andromache makes her only appearance here in the play's final instance of ignoring women's voices.

osd 5.3 seems to be an intimate indoor scene, early in the morning, though some directors have treated it as more public, either outside or in a great room of the palace. Aeneas had spoken of Hector's arming in 5.2, and the couple seem in the middle of their argument. Poel (1912) set up another Trojan tableau. One promptbook has all five characters on and posed, the other begins with only Hector and Andromache and follows conventional entrance directions. Shaw (1954) gave Andromache two ladies-in-waiting, though no attendants are called for, even to help Hector arm. In Hands she wailed non-stop, her anguish 'over-done' (John Bunker, *DT*). All Barton's productions elaborated the scene. In 1960 there were three banner bearers and three armourers upstage of the sandpit. In 1968 smoke billowed and two men with fans stood downstage. The Trojan emblem was brought on and Antenor, Paris and ten attendants entered and saluted it in 1976 (F. Shirley notes).

4ff Andromache often kneels or hangs onto Hector. Derek Godfrey established himself as 'cold and boastful' in Hall and Barton, and there was no pity at his death (*LT*, 21 August 1962, p. 11). In 1954 Hector tried to hand her off to her attendants, but she clung.

8sd At Stratford, CT, 1961, Andromache (Lois Kibbee), Priam, Troilus and Hector were grouped stage left in front of the mansion, while Cassandra took the stage-right plinth, hands raised. Miller's BBC 1981 Cassandra was much more in control here than in 2.2. Her hair was pinned up, a conventional indication of rationality, as compared to 'her hair about her ears' at 2.2.100. At 10, following Andromache's bidding, she joins her in kneeling to Hector. She is almost always in

CASSANDRA   Where is my brother Hector?
ANDROMACHE Here sister, armed and bloody in intent.
          Consort with me in loud and dear petition,
          Pursue we him on knees, for I have dreamt   10
          Of bloody turbulence and this whole night
          Hath nothing been but shapes and forms of slaughter.
CASSANDRA O 'tis true.
HECTOR   Ho! Bid my trumpet sound.
CASSANDRA No notes of sally, for the heavens, sweet brother.
HECTOR Be gone, I say, the gods have heard me swear.   15
CASSANDRA The gods are deaf to hot and peevish vows:
          They are polluted off'rings, more abhorred
          Than spotted livers in the sacrifice.
ANDROMACHE O be persuaded – do not count it holy
          To hurt by being just. It is as lawful,   20
          For we would give much, to use violent thefts
          And rob in the behalf of charity.
CASSANDRA It is the purpose that makes strong the vow,
          But vows to every purpose must not hold.
          Unarm, sweet Hector.
HECTOR   Hold you still I say.   25
          Mine honour keeps the weather of my fate.
          Life every man holds dear, but the dear man
          Holds honour far more precious-dear than life.

                    Enter TROILUS

          How now, young man, mean'st thou to fight today?
ANDROMACHE Cassandra, call my father to persuade.   30
                                        Exit Cassandra
HECTOR No, faith, young Troilus, doff thy harness, youth.
          I am today i'th'vein of chivalry.
          Let grow thy sinews till their knots be strong
          And tempt not yet the brushes of the war.
          Unarm thee, go, and doubt thou not, brave boy,   35
          I'll stand today for thee and me and Troy.
TROILUS Brother, you have a vice of mercy in you
          Which better fits a lion than a man.

black, and Andromache often in a contrasting colour (pale green in Davies 1985; red with a green
coat in OX 1999).

13b Hector may call his order off stage. In 1960 the armourer exited, returing when Troilus entered; in
     NT 1976 a boy was sent to command the trumpet.

37ff The focal circle on Mendes' Swan stage was closed and Hector stood there for Troilus' lecture
      (F. Shirley notes). Barton had him exercising and flexing his muscles in 1968.

HECTOR What vice is that? Good Troilus, chide me for it.

TROILUS When many times the captive Grecian falls,   40
      Even in the fan and wind of your fair sword,
      You bid them rise and live.

HECTOR O 'tis fair play.

TROILUS   Fool's play, by heaven, Hector.

HECTOR How now? how now?

TROILUS   For th'love of all the gods,
      Let's leave the hermit Pity with our mother,   45
      And when we have our armours buckled on
      The venomed vengeance ride upon our swords,
      Spur them to ruthful work, rein them from ruth.

HECTOR Fie, savage, fie!

TROILUS   Hector, then 'tis wars.

HECTOR Troilus, I would not have you fight today.   50

TROILUS Who should withhold me?
      Not fate, obedience, nor the hand of Mars
      Beck'ning with fiery truncheon my retire;
      Not Priamus and Hecuba on knees,
      Their eyes o'ergallèd with recourse of tears;   55
      Nor you, my brother, with your true sword drawn
      Opposed to hinder me, should stop my way
      But by my ruin.

Enter PRIAM *and* CASSANDRA

CASSANDRA Lay hold upon him, Priam, hold him fast;
      He is thy crutch – now if thou lose thy stay,   60
      Thou on him leaning and all Troy on thee,
      Fall all together.

PRIAM   Come, Hector, come, go back.
      Thy wife hath dreamt, thy mother hath had visions,
      Cassandra doth foresee, and I myself
      Am like a prophet suddenly enrapt   65

51ff   In the very physical 1968 staging, Hector and Troilus challenged each other, and Troilus knocked
     Hector's sword up (F. Shirley notes). Judge (RSC 1996) also had Troilus draw his sword and
     challenge Hector seriously.

58SD No matter how frail he had seemed in 2.2, Priam walks in here, perhaps leaning on Cassandra, so
     as not to distract the focus from Hector, but adding himself (and Hecuba) to the list of people
     whose premonitions Hector dismisses. At OX 1999 he was gasping. In 1990 he had donned a
     white uniform with black knee boots as if also preparing for war (F. Shirley notes). Barton (1968)
     had Hector and Troilus fighting again as Priam entered, and Hector pushed Andromache away
     when she tried to restrain him.

                        To tell thee that this day is ominous.
                        Therefore, come back.
    HECTOR   Aeneas is afield
                        And I do stand engaged to many Greeks
                        Even in the faith of valour to appear
                        This morning to them.
    PRIAM   Ay, but thou shalt not go.   70
    HECTOR   I must not break my faith.
                        You know me dutiful; therefore dear sir
                        Let me not shame respect, but give me leave
                        To take that course by your consent and voice
                        Which you do here forbid me, royal Priam.   75
    CASSANDRA O Priam, yield not to him!
    ANDROMACHE   Do not dear father.
    HECTOR   Andromache, I am offended with you –
                        Upon the love you bear me get you in.

                                            Exit Andromache

    TROILUS This foolish, dreaming, superstitious girl
                        Makes all these bodements.
    CASSANDRA   O farewell, dear Hector!   80
                        Look how thou diest, look how thy eye turns pale,
                        Look how thy wounds do bleed at many vents,
                        Hark how Troy roars, how Hecuba cries out,
                        How poor Andromache shrills her dolours forth!
                        Behold: Distraction, Frenzy, and Amazement,   85
                        Like witless antics, one another meet
                        And all cry 'Hector, Hector's dead! O Hector!'
    TROILUS Away, away!
    CASSANDRA Farewell – yet soft; Hector, I take my leave,
                        Thou dost thyself and all our Troy deceive.   *Exit*   90
    HECTOR   You are amazed, my liege, at her exclaim;
                        Go in and cheer the town. We'll forth and fight,
                        Do deeds worth praise and tell you them at night.

80ff   Cassandra fell to the ground in a peak of emotion for Shaw, and Hector helped her up. In 1961
       Jessica Tandy stood in full control on the plinth beside Landau's mansion steps, describing her
       vision. Her last couplet in Shaw's 1954 production was spoken as an afterthought. Often she has
       embraced Hector at her final speech, and the couplet resounds as unrhymed lines would not. In
       1968 the attendants moved in and armed Hector during her speech, which she spoke as if
       keening, and there was an echo. Judge had her silhouetted in the doorway against the red light
       behind the massive metal wall in 1996.

91–2   Hector often finishes arming here. In modern-dress versions, he buckles on a pistol, while in
       Stratford, CT, and other Civil War and period renditions it is a sword belt. In classically garbed
       productions, he takes up sword and shield. Priam helplessly embraces him before his last speech.

PRIAM Farewell, the gods with safety stand about thee.

[*Exeunt Priam and Hector separately*]

Alarum

TROILUS They are at it – hark! Proud Diomed, believe   95
I come to lose my arm or win my sleeve.

Enter PANDARUS

PANDARUS Do you hear my lord, do you hear?

TROILUS What now?

PANDARUS Here's a letter come from yond poor girl.

TROILUS Let me read.   100

PANDARUS A whoreson phthisic, a whoreson rascally phthisic so trou-
bles me, and the foolish fortune of this girl, and what one thing,
what another, that I shall leave you one o'these days; and I have a
rheum in mine eyes too and such an ache in my bones that unless
a man were cursed I cannot tell what to think on't. What says she   105
there?

TROILUS Words, words, mere words, no matter from the heart.
Th'effect doth operate another way. [*Tearing and scattering
the letter*]
Go, wind, to wind, there turn and change together.
My love with words and errors still she feeds,   110
But edifies another with her deeds.

Exeunt [*separately*]

96SD Troilus has heard the alarum at 94 and is leaving to fight when Pandarus enters, unaware of the
action in 5.2. In 1956 he sat, downstage, as if expecting another pleasant interchange. Often
modern productions make Pandarus' reference to his health (101) obvious, reflected in costume
and demeanor. In 1985, he moved in slowly on a cane, coughing. In 1996 he wore a shabby robe,
in contrast to his earlier camp finery. At SFC 2003, sparsely grey-haired without his wig, he was
coughing and covering his mattering eyes (Kidnie). In BBC 1981, there was a stream of people
heading to war, and Pandarus had to thread his way through them to Troilus.

111SD Pandarus often picks up the pieces of the letter before he exits. Troilus may add a shove (Davies
1985) or he may throw the letter at Pandarus (SMT 1948). Where this is Pandarus' last
appearance, 5.11.32–4 are added as a dismissal by Troilus. In SMT 1954; NYTh
1958; RSC 1998; and OSF 2001 he stayed on here to speak his epilogue, which seemed to flow
from Troilus' behaviour toward him as easily as at 5.11. In RSC 1985 he moved under the balcony
to the piano stool. He played through the ensuing scenes, with only occasional pauses, while
noises of battle – guns, crashes – could be heard and flashes became visible through the large
window on the stair landing and through the back door under the balcony.

ACT 5, SCENE 4

[5.4] *Alarum. Enter* THERSITES. *Excursions.*

The play's final series of vignettes (divided into eight scenes by editors) were dismissed as disorganized and ineffectual by early critics expecting one or two scenes with conventionally developed climactic action. No scene is longer than fifty lines; most are shorter, and often further divided. The sequence is ideally suited to film, with its ability to make quick cross cuts, or to the neutral location of the Elizabethan stage. Modern directors treat the scenes as a single movement, with players moving seamlessly on and off. The speed helps create the confusion and 'fog of war' on the fields outside Troy. Fry cut these scenes heavily. Poel also abridged his 'Finale' and gradually took the limelights through the day to sunset in 5.9. Macowan called the sequence 'War on the Greek and Trojan Fronts' (Programme, 1938) and added the sounds of modern battle. Directors have allowed opportunity for slightly expanded combat when stage directions merely say 'exeunt fighting'. Since 1960 Stratford has habitually added smoke, no matter what the period of the staging, and Gareth Lloyd Evans found it distracting in 1968 (*SS* 22).

The 'warriors treat war as personal', and there is no discipline, merely a series of individual meetings to settle scores (Wain, p. 129). On large stages, there has been a temptation to bring in extra soldiers and choreograph elaborate fights, as Hands did in 1981. From 5.4 on, Hands had 'silver helmets, spotlights in darkness and a moaning wind [that] was spectacular, professional, and not exciting' (Mark Amory, *Spectator*). Yale in 1916 lined up large phalanxes who matched swords in a tentative way as background for individual fights. 'As Mr Woolley construed "Troilus and Cressida", certainly there was a hint of "La Belle Helene" in the angular manoeuvres of the battle with which the action ends' (H.T.P., *BET*, 19 June 1916). Trevor Nunn's actors 'captured the fierce energy' of battle, the Greeks 'burly desperados in heavy metal, the Trojans . . . Saracens, in white armor, all that is left of chivalry'. Dromgoole's men fought in slow motion. Both of Hall's sandpits were the sites of gymnastic fighting, though Harold Matthews found the 1960 combats 'balletic' (*TW*, October 1960). In 2001, after a 'trudging' production, the lively battles spilled out into the auditorium (Bruce Webber, 'Shakespeare Staged in a Sandbox', *NYT*, 16 April 2001). In Barton (1968, 1976) and Judge, among others, the Greeks and Trojans were in very skimpy clothes. Smallwood commented, 'Since a good many hefty and dangerous-looking swords and spears were being flashed around to provide distinctly realistic stage effects, it was impossible not to wonder why their users had gone to so much trouble to expose the maximum area of vulnerable flesh' (*SS* 50, p. 212). 'The battles are never climactic. The play is about 'the

THERSITES Now they are clapper-clawing one another, I'll go look on. That dissembling, abominable varlet, Diomed, has got that same scurvy, doting, foolish, young knave's sleeve of Troy there in his helm. I would fain see them meet, that that same young Trojan ass, that loves the whore there, might send that Greekish whoremas-   5 terly villain with the sleeve back to the dissembling luxurious drab of a sleeveless errand. O'th't'other side, the policy of those crafty swearing rascals – that stale old mouse-eaten dry cheese, Nestor, and that same dog-fox, Ulysses – is proved not worth a blackberry: they set me up in policy that mongrel cur, Ajax, against that dog   10 of as bad a kind, Achilles, and now is the cur Ajax prouder than the cur Achilles and will not arm today; whereupon the Grecians begin to proclaim barbarism and policy grows into an ill opinion.

futility of war', and OSF 2001 shows this in 'a farcically grand afterthought' that Thersites 'savagely deconstructs' (Stephen Winn, 'Troilus Triumphs in Ashland', *San Francisco Chronicle*, 19 June 2001, p. E1). In 2001 Hall brought back the skeletons and bodies that had been visible during the Prologue and in 2003 Monette used technical effects – sound and light – to influence audience reactions.

OSD Mendes 'placed Ulysses, Agamemnon and Thersites . . . [in] the upper gallery, Thersites in a top hat, directing the show' (Holland, p. 74). At this point, however, he was still on the main stage for his soliloquy and meeting with Hector, and he occasionally returned from his post above (F. Shirley notes). The circle was now covered with a grate and light shone up to illuminate some of the combatants. On the small Swan stage there were short, fierce struggles between the named combatants. Beale called it a 'deadly circus act' at the time of the first Gulf War, with combatants at the rear and moving forward when their turn came to fight. In Guthrie 1956 Thersites had a camera and was onstage to photograph all the action (Wood and Clarke). Boyd had 'guns . . . on the stage . . . and shells were heard exploding off it'. In 1985 the piano remained as an artifact from a more gracious life as the battle surged through Davies' mansion. Pandarus, like the house, 'will prove a helpless civilian in the face of war' (Rose Asquith, 'Across the Trojan Line', *Obs*, 30 June 1985). He played 'the listless waltzes and hollow polonaises of Ilona Sekacz's music' (David Nice 'At the Barbican', *PP*, July 1986, p. 26). Flashes and sounds of gunfire were outside the mansion, and Billington found it 'close to Verdun' (*Gdn*, 8 May 1986).

In 1965 Papp had battering rams on stage as part of the siege. At Contact-Tara in 1993, with its tiny, partly cross-dressed cast, drumming staves produced the battle noise. Tension was created without blows being struck. In 1968 Barton mixed circus and formality, as Thersites entered with the tambourine and a boomerang and sprang through a hoop while warriors formed a temporary frieze of spear- and emblem-carriers at the rear. In 1996 the rear gates of Judge's great wall opened and the Greeks appeared as Thersites, a sort of temporary master-of-ceremonies, mentioned them.

Enter DIOMEDES *and* TROILUS

Soft, here comes sleeve and t'other.
TROILUS Fly not, for shouldst thou take the river Styx,   15
I would swim after.
DIOMEDES   Thou dost miscall retire:
I do not fly, but advantageous care
Withdrew me from the odds of multitude –
Have at thee!
THERSITES Hold thy whore, Grecian! Now for thy whore, Trojan! –   20
now the sleeve, now the sleeve!
[*Exeunt Troilus and Diomedes fighting*]

Enter HECTOR

HECTOR What art, Greek, art thou for Hector's match?
Art thou of blood and honour?
THERSITES No! No, I am a rascal, a scurvy railing knave, a very filthy
rogue.   25
HECTOR I do believe thee, live.   [*Exit*]
THERSITES God-a-mercy that thou wilt believe me! But a plague break
thy neck for frighting me. What's become of the wenching rogues?
I think they have swallowed one another – I would laugh at that
miracle; yet in a sort, lechery eats itself. I'll seek them.   *Exit*   30

13SD Two Myrmidons came on with banners in Shaw 1954 and remained through the whole final
sequence. In 1948 Thersites sat as Diomedes and Troilus fought in front of Quayle's broken
blocks and stubs of columns that were tilted to suggest a classical ruin. In Stratford, CT, cannon
were wheeled in beside the southern mansion and from this point on there were occasional
shots, Landau's version of rebel yells, and rifle fire. The pillars of the mansion partially collapsed
and 'destruction becomes distraction' as the 'fraternal bloodbath' begins (Judith Crist, *NYHT*,
24 July 1961). Motley provided two-handed swords for Troilus and Diomedes, though Civil War
swords were smaller and less dramatic. Roger Planchon, at Theatre de la Cité in 1964 used a
folding screen on a central axis that could be turned rapidly. During the battle, its walls seemed to
split apart, becoming panels, sections and hollow frames that the actors stumbled through
(*LT*, 5 February 1964).

30 Guthrie had brought the Myrmidons up from the pit during Thersites' speech, and they attacked a
couple of extras as the scene ended.

ACT 5, SCENE 5

[5.5] *Enter* DIOMEDES *and* SERVANT

DIOMEDES Go, go, my servant, take thou Troilus' horse,
    Present the fair steed to my lady Cressid.
    Fellow, commend my service to her beauty;
    Tell her I have chastised the amorous Trojan
    And am her knight by proof.
SERVANT   I go my lord.   *[Exit]*   5

Enter AGAMEMNON

AGAMEMNON Renew, renew! The fierce Polydamas
    Hath beat down Menon, bastard Margarelon
    Hath Doreus prisoner,
    And stands colossus-wise waving his beam

Often some of the heightened descriptions are slightly cut and the focus is on Patroclus' name. Ulysses increases the sense of speed when he announces that Achilles is already arming in response to Patroclus' death. Ajax has also been transformed from a holdout (5.4.12) to a foaming battler at 5.5.36 by the death of a friend.

OSD   Shakespeare concentrated on the results of Patroclus' death. Directors sometimes add details here, before or after Diomedes' orders to his servant that inform the audience of the outcome of his first fight with Troilus. In 1960 Barton and Hall staged a major fight between 5.4 and 5.5, and as the soldiers were going off, Patroclus screamed. Barton was more explicit in 1968. Patroclus came from upstage between 5.4 and 5.5 and challenged Hector and his spearmen. Hector killed him, then fought his way out against other Greeks. Thersites, who had been watching, spat on Patroclus' body. Agamemnon's speech was cut and Nestor came on, spotted the body and ordered it borne off (RSC promptbook). In 1996 'We saw . . . Hector kill the unarmed Patroclus; we saw Achilles discover the body and cradle it lovingly in his arms' (Smallwood, *SS 50*, p. 215). Boyd made the most radical changes in 1998. He added 'the death of Patroclus . . . [as] a mimed assassination, one pistol shot by Diomed, organized by Ulysses, their final card in the attempt to bring Achilles back into the fray' (Smallwood, *SS 53*, p. 260). The BBC 1981 brought in the news of Patroclus as a dispatch. In contrast to the fashion to have scantily clad classical warriors, at BOV 1979 Richard Cottrell brought in well-armed and fully clothed soldiers at this point to fight and stand guard through 5.8.

Upon the pashèd corpses of the kings,   10
Epistrophus and Cedius. Polyxenes is slain,
Amphimachus and Thoas deadly hurt,
Patroclus ta'en or slain, and Palamedes
Sore hurt and bruised. The dreadful Sagittary
Appals our numbers – haste we, Diomed,   15
To reinforcement, or we perish all.

Enter NESTOR [*and others*]

NESTOR Go, bear Patroclus' body to Achilles,
And bid the snail-paced Ajax arm for shame.
There is a thousand Hectors in the field:
Now here he fights on Galathe his horse,   20
And there lacks work; anon he's there afoot,
And there they fly, or die, like scaling schools
Before the belching whale; then is he yonder,
And there the strawy Greeks, ripe for his edge,
Fall down before him like a mower's swath.   25
Here, there, and everywhere he leaves and takes,
Dexterity so obeying appetite
That what he will he does, and does so much
That proof is called impossibility.

Enter ULYSSES

ULYSSES O courage, courage, princes, great Achilles   30
Is arming – weeping, cursing, vowing vengeance.
Patroclus' wounds have roused his drowsy blood,
Together with his mangled Myrmidons
That noseless, handless, hacked and chipped, come to him

16SD Soldiers have sometimes accompanied Nestor with Patroclus' body, which he then orders carried off (NYSF 1965; NT 1976). Guthrie's Myrmidons brought it in on a stretcher, with Thersites escorting them (F. Shirley notes). In Shaw 1954 Patroclus staggered on and fainted, and Nestor's soldiers bore him off. Nestor may also stagger a bit, as he did in SMT 1948, though he is no longer a figure of comedy. Judge made a major cut in the action. Patroclus' body was carried on and off, and Hector was brought in on a platform at the rear where he stood elevated as a symbol while Nestor talked about him. Hector was seen fighting with a knight in fancy armour, then he threw down his sword and shield and the action moved on to 5.9 (RSC 1996 promptbook).

29SD In 1985 Ulysses entered the mansion and smoke billowed in, while Pandarus continued to play 'like a brothel-musician in a revolution' (Billington, *Gdn*, 8 May 1986). Achilles' tent area was on the balcony, and Patroclus' body was carried up to him. Ulysses came back out from the curtains and announced from the stair landing that Achilles was arming. Achilles could be heard roaring.

Crying on Hector. Ajax hath lost a friend   35
And foams at mouth, and he is armed and at it,
Roaring for Troilus who hath done today
Mad and fantastic execution,
Engaging and redeeming of himself
With such a careless force and forceless care   40
As if that lust, in very spite of cunning,
Bade him win all.

Enter AJAX

AJAX Troilus, thou coward, Troilus!   *Exit*
DIOMEDES   Ay there, there!   *Exit*
NESTOR So, so we draw together.

Enter ACHILLES

ACHILLES   Where is this Hector?
Come, come, thou boy-queller, show thy face,   45
Know what it is to meet Achilles angry.
Hector! Where's Hector? I will none but Hector.

[*Exeunt*]

44SD   After Ajax and Diomedes have charged through, Achilles enters. At GC in 1973 he was holding the
rigid body of Patroclus in his arms. In 1981 he carried the body over his shoulder and roared with
rage. In 1985 he rushed down the steps and spun across the stage in his anger. Where the war is
made a subject of cynical fun, he may come on inappropriately dressed. At NYSF 1973 he was
wearing a green-spotted feather boa and matching trunks.

[**5.6**] *Enter* AJAX

AJAX Troilus, thou coward Troilus, show thy head!

Enter DIOMEDES

DIOMEDES Troilus I say, where's Troilus?
AJAX   What wouldst thou?
DIOMEDES I would correct him.
AJAX Were I the general, thou shouldst have my office
      Ere that correction. Troilus I say, what, Troilus!   5

Enter TROILUS

TROILUS O traitor Diomed, turn thy false face, thou traitor,
      And pay the life thou ow'st me for my horse.
DIOMEDES Ha, art thou there?
AJAX I'll fight with him alone – stand, Diomed.
DIOMEDES He is my prize, I will not look upon.   10
TROILUS Come both you cogging Greeks, have at you both!

Enter HECTOR

Exit Troilus [*fighting with Ajax and Diomedes*]
HECTOR Yea Troilus, O well fought, my youngest brother!

Ajax and Diomedes have occasionally been treated as comic prima donnas as they argue about who will engage revenge-bent Troilus. Hector's fight with Achilles has ranged from a few short strokes to a long enough fight to demonstrate the Greek's lack of conditioning. In modern-dress productions, the sumptuous armour segment is often cut, for want of suitable trophy accoutrements.

OSD   Ajax and Diomedes often enter together. In RSC 1968 they had attendants carrying bull emblems and when Troilus came on he had an attendant with a sphinx emblem.

11SD Moshinsky let Hector engage Ajax when he entered, giving Troilus a better chance, as he fell and rose to continue fighting Diomedes. In 1968 Diomedes and Troilus had the main fight, and Ajax moved in, was slightly wounded, and exchanged a few strokes with Hector as he left. Hector then drove out the men carrying the bull emblems (F. Shirley notes).

Enter ACHILLES

ACHILLES Now do I see thee, ha! have at thee, Hector.
     [*They fight; Achilles is subdued*]
HECTOR Pause if thou wilt.
ACHILLES I do disdain thy courtesy, proud Trojan.   15
   Be happy that my arms are out of use.
   My rest and negligence befriends thee now,
   But thou anon shalt hear of me again.
   Till when, go seek thy fortune.   *Exit*
HECTOR   Fare thee well.
   I would have been much more a fresher man,   20
   Had I expected thee.

Enter TROILUS

     How now my brother!
TROILUS Ajax hath ta'en Aeneas – shall it be?
   No, by the flame of yonder glorious heaven,
   He shall not carry him. I'll be ta'en too,
   Or bring him off. Fate hear me what I say,   25
   I reck not though I end my life today.   *Exit*

Enter one in [*sumptuous*] *armour*

13ff In 1960 Achilles and Hector were fully armed, with greaves, breastplates, wrist-guards and shields. Hector had a crested helmet and short cape, while Achilles had a plumed helmet and long cape as they moved about the sandpit. In later Barton productions, the men had almost no armour except their helmets, swords and shields. In 1990 the fights were intense but made difficult by two-handed swords on the small Swan stage. Hector and Achilles engaged in a long fight in SFC 1963. Hector (John Colicos) and Achilles (Leo Ciceri) started with swords and shields, and moved around the entire stage, very close to the audience (F. Shirley notes). Achilles lost his sword and shield and drew a bullwhip from his belt before retreating. Achilles collapsed in 1985. He managed a long fight in OX 2000 (F. Shirley notes). Hector and Achilles sat after their fight in 1968 and Barton transposed 5.8.4–12 to 5.6.21 and moved the sumptuous armour to the end of 5.7 (promptbook). Poel moved lines 15–19 to the end of 5.7, where Achilles spoke, left and returned with his Myrmidons for 5.9.

26SD In classically garbed productions, the rich armour is usually gold and includes breast and back plates, helmet and shield. Moshinsky added a gold-lined cloak. In scantily clad productions, the full armour is doubly striking. Despite his fatigue, Hector gives no quarter to the elaborately clad figure, showing himself susceptible to greed.

HECTOR Stand, stand, thou Greek, thou art a goodly mark.
        No? wilt thou not? I like thy armour well:
        I'll frush it and unlock the rivets all,
        But I'll be master of it.

                        [*Exit the one in sumptuous armour*]
                    Wilt thou not, beast, abide?   30
        Why then, fly on: I'll hunt thee for thy hide.   *Exit*

ACT 5, SCENE 7

[5.7] *Enter* ACHILLES *with Myrmidons*

ACHILLES Come here about me, you my Myrmidons,
        Mark what I say. Attend me where I wheel,
        Strike not a stroke, but keep yourselves in breath;
        And when I have the bloody Hector found,
        Empale him with your weapons round about,   5
        In fellest manner execute your arms.
        Follow me sirs, and my proceedings eye:
        It is decreed Hector the great must die.

                                    [*Exeunt*]

The Myrmidons have been called 'The Dirty Tricks Squad'. In several productions they have already been present to serve Achilles, most notably in Quayle, with their polka-dotted shirts and ear-flap caps, where they did not look particularly fierce, and Barton's 1968 and 1976 productions. Generally they have been in black, large and coarse-looking, and, if classically garbed, with helmets that hide their eyes and depersonalize them into killing machines. Recent modern-dress productions have used culturally typed street gangs or bikers, often in studded leather (BR 1963; SFC 1987). They may look beaten up (see 5.5.33–5a) and eager for revenge. The moves of 5.9 are orchestrated here, as Achilles exhibits 'low professional cunning' (*LT*, 17 March 1940, p. 6, referring to the Marlowe Society under George Rylands).

OSD   Originally Guthrie planned to isolate this from the battle scenes by dropping the curtain and having them on the fore-stage, but changed his mind (1956 promptbook). In Woolley's Yale production, the Myrmidons crouched servilely (H.T.P., *BET*, 19 June 1916). Barton arranged ten Myrmidons in a horseshoe downstage from Achilles in 1968. In BOV 1979, they stood in distinctive spiked helmets and cheek-pieces that revealed only their eyes and noses. In 1985 Davies had just five Myrmidons ringed around Achilles, and his speech was accompanied by pyrotechnic flashes of offstage battle. In 1990 Mendes had the meeting of the Myrmidons upstage, away from the fighting area, followed immediately by the entrance of Thersites and a comic semi-fight between him and Margarelon. The silent meeting of Paris and Menelaus had been cut. At the BBC 1981, Miller used his camera to advantage, making this a closeup. Achilles calmly trimmed his beard, using a hand mirror, as he instructed the Myrmidons, who stood behind him in his tent.

ACT 5, SCENE 8

[5.8] *Enter* MENELAUS *and* PARIS [*fighting, and*] THERSITES [*watching*]

THERSITES The cuckold and the cuckold-maker are at it! Now bull,
  now dog! 'Loo Paris 'loo! Now my double-horned Spartan! 'Loo
  Paris 'loo! The bull has the game: ware horns, ho!
                                        [*Exeunt*] *Paris and Menelaus*

          Enter Bastard [MARGARELON]

MARGARELON Turn, slave, and fight.
THERSITES What art thou?   5
MARGARELON A bastard son of Priam's.
THERSITES I am a bastard too, I love bastards! I am bastard begot,
  bastard instructed, bastard in mind, bastard in valour, in everything
  illegitimate. One bear will not bite another, and wherefore should
  one bastard? Take heed, the quarrel's most ominous to us: if the   10
  son of a whore fight for a whore, he tempts judgement. Farewell,
  bastard.   [*Exit*]
MARGARELON The devil take thee, coward.   *Exit*

Thersites helps the audience keep track of the combatants and his comments also serve as stage
directions, for he says Menelaus has the advantage, though again there is no conclusion to the
struggle. Guthrie cut the scene. Moshinsky and Mendes cut Paris and Menelaus and began at
line 4.

OSD In 1976 NT, Thersites had been sitting on the cockpit wall, occasionally shifting his position, as he
watched the fighting. He moved slightly but did not come down at Margarelon's challenge.
Thersites is always unarmed. If a correspondent, he usually had a camera or notebook.

13 Papp rearranged the lines so Thersites closed the scene with 'Farewell bastard'. In BBC 1981
Thersites gave Margarelon a raspberry. Thersites usually has left here and presumably survives,
though in Connecticut 1961, he was riddled with bullets and at NYTh in 1987 he died in a Middle
Eastern hospital amid other victims of the fighting.

[5.9] *Enter* HECTOR

HECTOR Most putrefièd core, so fair without,
        Thy goodly armour thus hath cost thy life.
        Now is my day's work done, I'll take my breath.
        Rest sword, thou hast thy fill of blood and death.
                           [*He disarms*]

Enter ACHILLES *and* MYRMIDONS

The lighting has often suggested sunset on the play's third day. After the swirl of short inconclusive episodes, directors have usually taken pains to stage the scene impressively and for shock value. Fry was an exception in 1907, when he had Troilus merely announce details in the manner of a Greek messenger reporting a death. Carados found all his cuts excusable except this one (*The Referee*, 2 June 1907). Occasionally the Myrmidons have been omitted, and Achilles actually does the killing he brags of, but always in an unfair manner. In OX 2000 Hector was sitting on the ground and Achilles pulled back his head from behind and slit his throat (F. Shirley notes). In Barton 1968 the Myrmidons started the attack, then Achilles finished Hector off, making his brag truthful. The same year, in HSSR Achilles, 'a cruel hulk', looking like 'an Andy Warhol movie sadist' in his shining black overalls, slashed Hector's throat to finish the job (Roderick Nordell, *CSM*, 7 August 1968; Stephen Mindick, *Boston After Dark*, 14 August 1968). The black garb of the Myrmidons echoes the 'dark'ning of the sun' (7).

osd Where the knight whose fancy armour covers deep rot has been kept, Hector may carry in the clad body (RSC 1968), a skull in the fancy helmet (RSC 1981) or just the armour (RSC 1990). He has examined it, or perhaps removed some part of it during his comments at 1–2, then taken off his own arms.

4sd The Myrmidon entrance has generally been highly dramatic, and may resemble a choreographed dance movement. V. C. Clinton-Baddeley wrote of the 1922 Marlowe Society production: 'They . . . crept in from all directions raising their cloaks like bats' wings and surrounded Hector who was killed invisibly and then they retreated leaving him lying there' (Sprague, p. 83). In his second production, Birch placed Hector on the steps under the 1932 bridge-like construction, with six Myrmidons confronting him and five more leaning over the arch parapet above. Achilles,

ACHILLES Look Hector, how the sun begins to set,   5
                How ugly night comes breathing at his heels;
                Even with the vail and dark'ning of the sun
                To close the day up, Hector's life is done.
HECTOR I am unarmed, forgo this vantage, Greek.
ACHILLES Strike, fellows, strike, this is the man I seek.   10
                          [*They kill Hector*]

bearing a shield with his name in Greek letters, stood behind Hector's right shoulder, and
Hector's labelled shield and some weapons leaned against the left side of the arch. Hector
stretched out his arms, as if crucified, and Achilles raised his arm to signal the attack with daggers
(production photo). In 1948 Quayle provided a small trough of water, and Hector doused his
head while five Myrmidons slipped in from various directions and Achilles crept down to a nearby
broken pillar and put his foot on Hector's sword (promptbook). In Ottawa (1978), Ray Jervas was
also washing when the solid phalanx of Greeks moved in, their shields reflecting the coppery
light. On Guthrie's 1956 battlefield, lines 1–4 were cut and the lights came up on Hector sitting on
a bench as the Myrmidons entered. Barton and Hall had him squatting in the center of the
sandpit, his helmet, sword and shield out of reach beyond the rim. In NYSF 1965 the Myrmidons
had no shields, only long spears, as they did at BOV in 1979 and RSC in 1996, where Achilles
watched from centre-stage as the Myrmidons raised Hector on their spears on the stage right
platform. In 1968 Barton employed very heavy smoke and twelve Myrmidons materialized out of
it and closed into a tight circle. In 1976, at the NT, as Hector rose unarmed, seven Myrmidons
attacked from the stage rear platform. At the RSC 'The savage murder of Hector releases a
barbarity out of all control and proportion . . . Achilles appears in black leather gear, with wings, a
bird of prey out of some Kenneth Anger nightmare' (Mairowitz, *PP*, October 1976, p. 21). In
Hands' elaborately staged last act, the Myrmidons wore long shiny dark cloaks and had long,
horn-like feathers on their helmets. They went toward Hector with dance-like movements. In
1987 SFC Robert Cross of the *Toronto Star* was sure William's biker Myrmidons said 'vroom,
vroom' as they came on! That year the Berliner Ensemble Achilles 'treats Hector like a rabid dog
at the end'. There was no horror, but when Hector backed into the curtain and was stabbed, the
spears were 'fixed like porcupine quills' (Graham Braddock, *TLS*, 4 September 1987, p. 957).

10ff   Hector has accepted his death in some productions and fought back in others. In Hands' 1981
production he was dressed in white and fatalistically ran headlong onto their spears. Quayle
moved the Myrmidons in step, they struck simultaneously and Hector collapsed into the trough.
Achilles then came close and pulled out his sword. At the NYSF 1965 Achilles directed from the
rear while the Myrmidons stabbed and then seemed to lift Hector's body up on their spears. They
did the same in 1996, impaling Hector 'like a stuck pig before lifting him on high' (Smallwood, *SS
50*, p. 215). Dorn staged the death 'magnificently' on a debris-filled battlefield. He seemed to be
raised up on the Myrmidon spears, 'his arms out-stretched in a Christ-like pose'. Achilles watched
from above, his hands in his pockets (Hortmann, p. 326). John Russell Brown complained of

So Ilium, fall thou next, come, Troy, sink down.
Here lies thy heart, thy sinews, and thy bone.
On Myrmidons, and cry you all amain:
'Achilles hath the mighty Hector slain.'

Retreat [*sounded*]

Hark, a retire upon our Grecian part.   15

[*Another retreat sounded*]

A MYRMIDON The Trojan trumpets sound the like, my lord.
ACHILLES The dragon wing of night o'erspreads the earth,
　　　And stickler-like the armies separates.
　　　My half-supped sword that frankly would have fed,
　　　Pleased with this dainty bait, thus goes to bed. [*Sheathes his*   20
　　　sword]

added actions that broke the momentum in 1960. After the killing in the sandpit, Achilles had a long pause in his last short speech to turn over Hector's body with his foot. There was another delay as one of the Myrmidons examined Hector's cloak (*SS* 14, p. 130) before they dragged him out. In 1968 Barton had the Myrmidons 'blood' Hector, then draw back so Achilles could deliver the final blow. In 1976, Barton and Kyle's Myrmidons hacked Hector savagely with their swords. Moshinsky had one Myrmidon garrotte Hector while the others stood around. Miller (BBC 1981) staged the scene as if Achilles alone confronted Hector then, at his signal, the Myrmidons entered from behind and bludgeoned him. The cameras focused on the maces coming down. In 1985, as the exhausted Hector stood on the balcony, the Myrmidons lined up like a firing squad and shot when Achilles signalled from the stair landing. Berry likened it to 'the execution of the Emperor Maximilian' (*On Directing Shakespeare*, p. 21).

The killing has been graphically brutal, as with Harrison's coshes and chains in the hands of a motorcycle gang at BR 1963, or in Hall's 2001 sandpit, where the Myrmidons first beat Hector senseless with their shields, then repeatedly stabbed him with their spears, finally backing away from a blood-soaked body (Kastan). Or it has become partly symbolic. At TR 1971 the Myrmidons pelted Hector with sponges soaked in 'blood' and he and the stage were spattered (F. Shirley notes). At the Newhouse in NYSF 1973, a walkway five feet above the stage rear was 'filled by a sheet of plexiglass, backlit and hosed down from behind with "blood" which spattered and dripped down' (Comtois, p. 405). There were ritual overtones in 1990, with drums and shouts offstage. Hector had faced rear and was killed in slow motion. He was laid on the circle where Patroclus' body had been earlier, and Achilles rose from a crouch to stand behind him (F. Shirley notes).

There has occasionally been attempted resistance. In 1956 Guthrie had Hector reach for his sword as Achilles moved around his bench and a Myrmidon struck the sword away. Nunn staged the longest struggle. Hector grabbed a spear and fought back, was stabbed repeatedly, and tried to rise several times before giving up (NT 1999 promptbook). Boyd had an unusual treatment in his greatly rewritten fifth act. 'There were no Myrmidons, the necessary touring economy most

> Come, tie his body to my horse's tail,
> Along the field I will the Trojan trail.

Exeunt [dragging out the body]

curiously explained by presenting an Achilles with a leaning to voodoo, sprinkling chicken's blood around the stage and calling on the Myrmidons in the sky for assistance with his bloody purpose against Hector, whose heart he cut out after gunning him down' (Smallwood, *SS* 53, p. 260). In 1990 Beale asked to remain on for 5.9 and screamed as he watched. 'Achilles was not fulfilling his heroic potential' and at first it was a scream of pain, but later in the run became triumphant (Beale, pp. 165–6). At SFC 1963, Cassandra's prophetic words were replayed on a loudspeaker as the Myrmidons moved in (Howard Taubman, *NYT*, 19 June 1963).

22SD   After Achilles' final directions to tie Hector to his horse's tail, the Myrmidons usually bear the body off. At HSSR in 1968 the body was left hanging against a red glow 'in Sebastian Melmot's timeless blasted Moonscape' setting, before a blackout. In 1976 Moshinsky had them wrap him in a cloak before carrying him out. At BOV 1979, they carried him out on their shoulders, one supporting his head. In 1985 three Myrmidons went up the mansion stairs and two carried Hector down, followed by the third. Pandarus had put his head down during the killing, then resumed playing as the body was carried out (RSC promptbook). The shameful treatment that Achilles decrees has occasionally begun onstage with the attitude toward the body. He was picked up by the legs in Barton 1968, and dragged off in 1960, 1990 and at NT 1999.

ACT 5, SCENE 10

[**5.10**] *Sound Retreat. Enter* AGAMEMNON, AJAX, MENELAUS, NESTOR, DIOMEDES, *and the rest, marching* [*to the sound of drums*]. *Shout* [*within*]

AGAMEMNON Hark, hark, what shout is that?
NESTOR Peace, drums.
SOLDIERS (*Within*) Achilles! Achilles! Hector's slain! Achilles!
DIOMEDES The bruit is Hector's slain, and by Achilles.
AJAX If it be so, yet bragless let it be: 5
    Great Hector was as good a man as he.
AGAMEMNON March patiently along; let one be sent
    To pray Achilles see us at our tent.
    If in his death the gods have us befriended,
    Great Troy is ours, and our sharp wars are ended.   10

Exeunt

OSD   The scene has often been reasonably static, with offstage shouts providing the excitement, but some producers have embellished the ten lines. Poel merely began to lower the limelights. Quayle brought the Myrmidons across the stage shouting as the Greek leaders gathered. Guthrie 1956 and Barton 1968 added Ulysses among 'the rest', though he for once has no lines. Several promptbooks (NT 1976; RSC 1981) have no marking for this scene and may, like Miller, have skipped it to focus on the Trojan reaction.

2   Ulysses, a fan bearer and the emblem bearers with the bulls came on for Barton in 1968 and the soldiers shouted. The generals were excited and embraced Menelaus. Ulysses was the last to leave, looking over the battlefield (F. Shirley notes).

[5.11] *Enter* AENEAS, PARIS, ANTENOR, *and* DEIPHOBUS

AENEAS Stand, ho! Yet are we masters of the field.

Enter TROILUS

TROILUS Never go home, here starve we out the night:
        Hector is slain.
ALL   Hector? The gods forbid!
TROILUS He's dead, and at the murderer's horse's tail
        In beastly sort dragged through the shameful field.   5
        Frown on, you heavens, effect your rage with speed,
        Sit, gods, upon your thrones and smile at Troy!
        I say at once, let your brief plagues be mercy,
        And linger not our sure destructions on.
AENEAS My lord, you do discomfort all the host.   10

osd Fry and Poel cut the scene heavily and concentrated on an added tableau of Troilus mourning Hector. Poel added blue lights and music to accompany Troilus' weeping, and Cassandra came on. At The Players in 1932 Herbert brought on Hecuba and Priam to illustrate the effect of the news. Quayle and Shaw omitted the static tableau but ended the play at 31. In 1998 Boyd transmuted this practice by having the Catholic priest (Helenus) perform a Christian funeral service. Cassandra prayed and Paris wept over the body (RSC promptbook). In 1960 Hall and Barton began the scene with Trojans, including extras, dancing around their emblem to celebrate supposed victory. By contrast, Moshinsky limited the Trojans to Troilus and Aeneas in 1976. In 1985, Pandarus played a last slow waltz until 31, when the other Trojans left. In 1990 light came through the grid covering the stage circle and the horizontal bars at the rear cast shadows over Troilus and the Trojans. Troilus brought in two swords in 1996; presumably one was Hector's. Miller's cameras focused on bodies on stretchers and moans accompanied Troilus' words. The wounded remained as a background for Pandarus. A bit more of the southern mansion façade crumbled in 1961 as Troilus entered.

2ff In 1960 Troilus stooped and wiped his hand on some blood in the sandpit, circled and stopped, facing Paris for his speech. The warriors sat on the rim of the sandpit or in the sand, their mood suddenly completely changed (F. Shirley notes).

TROILUS You understand me not that tell me so.
I do not speak of flight, of fear, of death,
But dare all imminence that gods and men
Address their dangers in. Hector is gone:
Who shall tell Priam so, or Hecuba? 15
Let him that will a screech-owl aye be called
Go in to Troy and say there, 'Hector's dead.'
There is a word will Priam turn to stone,
Make wells and Niobes of the maids and wives,
Cold statues of the youth, and in a word 20
Scare Troy out of itself. But march away;
Hector is dead, there is no more to say.
Stay yet! You vile abominable tents,
Thus proudly pitched upon our Phrygian plains,
Let Titan rise as early as he dare, 25
I'll through and through you; and thou great-sized coward,
No space of earth shall sunder our two hates.
I'll haunt thee like a wicked conscience still
That mouldeth goblins swift as frenzy's thoughts.
Strike a free march to Troy, with comfort go: 30
Hope of revenge shall hide our inward woe.

Enter PANDARUS

24–31 As they slowly left, Barton and Hall's soldiers saluted the emblem. In 1990 Troilus picked up
Hector's armour that had lain downstage where he left it in 5.9, then took just the sword. At 26 he
stood, arms outstretched and a sword in each hand, to speak his threat of vengeance. In 1998 he
'intoned', over and over, 'in a frenzy', 5.6.26: 'I reck not though I end my life today' (Smallwood,
SS 53, p. 257). (See Dawson's edition for details of the textual problems of 21–54.)

31SD In the earlier productions Pandarus' appearance as epilogue was omitted. In 1956 Guthrie
presented him in a hat and overcoat with two suitcases, the refugee familiar from Second World
War photographs. One wondered if he was about to join his niece and Calchas (F. Shirley notes).
Rogers sang his verses seriously, 'the sting at the tail' so . . . 'the taste left at the end of the play
was of bitter disillusion and disgust, a shock perhaps the more rude on account of the frivolity
and fun that had gone before' (Wood and Clarke). His entry has become more degraded over the
years. In 1960 his hair was unkempt and he was wrapped in a cloak, his zest transformed to
disgust. Occasionally he is a grubbier refugee – in 1985 his suit was rumpled and dirty. Disease
also became apparent. In Strachan 1998 he was in stained trousers, his skin splotched, and in
1990 he was dirty and ill. At times he has crawled on, as Clive Francis did in 1996, apparently an
AIDS victim, and Hall 2001 gave him the distinctive spots of Kaposi's sarcoma (Kastan).

In some performances, Thersites has shared the stage, either from the beginning, or as
Pandarus enters at 31. He may be silent or repeat an earlier line or two. In Barton 1968

PANDARUS But hear you, hear you –
TROILUS Hence broker-lackey! [*Strikes him*] Ignomy and shame
        Pursue thy life and live aye with thy name.

                         Exeunt all but Pandarus

PANDARUS A goodly medicine for my aching bones. O world, world –   35
    thus is the poor agent despised. O traitors and bawds, how
    earnestly are you set a-work and how ill requited! Why should
    our endeavour be so loved and the performance so loathed? What
    verse for it? What instance for it? Let me see,   40
        Full merrily the humble-bee doth sing   40
        Till he hath lost his honey and his sting,
        And being once subdued in armèd tail,

David Waller (Pandarus) and Norman Rodway (Thersites) 'left together with the symbols of war and lechery' (Sprague, p. 49). In OSF 2001 Thersites came in to balance his opening position as Prologue. A couple of times Cressida has reappeared, a silent witness, lost in a sort of no-man's land not of her making. In Utah, Cassandra, Thersites and Pandarus uttered the farewell 'as a choric chant' (Aggeler, p. 232), recalling their appearance in the Prologue. In Nunn, the stage gradually darkened, and Pandarus entered in a cream robe and shawl, Cressida heavily made up behind him, and he presented her to Troilus, who rejected them both (promptbook).

33–4 Troilus has occasionally merely spat his words at Pandarus, as in 1985 and BBC 1981. More often he has struck him, though there is no textual indication for physical abuse. In 1960 Troilus was leaving, but returned to kick Pandarus. In 1996 he booted the crawling figure down the three steps of the stage-right platform. When Troilus left, the gates representing Troy's walls at FTG 1983 slammed shut, leaving Pandarus outside in no-man's land. In 1981 Hands had added barbed wire to the muddy stage cloth for the battle scenes and Troilus pushed Pandarus into it, so he spoke his last speeches with his hands entangled, with Thersites and an armed corpse sharing the stage (RSC promptbook). Thersites entered in Nunn to return Cressida's glove token.

35ff In 1985 Pandarus spoke the prose lines from his piano stool, turned to the keyboard for a final riff, and then walked up toward the balcony for 40–54 while a player piano took over and the lights slowly dimmed (RSC promptbook). He was coughing and ill in BBC 1981, but sang 40–3 in a broken voice, surrounded by the wounded. In 1990 Pandarus stretched his arms to the surrounding Swan Theatre audience at 'bequeath'. Thersites first returned to accompany Pandarus in the 1960s – with the Prologue at the 1960 sandpit and alone in BR 1963. Barton added a grotesque celebratory note in 1968 when Thersites banged the tambourine and they circled in a mock dance. The lights went black at a final bang of the tambourine at 54 (F. Shirley notes). In 2003, Monette's use of 'the Nine Inch Nails clip tried to relate the production's normalizing moral attitudes to sex to the audience's world and sexualities, thus offering one last "answer", this time to questions of Shakespeare's modern relevance' (Kidnie).

Sweet honey and sweet notes together fail.
Good traders in the flesh, set this in your painted cloths:
As many as be here of panders' hall, 45
Your eyes, half out, weep out at Pandar's fall.
Or if you cannot weep, yet give some groans,
Though not for me yet for your aching bones.
Brethren and sisters of the hold-door trade,
Some two months hence my will shall here be made. 50
It should be now, but that my fear is this:
Some gallèd goose of Winchester would hiss.
Till then I'll sweat and seek about for eases,
And at that time bequeath you my diseases. [*Exit*]

FINIS

BIBLIOGRAPHY

Promptbooks

Albers, Kenneth. Promptbook for OSF, 2001, now in OSF Archives.

Barton, John. Promptbook for RSC, Stratford, 1968, now in SCL.

    Promptbook for RSC, Aldwych, 1969, now in SCL.

    Promptbook for RSC, European tour, 1969, now in SCL.

Barton, John, and Barry Kyle. Promptbook for RSC, Stratford, 1976, now in SCL.

    Promptbook for RSC, tour and Aldwych, 1977, now in SCL.

Boyd, Michael. Promptbook for RSC Swan, Pit and English tour, 1998–9, now in SCL.

Davies, Howard. Promptbook for RSC, Stratford, 1985, now in SCL.

Guthrie, Tyrone. Promptbook for Old Vic, London and tour, 1956–7. Three copies now in Bristol University Theatre Collection.

Hall, Adrian. Promptbook for Trinity Repertory Company, 1971, at TR.

Hall, Peter, and John Barton. Promptbook for SMT, Stratford, 1960, now in SCL.

    Promptbook for RSC, Edinburgh and Aldwych, 1962, now in SCL.

Hands, Terry. Promptbook for RSC, Aldwych, 1981, now in SCL.

Harrison, John. Promptbook for BR, Birmingham, 1963, in Sir Barry Jackson Archives, Birmingham.

Judge, Ian. Promptbook for RSC, Stratford, 1996, now in SCL.

Kemble, John Philip. Promptbook c. 1800, now in Folger Shakespeare Library.

Landau, Jack. Prompt typescript for ASF, 1961, now in Harvard Theatre Collection.

Langham, Michael. Promptbook for SFC, 1963, now in SFC Archives.

Mendes, Sam. Promptbook for RSC, Stratford, 1990, now in SCL.

Moshinsky, Elijah. Promptbook for NT, 1976, now in NT Archives.

Nunn, Trevor. Promptbook for NT, 1999, now in NT Archives.

Payne, Ben Iden. Promptbook for SMT, 1936, now in SCL.

Poel, William. Promptbook, 1912, two copies now in Enthoven Collection, British Theatre Museum.

Quayle, Anthony. Promptbook for SMT, 1948, now in SCL.

Sandoe, James. Promptbook for OSF, 1958, now in OSF Archives.

Shaw, Glen Byam. Promptbook for SMT, 1954, now in SCL.
Turner, Jerry. Promptbook for OSF, 1972, now in OSF Archives.
White, Richard E. T. Promptbook for OSF, 1984, now in OSF Archives.
William, David. Promptbook for SFC, 1987, now in SFC Archives.

Videotapes of productions

Boyd, Michael. RSC Swan, 1998, now in SCL.
Davies, Howard. RST, 1985, now in SCL.
Judge, Ian. RST, 1996, now in SCL.
Mendes, Sam. RSC Swan, 1990, now in SCL.
Miller, Jonathan. BBC / Time-Warner, 1981.
Moshinsky, Elijah. NT at National Youth Theatre, 1976, now in NT Archives.
Nunn, Trevor. NT Olivier, now in NT Archives.
William, David. SFC, 1987, now in SFC Archives.

Editions and adaptations

William Shakespeare's Comedies, Histories, & Tragedies, London, 1623.
    Facsimile prepared by Helge Kökeritz, New Haven: Yale, 1954.
Beckerman, Bernard and Joseph Papp. *The Festival Shakespeare Troilus and Cressida*. New York, 1967.
Bell's British Theatre, Vol. xii. London, 1780.
Clark, W. G. and William Aldus Wright. Cambridge Edition, 1865.
Collier, J. Payne. Shakespeare *Plays*, 1853.
Craig, W. J. *Troilus and Cressida*. London, 1905.
Daniel, George. Remarks, *Troilus and Cressida*, Adapted for stage presentation, Cumberland's British Theatre (No. 385).
Dawson, Anthony B. The New Cambridge Shakespeare *Troilus and Cressida*. Cambridge: Cambridge University Press, 2003.
Dick's *Complete Edition of Shakespeare's Works*. London, n.d.
    Standard Drama, *Troilus and Cressida* (No. 133). London. n.d.
Dryden, John. *Troilus and Cressida: or, Truth Found too Late, The Comedies, Tragedies, and Operas*, Vol. ii. London, 1701.
Dyce, Alexander. Shakespeare, *Works*, London, 1875.
Greenblatt, Stephen, Walter Cohen, et al. *The Norton Shakespeare*. New York: W. W. Norton, 1997.
Hillebrand, Harold N. and T. W. Baldwin. *A New Variorum Edition of Shakespeare: Troilus and Cressida*. Philadelphia: J. B. Lippincott, 1953.

J. R. *Troilus and Cressida, 'Altered from Shakespeare and Dryden, 5 December 1810'*. Copy in Folger Shakespeare Library.

Johnson, Samuel. *The Plays of William Shakespeare*, Vol. VII. London, 1765.

Johnson, Samuel and George Steevens. *The Plays of William Shakespeare*, Vol. IX, 1773.

Rowe, Nicholas. *William Shakespeare: Collected Works*, Vol. IV. London, 1709.

Seltzer, Daniel. *Troilus and Cressida*. New York: New American Library, 1963.

Troilus and Cressida. A Tragedy, By Mr. William Shakespeare. London: J. Tonson, 1734.

Standard reference works

A Biographical Dictionary of Actors, Actresses, Musicians, Dancers & Other Stage Personnel in London, 1660–1800. Ed. Philip H. Highfill, Jr, Kalman A. Burnim and Edward A. Langhans. Carbondale: Southern Illinois University Press, 1973–8.

The London Stage, 1660–1800. Parts 1–3. Ed. William van Lennep, et al. Carbondale: Southern Illinois University Press, 1960–5.

Other works

Aggeler, Geoffrey. 'Utah Shakespeare Festival'. *Shakespeare Quarterly* 36 (1985): 230–2.

Alexander, Peter. '*Troilus and Cressida*, 1609'. *Library* 9 (1928–9): 267–86.

Asp, Carolyn. 'In Defense of Cressida'. *Studies in Philology* 74 (October 1977): 406–17.

'Transcendence Denied: The Failure of Role Assumption in *Troilus and Cressida*'. *Studies in English Literature* 18 (Spring 1978): 257–74.

Beale, Simon Russell. 'Thersites in Troilus and Cressida'. In *Players of Shakespeare 3: Further Essays on Shakespearean Performances*. Ed. Russell Jackson and Robert Smallwood. New York: Cambridge University Press, 1993, pp. 160–73.

Berry, Ralph. *On Directing Shakespeare: Interviews with Contemporary Directors*. London: Hamish Hamilton, 1989.

Shakespeare and the Awareness of Audience. London: Macmillan. 1985.

Boas, Frederick S. *Shakespeare and his Predecessors*. New York: Charles Scribners Sons, 1896.

Boling, Ronald J. 'Stage Images of Cressida's Betrayal'. *Essays in Theatre* 14 (1955–6): 147–58.

Bowen, Barbara E. *Gender in the Theater of War: Shakespeare's Troilus and Cressida*. New York: Garland Publishing Company, 1993.

Bratton J. S. 'Theatre of War: The Crimea on the London Stage, 1854–55'. In *Performance and Politics in Popular Drama: Aspects of Popular Entertainment in Theatre, Film and Television, 1800–1976*. Ed. Louis James and Bernard Sharrett. Cambridge: Cambridge University Press, 1980.

Brockbank, Philip. '"Troilus and Cressida": Character and Value, 1200 BC to AD 1985'. In *On Shakespeare: Jesus, Shakespeare and Karl Marx and Other Essays*. London: Blackwell, 1989, pp. 30–59.

Brown, Ivor. *Shakespeare Memorial Theatre 1954–56: A Photographic Record*. London: Max Reinhardt, 1956.

Brown, John Russell. 'Three Directors: A Review of Recent Productions'. *Shakespeare Survey 14*. Cambridge: Cambridge University Press, 1961, pp. 129–37.

Bullough, Geoffrey, ed. *Narrative and Dramatic Sources of Shakespeare*, Vol. VI. London: Routledge and Kegan Paul, 1966.

Bulman, James C, ed. *Shakespeare, Theory and Performance*. New York: Routledge, 1996.

Byrne, Muriel St. Claire. 'Fifty Years of Shakespearian Production: 1898–1948'. *Shakespeare Survey 2*. Cambridge: Cambridge University Press, 1949, pp. 1–20.

Chambers, Edmund K. *Shakespeare: A Survey*. New York: Oxford University Press, 1926.

Charney, Maurice. *Shakespeare on Love and Lust*. New York: Columbia University Press, 2000.

Coleridge, Samuel Taylor. *Shakespearean Criticism*, Vol. II. Ed. Thomas Middleton Raysor. London: Dent [1960].

Comtois, M. E. 'New York Shakespeare Festival, Lincoln Center, 1973–74'. *Shakespeare Quarterly* 25 (Autumn 1974).

Cook, Carol. 'Unbodied Figures of Desire'. In *Performing Feminisms: Feminist Critical Theory and Theatre*. Ed. Sue Ellen Chase. Baltimore: Johns Hopkins University Press, 1990.

Crosse, Gordon. Unpublished Notebooks, at Birmingham Public Library; on Microfilm at Folger Shakespeare Library.

David, Richard. 'Drams of Eale: A Review of Recent Productions'. *Shakespeare Survey 10*. Cambridge: Cambridge University Press, 1957, pp. 126–34.

'Stratford, 1954'. *Shakespeare Quarterly* 5 (1954).

Designing Shakespeare: An Audio Visual Archive 1960–2000. www.pads.ahds.ac.uk

Dessen, Alan. 'What's New? Shakespeare on Stage in 1986'. *Shakespeare Quarterly* 38 (1987): 90–6.

Dryden, John. 'On The Grounds of Criticism in Tragedy'. *The Comedies, Tragedies, and Operas*, Vol. II. London: 1702.

Dusinberre, Juliet. '"Troilus and Cressida" and the Definition of Beauty'. *Shakespeare Survey 36*. Cambridge: Cambridge University Press, 1983, pp. 85–95.

Ellis-Femor, Una. *The Frontiers of Drama*. London: Methuen, 1948.

Elton, W. R. *Shakespeare's Troilus and Cressida and the Inns of Court Revels*. Brookfield, VT: Ashgate, 2000.

Evans, Gareth Lloyd. 'The Reason Why: The Royal Shakespeare Season Reviewed'. *Shakespeare Survey 22*. Cambridge: Cambridge University Press, 1969, pp. 135–44.

Foakes, R. A. '*Troilus and Cressida* Reconsidered'. *University of Toronto Quarterly* 32 (January 1963): 142–54.

Forbes, Brian. *Dame Edith Evans*. Boston: Little, Brown and Co, 1977.

Greene, Gayle. 'Shakespeare's Cressida: "A Kind of Self"'. In *The Woman's Part*. Ed. Carolyn Swift Lenz, et al. Urbana: University of Illinois Press, 1980, pp. 133–49.

Grigely, Joseph. *Textuality: Art, Theory and Textual Criticism*. Ann Arbor: University of Michigan Press, 1995.

Hazlitt, William. 'Characters in Shakespeare's Plays'. *Complete Works*, Vol. IV. Ed. P. P. Howe. London: Dent, 1930.

Helms, Lorraine. 'Playing the Woman's Part: Feminist Criticism and Shakespearean Performance'. In *Performing Feminisms: Feminist Critical Theory and Theatre*. Ed. Sue Ellen Chase. Baltimore: Johns Hopkins University Press, 1990.

Hobson, Harold. *Theatre 2*.

Hodgdon, Barbara. 'He do Cressida in Different Voices'. *English Literary Renaissance* 20 (1990): 254–86.

Holland, Peter. *English Shakespeares: Shakespeare on the English Stage in the 1990s*. Cambridge: Cambridge University Press, 1997.
    'Shakespeare Performances in England, 1989–1990'. *Shakespeare Survey 44*. Cambridge: Cambridge University Press, 1992, pp. 157–90.

Hook, Lucyle. 'Shakespare Improv'd, or A Case for the Affirmative'. *Shakespeare Quarterly* 4 (1953): 289–99.

Hortmann, Wilhelm. *Shakespeare on the German Stage: The Twentieth Century*. Cambridge: Cambridge University Press, 1998.

Kastan, David Scott and Tom Dale Keever. 'Sir Peter Hall's Troilus and Cressida and the Tradition of the Play'. Theatre for a New Audience web site. www.tfana.org/2001/troilus

Kaula, David. 'Will and Reason in Troilus and Cressida'. *Shakespeare Quarterly* 12 (1961).

Kimbrough, Robert. 'The Origins of Troilus and Cressida: Stage, Quarto and
Folio'. *PMLA* 77 (June 1962): 194–9.
'The Troilus Log: Shakespeare and "Box-Office"'. *Shakespeare Quarterly* 15
(1964): 201–9.
Knight, G. Wilson. *Principles of Shakespearian Production With Especial
Reference to the Tragedies*. London: Faber and Faber [1936].
The Wheel of Fire. New York: Barnes and Noble, 1965.
Kott, Jan. *Shakespeare Our Contemporary*. Trans. Boleslaw Taborska. Garden
City, NY: Anchor Books, 1966.
Lawrence, William W. *Shakespeare's Problem Comedies*. New York: Macmillan,
1931.
Lennox, Charlotte. 'The Fable of "Troilus and Cressida"'. *Shakespeare
Illustrated*, Vol. III. London, 1754.
Lundstrom, Rinder F. *William Poel's Hamlet: The Director as Critic*. Ann
Arbor: University of Michigan Research Press, 1981.
Mahon, John and Ellen. *Shakespeare Bulletin*. November–December,
1983.
McAlindon, Tom. 'Language, Style and Meaning in Troilus and Cressida'.
PMLA 84 (January 1969): 29–43.
McGlinchee, Claire. 'Stratford, Connecticut Shakespeare Festival, 1961'
Shakespeare Quarterly 12 (1961): 421–2.
McManaway, James G. 'Additional Prompt-Books of Shakespeare from the
Smock Alley Theatre'. *Modern Language Review* 45 (1950): 64–5.
Miller, Edward Haviland. 'Shakespeare in the Grand Style'. *Shakespeare
Quarterly* 1 (1950): 243–6.
Monck, Nugent. 'The Maddermarket Theatre and the Playing of Shakespeare'.
Shakespeare Survey 12. Cambridge: Cambridge University Press, 1959,
pp. 71–5.
Muir, Kenneth. 'Troilus and Cressida'. *Shakespeare Survey 8*. Cambridge:
Cambridge University Press, 1955, pp. 28–39.
Mullin, Michael. *Theatre at Stratford-upon-Avon*. 2 vols. Westport, CT, 1980.
Newlin, Jeanne T. 'The Darkened Stage: J. P. Kemble and *Troilus and Cressida*'.
In *The Triple Bond: Plays, Mainly Shakespearean, In Performance*. Ed.
Joseph G. Price. University Park: Pennsylvania State University Press,
1975, pp. 190–202.
'The Modernity of Troilus and Cressida: The Case for Theatrical Criticism'.
Harvard Library Bulletin, 17 (1969): 353–75.
Nosworthy, J. M. *Shakespeare's Occasional Plays*. New York: Barnes and Noble,
1965.
Oates, Joyce Carol [J. Oates Smith]. 'Essence and Existence in Shakespeare's
Troilus and Cressida'. *Philological Quarterly* (1967): 167–85.

O'Connor, Marion. 'William Poel to George Bernard Shaw'. *Theatre Notebook*
 54:3 (2000): 167–76.
Papp, Joseph. 'Directing Troilus and Cressida'. In *The Festival Shakespeare
 Troilus and Cressida*. New York, 1967.
Poel, William. *An Account of the Elizabethan Stage Society*. Private Printing,
 1898.
 Shakespeare in the Theatre. London: Sidgwick and Jackson, 1913.
Rossiter, A. P. 'The Modernity of "Troilus and Cressida"'. Lecture at
 Stratford, 25 August 1954.
Roy, Emil. 'War and Manliness in Shakespeare's Troilus and Cressida'.
 Comparative Drama 7 (1973): 107–20.
Russell, Barry. 'Midlands: Anti Heroes'. *Drama* 4 (1985).
Rutter, Carol. *Enter the Body: Women and Representation on Shakespeare's Stage*.
 London: Routledge, 2001.
Schoenbaum, Samuel. *William Shakespeare: A Documentary Life*. New York:
 Oxford University Press, 1975.
Sedgwick, Eve Kosofsky. *Between Men: English Literature and Male Homosocial
 Desire*. New York: Columbia University Press, 1985.
Shaw, George Bernard. 'Ibsen Ahead'. In *Our Theatres in the Nineties*, vol. 2.
 London: Constable and Company, 1932.
Shaw, William. 'Meager Lead and Joyous Consequences: RSC Triumphs
 Among Shakespeare's Minor Plays'. *Theatre Survey* 27 (May 1986):
 37–67.
Shirley, Frances A. *Shakespeare's Use of Off-Stage Sounds*. Lincoln: University
 of Nebraska Press, 1963.
Shrimpton, Nicholas. 'Shakespeare Performances in London and
 Stratford-upon-Avon'. *Shakespeare Survey 39*. Cambridge: Cambridge
 University Press, 1986, pp. 191–206.
Slights, Robert C. 'The Parallel Structure of *Troilus and Cressida*'. *Shakespeare
 Quarterly* 25 (1972): 42–51.
Smallwood, Robert. 'Shakespearean Performances in England, 1996'.
 Shakespeare Survey 50. Cambridge: Cambridge University Press, 1997,
 pp. 201–24.
 'Shakespearean Performances in England, 1999', *Shakespeare Survey 53*.
 Cambridge: Cambridge University Press, 2000, pp. 244–73.
Speaight, Robert. *Shakespeare on Stage*. Boston, 1973.
 William Poel and the Elizabethan Revival. London: William Heinemann,
 1954.
Spencer, Hazelton. *The Art and Life of William Shakespeare*. London: G. Bell,
 1947.

Shakespeare Improved: The Restoration Versions in Quarto and on the Stage.
Cambridge, MA: Harvard University Press, 1927.

Sprague, Arthur Colby and J. C. Trewin. *Shakespeare's Plays Today: Some Customs and Conventions of the Stage.* London: Sidgwick and Jackson, 1970.

Spurgeon, Caroline. *Shakespeare's Imagery and What it Tells Us.* Boston: Beacon Hill Press, 1961.

Styan, J. L. 'Political Cressida in Performance'. In *Shakespeare Worldwide.* Ed. Yoshiko Kawachi. Tokyo: Yoshodo, 1995, pp. 263–6.

Tatlock, J. S. P. 'The Siege of Troy in Elizabethan Literature, Especially in Shakespeare and Heywood'. *PMLA* 30 (1915): 673–770.

Taylor, Gary. '*Troilus and Cressida*: Bibliography, performance and Interpretation'. *Shakespeare Studies* 15 (1982): 99–136.

Trewin, John. *Going to Shakespeare.* London: G. Allen and Unwin, 1978.

Tylee, Claire M. 'The Text of Cressida and Every Ticklish Reader: *Troilus and Cressida*, The Greek Camp Scene'. *Shakespeare Survey 41.* Cambridge: Cambridge University Press, 1989, pp. 63–76.

Voth, Grant L. and Oliver H. Evans. 'Cressida and the World of the Play'. *Shakespeare Studies* 14 (1975): 231–9.

Wain, John. *The Living World of Shakespeare.* New York: Macmillan, 1964.

Walker, Alice. 'The Textual Problem of *Troilus and Cressida*'. *Modern Language Review* 45 (1950): 459–64.

Warren, Roger. 'Theory and Practice: Stratford, 1976'. *Shakespeare Survey 30.* Cambridge: Cambridge University Press, 1977, pp. 169–79.
'Interpretations of Shakespearean Comedy, 1981'. *Shakespeare Survey 35.* Cambridge: Cambridge University Press, 1982, pp. 141–52.

Williamson, Audrey. *Old Vic Drama 2.* London: Rockliffe, 1957.

Wood, Roger and Mary Clarke. 'Troilus and Cressida'. *Shakespeare at the Old Vic.* New York: Macmillan, 1957.

Worthen, W. B. 'Drama, Performativity and Performance'. *PMLA* 113 (October, 1998): 1093–107.

Yoder, R. A. 'Sons and Daughters of the Game: An Essay on Shakespeare's *Troilus and Cressida*'. *Shakespeare Survey 25.* Cambridge: Cambridge University Press, 1972, pp. 11–25.

INDEX

Adrian, Max 25, 36, 39, 93, 101, 149
Agate, James 16, 17, 25
Albers, Kenneth 80, 82, *82*, 156
Aldredge, Theoni 46
Aldredge, Tom 46
Alexander, Peter 2
Allan, Roger 76
Allen, Sheila 50
American Place Theatre, New York 79
American Shakespeare Festival, Stratford
    CT 35, 36, 39, *41*, 42, 140, 157, 161,
    189, 224, 232
Anderson, Georgine 43, 152
Annis, Francesca 55, 56, 193, 194
Appell, Libbey 90
Archer, William 10
Armstrong, Alun 60, 61, 124, 127, 139,
    173, 175
Ashbourne, Jayne 71, 185, 191
Asp, Carolyn 61
Atienza, Edward 57
Atkins, Robert 16, 18, 28, 30, 84
Atkinson, Brooks 19, 33, 111
Audley, Maxine 39
Ayrton, Randle 21, 93, 157

Bachman, Stefan 131, 134, 139
Ballard, Jamie 78
Balman, Rollo 125
Bamber, David 74, 75, 94
Barkhimer, Steven 85, 110
Barrett, Edith 18, 208
Barritt, Ian 78
Barton, Anne 48
Barton, John 36, *38*, 39, 40, 47, *49*, 50,
    54, 55, 56, 57, 59, 69, 70, 82, 91, 92,
    93, 94, 97, 98, 99, 100, 105, 108, 110,
    111, 112, 114, 116, 118, 120, 121,

124, 126, 131, 138, 139, 140, 141,
    142, 149, 151, 156, 157, 165, 166,
    173, 174, 175, 176, 179, 180, 184,
    186, 187, 189, 190, 192, 193, 194,
    198, 199, 204, 206, 207, 208, 209,
    212, 222, 223, 225, 229, 231, 233,
    234, 235, 236, 237, 238, 239,
    240
Baughan, E. A. 8, 21
Baylis, Lilian 16
BBC 57, 58, 131, 168, 180, 182, 189, 190,
    212, 225, 232, 240
Beale, Simon Russell 67, 68, 82, 124, 126,
    127, 139, 140, 173, 204, 205, 223,
    236
Belt, Wayne 83
Benesch, Vivienne 134
Berliner Ensemble 1, 64, 66, 76, 89, 94,
    125, 126, 148, 149, 155, 186, 191,
    209, 211, 234
Berry, Ralph 235
Betterton, Thomas 4
Billington, Michael 55, 223
Birch, Frank 13, 15, *15*, 23, 24, 92, 179,
    233
Birmingham Repertory Theatre
    Company 42, 44, 152, 231
Boas, Frederick S. 20
Bourton, Rayner 194
Boyd, Michael 71, 72, 76, 77, 84, 89, 100,
    105, 110, 124, 130, 131, 134, 149,
    156, 188, 194, 208, 223, 225, 235,
    236, 238
Brantley, Ben 72
Bratton, J.S. 27
Bresson, Adolphe 9
Brett, Jeremy 137, 208, 212
Bridges-Adams, W. 11